Vegetable Gardening

The Ultimate Guide for Growing Vegetables

Suzie Glendy

contained within this document, including, but not limited to, errors, omissions, or inaccuracies.

Table of Contents

Introduction

One of the most accessible and fulfilling hobbies anyone can pick up and maintain is gardening. It can be done anywhere, and the start-up costs are minimal. Growing your own produce at home offers a variety of benefits. Gardening is known to improve mood, strengthen the functioning of the immune system, promote better relationships, reduce stress, be a tool for recovery, and be therapeutic. A common misconception most have is that you need a green thumb to be a good gardener. Well, this is not a gift only a few are blessed with. You can learn about it and become good, too. As with any other skill in life, with consistency, practice, and patience, you can become an excellent gardener.

It is not a hobby that offers immediate gratification—instead, it needs to be done in steps. You cannot grow a garden from seeds and harvest brilliant produce overnight. It is a slow process, but is incredibly rewarding and nurturing. The act of working in a garden is known as gardening, and it is now known to be an activity that promotes stress management and is not restricted to a specific age group. You can also use gardening to reconnect with the environment and form a better bond with the ecosystem around you.

These days, gardening is steadily gaining popularity, and you don't need plenty of open space to start a garden. A variety of options are available as long as you are interested in them. From using containers to turning the windowsill into a full-fledged garden, there is a lot to choose from. Gardening is a sustainable agricultural practice utilizing small spaces of land to produce fresh vegetables, fruits, and more. It is practiced by different communities across the world. Regardless of whether you live in the city, suburban area, or the countryside, you can grow whatever you want. You can also turn your balcony, porch, or rooftop into a garden. If you have open space at home, turning it into a garden is a marvelous idea.

Gardening is nothing but the practice and the act of growing plants in a garden. A variety of tasks are included in it, such as preparing the soil, planting, weeding, and overall maintenance. It can be a part of your lifestyle, or even an engaging hobby. It is an excellent means to take care of the environment and your family, too. Since the dawn of civilization, humans have been planting seeds to help them survive and obtain the nourishment needed from the produce they harvest. Over time, it has developed into a craft involving a variety of techniques and tools. These days, gardening is not just an art but a science, too. With careful planning and preparation, a variety of techniques can be used to create a thriving garden at home. These techniques are designed to regulate and improve the yields obtained and grow a variety of healthy plants. Modern gardens provide an opportunity to express yourself through a variety of plants and the garden you create. It is a unique, fun, and engaging activity. Regardless of whether you are a hobbyist or a newbie, it is never too late to start gardening.

More and more people these days are trying their hand at gardening. It is an enjoyable hobby. By growing your produce at home, you'll not only have freshly harvested ingredients, but will also end up saving on your food bill, too. If you are eager to learn about gardening and want to get started, then this is the perfect book for you. This book will act as your guide every step of the way, and will introduce you to all the information required to create a thriving garden.

The information given in this book has been divided into three parts for your convenience:

- The first part of the book deals with the basics of gardening.

- The second part of the book deals with a variety of vegetables you can grow at home and how to grow them.

- The final part of the book is all about maintaining and tending to your garden.

When you put all this information together, you are armed with everything required to get started. When it comes to learning about something new, focusing on the benefits it offers will automatically improve the motivation to get started. Once you know what to do, gardening is easy.

You will learn about the different types of gardens you can start at home—from a conventional in-soil garden and raised beds to using planter boxes and vertical gardening, the choices are truly endless. A few basic considerations you must remember before getting started include the ease of access, soil condition, sun and shade requirements, maintenance, plant size, tools needed, and fencing. This book will introduce you to detailed information about each of these aspects. You will also learn about the nutrition requirements of plants, improving the quality of the soil, basic tools, and the steps needed to start planting and growing. With a little planning and preparation, the overall process will become doubly rewarding. Gardening is not an act you can accomplish overnight. It is a sweet labor of love and patience. Once you start committing to this process, the results will blow your mind!

This book will introduce you to different types of vegetables you can grow at home. From leafy vegetables and bulbs to roots, tubers, and flowers—you have a lot to choose from. You will learn in detail about the requirements for growing different varieties of plants—from the temperature they need to other growth factors and harvesting, this book will be your guide. It is not just about starting a garden; you must tend to it as well. This is where the final part of the book steps into the picture. You will be introduced to common challenges most gardeners face and tips to overcome them. You will also come across a variety of solutions to deal with common insects, pests, and diseases that plague vegetable gardens. And finally, you will discover the secrets to increasing the yield from your garden.

Once you are armed with all this information, the next step is to simply get started. Remember, this process takes commitment, consistency, awareness, careful monitoring, love, and plenty of patience. If you commit to this, you can grow all the vegetables you want! You can enjoy the delicious harvest from your garden and share your labor of love with others. This can also be a family activity that involves all members of your household. Imagine the joy of digging into a meal cooked using everything you grow in the garden! Wouldn't it be wonderful?

So, are you eager and excited to jump into the world of gardening? If yes, what are you waiting for? It is time to get started!

Part 1:

ABCs of Gardening

Growing your own vegetables at home must be quite an exciting notion. Well, before you can start gardening, it is important to understand the different aspects it entails. From the benefits it offers to the different considerations and planning, there is a lot to consider. The first part of this book will act as an introductory guide that will familiarize you with the different aspects of gardening.

Chapter 1:

Benefits of Gardening

Gardening probably sounds like a good pastime or hobby. Well, these are not the only benefits associated with it. Regardless of whether it is your hobby or you are a horticulturist by profession, the benefits of gardening cannot be overlooked. It doesn't matter whether you have an outdoor garden or a small container garden in the kitchen, these are all the benefits you stand to gain.

Improves Mood

A wonderful benefit of gardening is that it automatically improves your mood. Gardening is known to reduce anxiety, depression, and so much more—thus enhancing your overall mood. Marianne Thorsen Gonzalez (Gonzalez et al., 2011) conducted a study in order to to understand the many benefits of gardening. The study spanned several years, and the participants of this study consisted of individuals diagnosed with depression. Researchers made them participate in gardening for 12 weeks. They measured different aspects of the participants' mental health before and after this gardening intervention, including the intensity of their depressive symptoms. At the end of the study, the researchers discovered there was a significant improvement in their depressive symptoms. When the participants kept gardening even after the intervention ended, these levels only improved.

Strengthens Immune Function

Most do not even realize it, but we are more similar to plants than we believe. Plants produce energy through a process known as photosynthesis. In this process, they utilize sunlight to make the nutrients needed for their growth and development. Similarly, even the human body is adept at absorbing vitamin D. The best source of vitamin D is sunlight, and this vitamin is crucial in helping to strengthen your bones and supporting immune functioning. Exposing yourself to healthy sunlight daily is needed to reduce the risk of developing different types of cancer and multiple sclerosis.

Builds Connections

Humans are social beings, and we thrive in communities. Unsurprisingly, forming and maintaining relationships is needed for our overall sense of well-being. Gardening helps to foster personal connections, which in turn enhances the sense of well-being (Lam et al., 2019). In this study, students were asked to photograph their gardening efforts and share all that they learned. While doing this, they reported an enhanced sense of well-being from the relationships they formed with others during this process. Whether it is a community garden or interactions with other gardening enthusiasts online, it helps form relationships. These benefits can further be intensified if you think of gardening as a family bonding activity, too.

Improves Strength

Gardening is a physical exercise. There are different tasks associated with it, such as raking dried leaves, cutting grass, removing weeds, and so on. It is a light- to moderate-intensity physical activity, and certainly gets your muscles moving. Gardening regularly helps improve your strength, because most of the major muscle groups are exercised whenever you tend to plants. Weight gain is quite common as we age— from reduced physical activity to slowed metabolism, different factors are at play. Taking up gardening on a regular basis helps to reverse weight gain associated with aging (Litt et al., 2017).

Reduces Stress

These days we live in a world that is extremely stressful. Whether it is in our personal or professional lives, we are constantly bombarded by different worries and stressors. Therefore, learning to deal with stress is needed to ensure your overall well-being. Stress not only takes a toll on your mental health, but also harms your physical health as well. From the increased risk of cardiovascular disorders to digestion troubles, there are a lot of problems associated with chronic stress. Gardening regularly helps recuperate and improve your ability to deal with such stress. In fact, the levels of stress-inducing hormones decrease when you start gardening. Previously, it was mentioned that gardening also improves your overall mood. A combination of these factors helps manage stress and ensures that it does not get the best of you. Managing stress will work wonders for your professional and personal relationships as well.

Protects Memory

The next time you start gardening, understand that you are protecting and strengthening your memory while doing this. This is an incredible benefit associated with gardening. Any form of exercise is known to promote cognitive functioning. Gardening helps to protect memory, improve cognitive functioning, and reduce the risk of developing cognitive disorders (Park et al., 2019). The researchers of the study noticed that those who garden regularly had better brain nerve growth factors. This, in turn, is needed to enhance your memory functioning. Even if you keep the science part of it aside, here is a simple explanation for how it keeps your mind sharp—all of the activities involved need planning and attentiveness. Consistently watering the plants, mulching, or adding the required manure at specific times are all little aspects that you need to pay attention to. By regularly engaging the mental muscles, you are essentially strengthening your cognitive functioning.

Tool for Recovery

It might come as a surprise, but gardening is commonly used as a tool during addiction recovery programs or rehabilitation. Yes, it is an effective rehabilitation tool known as horticulture therapy. This is not a new age concept, and has been around for years now. Several addiction recovery programs use plants as a part of their regular agenda to help addicts on their way to a better life. Gardening is known to elicit positive emotions and feelings that help those tackling an addiction. It is also a means of natural recovery. A rehabilitation program that focuses on gardening has a higher completion rate for those who opted for this when compared to other activities.

Reduces the Risk of Cardiovascular Disorders

If you want to strengthen the health of your heart while reducing the risk of cardiovascular disorders, it is time to grab your gardening tools and head outdoors. Spending a couple of hours taking care of your garden is known to reduce stress and anxiety levels. It also stabilizes blood pressure levels. When combined, these factors automatically reduce the risk of strokes, heart attacks, and other coronary disorders.

Promotes Dexterity and Strength

Gardening is an activity that requires making a variety of precise movements. One benefit associated with this is that it increases the strength in your hands as well as their dexterity. These start reducing with age. To effectively tackle this, start gardening regularly since it is known to help develop and maintain the strength of your hands. It also improves how you work with them. The simple, repetitive movements associated with gardening promote strength and dexterity. All the different movements needed while tending to the plants—from sowing seeds to watering them, and even removing weeds—are helpful.

A Great Exercise

It's been repeatedly mentioned that gardening is a low- to moderate-intensity activity. Regardless of whether it's an indoor garden, an outdoor vegetable patch, or even raised beds—gardening is an effective aerobic exercise. Once you start gardening, you probably will not even realize when you break a sweat. From pulling weeds to watering plants and reaching for different gardening tools, there are different movements you will be performing repeatedly. This improves the flexibility, strength, and stamina of the different muscle groups involved in these processes. If you have been meaning to exercise regularly or have been avoiding it for some reason or the other, why don't you start gardening? You can attain the benefits associated with exercising while tending to your lovely garden.

Promotes Healthy Eating Habits

We all know that it's important to eat healthily. A simple effective means to do this is by growing your vegetables, fruits, and even herbs, at home. Most of the fresh produce available on the market these days has traces of insecticides, pesticides, and other chemical compounds and fertilizers added to promote their growth. Unfortunately, all these chemical compounds slowly but surely make their way into our systems as well. If you want to become more mindful of what you are eating and wish to start eating healthily, start growing vegetables and fruits at home. With a little extra effort, you can develop and maintain better eating habits.

Also, your relationship with food improves for the better when you are aware of where it comes from. When you are aware of all the effort that went into growing the fresh ingredients you cook with, you'll be more grateful for them. A combination of these factors promotes healthier eating habits.

Improves Self-Esteem

Self-esteem is incredibly important, but forgetting about it is also equally easy. A good thing about practicing any activity is that it makes you feel better about yourself. If you have never tried your hand at gardening, chances are you might be worried that you will not be good at it. However, when the seeds turn into saplings and then into healthy plants, you will feel better about yourself. In a way, gardening can help improve your self-esteem (Thompson, 2018). There are a lot of activities involved in tending to a garden. Regardless of its size, you will need to take care of it. From sowing seeds to watering them, fertilizing them, and weeding regularly, you have a lot to do. When you complete each task effectively and efficiently, it improves your self-confidence and self-esteem—and this is not just restricted to the garden, but it trickles into other aspects of your life as well.

Burns Calories

Previously, it was mentioned that gardening is believed to be a physical activity of varying intensity. If you have a larger garden, this is quite true. Doing light yardwork or even working in your garden is believed to help burn up to 330 calories per hour. This is quite a high calorie burn count. Participating regularly in gardening can reduce your body mass index, or BMI (Zick et al., 2013). In this study, the BMI of those who participated in community gardening programs was compared with the one who did not. It was noticed that those who took up gardening regularly had a lower BMI than their counterparts. So, if you want to shed those extra pounds and keep them away, start gardening immediately!

Strengthens Your Bones

A common age-related problem is a reduction in the strength and density of the bones, which become brittle as you age. The levels of vitamin D also reduce with age. This is one of the most important vitamins when it comes to maintaining the strength and integrity of the skeletal framework in the human body. In one of the previous points, it was mentioned that spending time outdoors gives your body the vitamin D it needs. The more time you spend outdoors soaking up the sunrays, the more vitamin D you are getting. This vitamin is also needed for better absorption of calcium in the body. A combination of these factors ensures your bones do not become weak or brittle. Also, the soft and warm rays of the sun early in the morning are helpful.

Reduces Blood Pressure

High blood pressure, or hypertension, is a risk factor for several cardiovascular disorders. Hypertension by itself is a problematic condition. That said, managing and fighting it is perfectly possible. You can not only reduce the risk of high blood pressure, but stabilize it as well, if you start gardening regularly. Thus, you can actually regulate your blood pressure. Are you wondering how this is even possible? Well, gardening helps reduce your anxiety and stress levels. It also improves your overall mood and enhances your physical health. When you feel better physically and mentally, stress reduces. Also, stress is a leading cause of high blood pressure. By regulating this, you can regulate your blood pressure, too. When the blood pressure reduces, stress on the arteries also reduces. This, in turn, improves your cardiovascular health.

Relieves Chronic Pain

Stiffness of the joints or muscle pain can make incredibly simple movements extremely painful. Chronic pain usually exists in the joints, and this results in joint stiffness. This, in turn, means those experiencing joint stiffness cannot move them much—which further worsens their stiffness and causes more pain. It is a vicious cycle that is quite easy to get stuck in. A simple way to relieve chronic pain is by gardening regularly. When you plant, water, and maintain your garden, you are required to perform simple movements. This is also a low-intensity exercise that does not stress your muscles or joints any further.

Gardening also reduces the pain you are experiencing by focusing on your mental well-being. Whenever you exercise or engage in an activity, feel-good hormones known as endorphins are released into the bloodstream. Endorphins increase your body's pain tolerance and make it easier to deal with any pain you experience. Gardening continuously improves your mood and reduces stress. A combination of the physical and mental factors mentioned until now helps relieve chronic pain.

Better Sleep at Night

Do you usually struggle to fall asleep or stay asleep at night? Well, this is a sign that you need to tire your body physically and mentally. A pleasant side effect of wearing yourself out is your ability to sleep at night. It also reduces any stress you are experiencing. A combination of these factors makes it easier to fall asleep—and the benefits of good quality sleep cannot be overlooked. From regulating stress to promoting a better mood, it does a lot. Sleep is also needed to promote your body's metabolism. Have you ever noticed that you feel better, more energetic, and more motivated after a good night's rest? If you make a habit of getting a good night's sleep every night, you can wake up refreshed and ready to take on the challenges of the day. By gardening daily, you can achieve this objective.

Saves Money

Gardening not only offers health benefits—it is good for your bank balance, too. Growing vegetables for your consumption automatically reduces your food bill. Even a small garden can produce a surprising quantity of vegetables. Whether it be herbs or vegetables you are harvesting, it will certainly reduce your food bill. If you want to eat healthier, you'll need to purchase wholesome vegetables and other ingredients—and these can be expensive. Even if you manage to grow a little bit of what you eat daily at home, the money spent will be reduced. Starting the garden is extremely simple, and the expenses involved are nominal. For instance, fertilizers can be fashioned out of the scraps from your kitchen—rainwater can even be harvested and used to water the plants. With a little extra effort, you can significantly reduce your grocery bills.

Promotes Good Bacteria

An unexpected health benefit of gardening is that it exposes you to a variety of good bacteria. Chances are, you imagine disease-causing pathogens the minute you hear the word bacteria. However, certain strains of bacteria are helpful. Some strains of bacteria found in garden soil stimulate the release of serotonin in your brain (Lowry et al., 2007). This is a feel-good chemical that improves immune functioning and elevates mental health. This hypothesis is known as the hygiene hypothesis, and refers to a connection between immune functioning and the brain. Since gardening improves them simultaneously, your overall sense of well-being will improve.

Encourages Creativity

Gardening is not just a physical activity, but it engages your mental muscles as well. A lot of planning is involved in this seemingly simple activity. Yes, you read it right. Gardening is not just something you can do on a whim. Instead, it requires careful consideration. From deciding where you want to grow the plants to their requirements, along with a combination of plants you want to grow, planning is needed. With a little planning, the overall health of your garden will improve. It also ensures you have a regular supply of fresh vegetables and other produce. If you have a small space at your disposal, you'll need to figure out the plants that will grow better together to maximize the output obtained. This involves creativity. If you are new to gardening, it means you will be learning a few new skills. Weeding, watering, and even growing plants are all skills you need to learn. With practice and conscious effort, you can become better at it. It essentially means you are engaging your creative muscles while gardening.

Practicing Mindfulness

Mindfulness is a simple act of staying present only in the moment, and nothing else. Most of us are constantly overwhelmed by thoughts about the future or the past. Due to this, we forget about the moment available right now—and that is the present. Unless you are 100% focused on the moment you have right now, you cannot make the most of your life or the opportunities available. You can achieve this state of mindfulness by gardening. Whatever the activity involved, you need to be fully focused on it. Whether it is planting in the right place, monitoring the growth of your plants, or weeding the garden regularly, you need to be focused on whatever you are doing. Tending to your garden ensures that you are focusing on only one activity at a time. This, in turn, makes it easier to practice mindfulness. It also ensures you're in a calmer and more balanced state of mind. This will trickle into all the other activities you perform as well. Mindfulness is known to reduce stress, improve concentration, and support problem-solving abilities. These are all benefits that come in handy in all aspects of your life, not just your garden.

Promotes Mental Clarity

There is a lot of information you must remember when it comes to gardening. The bigger the garden, the more information you will need to remember. In a way, doing all this exercises your mental muscles. As with any other muscle, the more you exercise your brain, the stronger it gets. This automatically translates to better memory and cognitive functioning. There are different tasks you need to remember and take note of while gardening (Hall & Knuth, 2019). From remembering where certain plants are planted, their needs and optimal planting schedule, and the best time to harvest, your mental muscles are engaged. The more parts of the brain used, the better your cognitive functioning. This, in turn, increases mental clarity. All of this coupled with the stress-busting benefits offered by gardening promotes mental strength and clarity.

Facilitates Family Bonding

If you are looking to create more opportunities to spend time with your family, consider gardening since it can become a family-bonding exercise. In today's digital world, most families are spending most of their time in front of blue screens and devices. Whether it is cell phones, tablets, video games, computers, laptops, or any other device—we are stuck staring at screens. You get an opportunity to cut down on screen time by gardening. You can get your family members involved in gardening, too.

For instance, allocate different tasks to the members of your household. From weeding, watering, mulching, or even harvesting—different members can perform their designated tasks. This gives you a chance to bond. If you have children at home, you can get them interested in this activity from a young age. It will make them more mindful of the food they eat, develop a healthier relationship with food in general, and teach them responsibility as well. When you get your entire family involved in gardening, even for a couple of hours per week, it gives you a chance to bond and catch up with each other. Another benefit of gardening is that you can find an activity associated with it for any age group.

Makes You Responsible

A commonly overlooked benefit of gardening is that it is a fun and stress-free way to become more responsible. For instance, forgetting to remove the weeds will quickly spoil any garden. Similarly, not watering the plants will result in wilting. You not only have a lot of tasks to complete, but should perform them in a timely fashion. This, in turn, automatically increases your sense of responsibility. After all, your garden depends on you. Your plants depend on you for their daily requirements—from obtaining water to fertilizers, they need your active involvement to thrive and flourish. Keeping the garden healthy results in a good harvest. Gardening gives you a chance to see your efforts result in gains. This by itself is quite fulfilling. Also, if you get children involved in gardening from a young age, you are teaching them the importance of responsibility, too.

Gives a Sense of Purpose

Gardening also gives you a sense of purpose. When you are responsible for taking care of something, it teaches accountability. Nurturing seeds into plants and seeing the results of your efforts is extremely satisfying. Over time, it increases your self-esteem and confidence while making you more responsible. These benefits aren't restricted to just your garden and plants. They also start influencing other aspects of your life. All this coupled with mindfulness automatically ensures you are doing your best. A combination of these factors increases your feel-good quotient. This gives you a sense of purpose and calmness.

So gardening is not just a hobby or a pastime. Instead, it offers a variety of physical, mental, and emotional health benefits. Chances are you are eager to get started with gardening. By learning all the different bits of information discussed in the subsequent chapters, you can start your garden at home and enjoy all the benefits discussed in this chapter!

Chapter 2:

Garden Ideas

From promoting clean eating to the money-saving benefit it offers, there is a lot you gain by starting the ever-increasing art of gardening. It also shows you exactly where the food you eat comes from. No wonder gardening has become popular again. It's not just the versatility of the benefits gardening offers, but there are also different types of gardens to choose from as well. Regardless of the space available, you'll find at least one type of garden idea that fits your needs and requirements. In this section, let's look at all the different ideas you can use to start and maintain a vegetable garden at home.

In-Soil Garden

An in-soil garden is the first thing that pops into your head when you visualize what a garden looks like. This is the basic and conventional type of garden anyone can opt for. As the name suggests, you will be growing plants in the soil. Whether it is an open space in front of your home or in your backyard, you can grow whatever you want in the soil. You simply need to clear out a specific portion of the space available and create the right conditions for the plants you wish to grow. This is about it.

Raised Beds

Raised bed gardens are steadily gaining popularity these days because of their aesthetic appeal. In this technique, you will essentially be using raised beds for growing vegetable plants of your choice, instead of directly planting them in soil. It has a clean aesthetic appeal without compromising functionality. Different vegetables can be grown in individual plant beds. For instance, leafy vegetables can be grown in one raised bed, while the other bed can be used for root vegetables. This helps separate the vegetables into different planters and focuses on the individual needs of the plants you wish to grow.

Pots and Containers

Growing vegetables at home is inexpensive. You don't need plenty of space—or even lots of money—to grow them. Simple pots and planters are ideal to do this. Even containers can be fashioned into homes for your beloved plants. A wonderful thing about opting for pots and containers is that you can even fashion the items available in your home to do this. It is a popular rustic trend that is extremely inexpensive, and can instantly elevate any of your surroundings. Even a mismatched collection of pots will come in handy for this. Depending on the size of the pots or containers you decide to use, the plants you can grow will differ.

Using Dividers

If you have small to medium sized lawns, then you can use a large bed with dividers. Using dividers also comes in handy for anyone who wants a fairly compact garden that facilitates the growth of a variety of vegetables. Instead of having multiple vegetable beds, this is a perfectly effective alternative. It does not require much space or effort. Creating dividers is not only inexpensive, but quite simple as well. You can use them to differentiate between the different plants you wish to grow. You can either purchase them from hardware stores, or even make them at home using wooden planks or timber. The plants essentially need to be set out to create a grid, and can be either secured with screws, nails, glue, or garden string. Once you have created the dividers, different boxes on the grid can be used for different plants.

Hanging Planters

Another excellent space-saving solution available at your disposal is to opt for hanging planters. You can either opt for multiple hanging planters or a few, depending on your requirements. This also depends on the space available. By using hanging planters, you can easily separate the vegetables you wish to grow. It also makes your life easier as a gardener, because you can cater to the varying needs of the plants without any worries. Planters can become heavy when filled. Therefore, opting for metal frames is the best option available in terms of strength as well as stability. The planters can be built from plastic, metal, or even wood. Depending on the kind of aesthetic you have in mind or the money you wish to spend, the options available will differ.

Gardening Boxes

One of the best options for urban gardeners and city dwellers is to opt for a big container box. A vegetable garden in the box is not only easy to maintain, but also doesn't require much space. The only space it will take up is the space needed to accommodate the box. The container size can be as big or small as you desire. You can place it on a balcony, terrace, outdoors in a small garden, or even on the windowsill. Depending on the space available, opt for a box accordingly. You might not be able to grow a variety of plants, but you can grow a couple of varieties easily. You can even maintain this garden throughout the year and indoors by using grow lights.

Planter Boxes

These types of boxes are an amazing way to enhance the overall aesthetics of your home. It's also an efficient means to create a garden within a small space. Whether it be vegetables, herbs, or even flowers—these boxes can be easily used. All you need to do is find some space that will fit the planter box of your choice. Whether it is the fire escape, deck, balcony, or patio, these boxes can pretty much go anywhere. Once you have the boxes ready, you simply need to fill them with the desired gardening soil and start planting.

Tiered Garden

If you have plenty of vertical space available at your disposal, it is time to make the most of it by creating a tiered garden. This essentially refers to a design wherein one or more retaining walls are used to create two or more levels that can be used to grow the plants of your choice. This is especially a good idea if your house is built on a hill, or if there is more vertical space than horizontal available. The best way to go about creating a tiered garden is by hiring the services of a professional who can do it. If you want to do it yourself, that is an option too—but it is more of an advanced DIY project that requires heavy equipment.

Planting Table

If you want a space-saving solution or want to reduce the physical effort involved in tending to the garden, then opt for a planting table. It essentially involves a raised box bed to grow plants. The garden itself looks like it's set on a tabletop. These tables are not difficult to construct, and can be done so in less than $50 and a couple of hours. You can also purchase a ready-made one. Once the raised garden bed table is ready, you'll need to fill it with the required soil or planting medium and select a specific irrigation system. Once all these things are taken care of and the bed is exposed to sufficient sunlight, start planting!

Roof Garden

If you don't have much space in your home but have a terrace or a rooftop, you can use it to create a garden. These types of gardens are ideal, because they expose your plants to sufficient sunlight. Before you decide to convert any portion of your roof or terrace into a garden, identify which part you desire to use. The plants you opt for must be hardy enough to withstand harsh weather conditions, especially sun and rain. Another benefit of turning your terrace into a garden is that it reduces the temperature within the house. From flowering plants to vegetables, you can grow anything you desire on the roof.

Balcony Garden

If you have a small balcony or live in an apartment with one, turn it into a gardening space. The first thing you must do is select plants that are ideal to be grown on your balcony depending on the sun, shade, and wind the said spot receives. In an enclosed balcony, the climatic conditions are usually controlled. Ensure that the plants you select are not cramped on the balcony. With a little extra planning and preparation, your balcony can turn into an aesthetically pleasing spot.

Green Wall

A green wall is essentially a vertical structure used to grow plants, and is becoming quite a popular trend these days. Whether it is indoors or outdoors, a freestanding green wall can be installed anywhere—it can also be attached to a wall. When you grow vegetation on or against a vertical surface, it is a green wall—they are quite similar to a vertical garden.

Vertical Garden

Who says a garden needs to be horizontal or in the soil? These days, vertical gardens have become all the rage. As the name suggests, you'll be using the vertical space available if you don't have much horizontal space at your disposal. Regardless of whether it is the balcony of your apartment or a wall, you can use it to create a garden. This is quite a beneficial type of garden, but it does require plenty of planning and maintenance. Planters can be used for meticulously growing any plant of your choice. Whether it's ornamental or vegetable plants, you can pretty much grow anything you desire. By simply installing containers on a wall or fence, you can start growing fresh produce.

Windowsill Garden

If you have any space on your windowsill, turn it into a garden. You can use planter boxes or any other containers to grow plants on your windowsill itself. If the window faces the sun, then this becomes an ideal spot to grow a variety of vegetable plants, as well as herbs. Also, this is an inexpensive option and is aesthetically pleasing, too.

Grow Bags

A grow bag is exactly what the name suggests. It is a planter that can be filled with growing medium and used as a pot to grow plants. Grow bags are more forgiving when compared to terracotta pots, especially if you forget to water the plants in the garden. They usually come with handles that can be used to move the plants toward sunlight or shade depending on their growing requirements. If you are running a little low on storage space, you can use these grow bags for additional storage and not just to grow plants.

Hydroponic Garden

Gardening is no longer restricted to plants that are grown in soil. Yes, you read it right. A popular technique to grow plants these days is known as hydroponic gardening. This is not a new technique, but has been around for centuries. However, it is only recently that this technique has been gaining popularity again. This is a method of growing plants without using any soil. You can use it to grow a variety of plants ranging from fruits to vegetables, and even herbs. These gardens can be created both indoors as well as outdoors, depending on the space requirement. A soilless medium is used for growing plants in water.

Greenhouse Garden

If you want to grow vegetables or fruits irrespective of the weather conditions including the temperature and the season, opt for a greenhouse. They create the ideal growing conditions for any plants you wish to grow, because you have complete control over regulating the factors involved. However, the initial cost of setting up a greenhouse is quite high. Also, it is an extremely time-consuming process. These gardens are ideal for gardening experts. You will need a large backyard or a farm to set up a greenhouse. This isn't ideal for small spaces, because it can make them look cramped. That said, these days you have an option to set up a mini greenhouse too, provided you have the required space available.

Regardless of the gardening idea that appeals to you, growing vegetables at home is simple. Once you commit to this process, you can reap the incredible benefits it offers. You'll be introduced to all the other aspects of starting your garden at home in the subsequent chapters. You can use that information and the ideas given in this chapter to create a garden that meets your needs and requirements.

Chapter 3:

Considerations Before Getting

Started

When most people think about growing vegetables at home, they usually consider the plants they want to grow or how the garden will look in general. However, there is so much more to designing a vegetable garden than just this. For instance, certain plants grow well together while others don't. Some vegetables produce substances that inhibit the growth of other plants around them. Similarly, if tall plants are grown next to short ones, the former can reduce the latter's sun exposure. Plants that belong to the same family also attract certain types of pests, and having a plan to deal with them is needed. The good news is that the growing requirements of most vegetable plants are pretty much the same. In this section, you'll be introduced to different factors you must take into consideration before starting a vegetable garden.

Sun and Shade

Environmental factors play a significant role in the growth of the plants you wish to add to your garden. The first thing you need to do is research the plants that are ideal for the local environment of the area you reside in. Whether it is the climatic conditions or the soil type, these are crucial factors that help determine the best plants for your garden.

Most vegetable plants require plenty of exposure to sunlight. They need around 6-8 hours of direct sunlight daily for their growth. On the other hand, leafy green vegetables require less sun, and some prefer to grow in colder weather—such as lettuce. Paying attention to the sunlight requirements of the plants is needed for selecting an ideal spot to start the vegetable garden—this also gives you better insight into selecting the ideal season to start growing.

Along the same lines, you should also consider the amount of shade the plants you wish to grow require. Doing this is needed to ensure the plants in your garden are not subjected to undue stress or heat. For instance, when you opt for shade-loving plants, the ideal location would be anywhere where there's plenty of shade—such as under fully grown trees.

Ease of Access

Paying attention to ease of access is one factor most gardeners overlook. This is incredibly important, however, because it determines the maintenance requirements of the plants. Ideally, opt for a location that is close to a water source if you wish to grow vegetables. Most vegetable plants must be watered regularly. An erratic watering pattern means the plants might wither and die, become prone to pests, or even struggle to flower and produce vegetables. To ensure all this doesn't happen, paying attention to the accessibility of the garden is needed.

You must also take into consideration how easily you can cater to the maintenance requirements of the vegetable garden. Whether it is mulching, weeding, amending the soil, or even watering—all these tasks require manual effort. If you cannot easily access the plants, then doing these things becomes incredibly difficult. Watering the plants becomes tricky if they are far from a watering source. For instance, if the raised beds are too wide or high, then reaching the plants becomes unnecessarily tricky.

Soil Conditions

One of the most important factors in any garden is the soil. Most vegetable plants spend their entire growing season producing flowers and fruits. Such plants are heavy feeders, and require soil rich in nutrients needed for their growth. The nutrients present in the soil also determine the ability of the plants to fight diseases and pests. One of the most basic requirements for growing vegetable plants is to ensure the soil is rich in organic matter. Whether it is organic manure or compost, adding it during spring or fall ensures the soil is ideal for growing the vegetables you want. Before you decide to start a garden using the existing soil, ensure that you get it tested. The test results will help determine if the soil has to be amended. Similarly, it will also show whether the soil pH must be adjusted to fit the growing requirements of the plants.

Consider the drainage and runoff, too, while selecting the soil for your vegetable garden. This matters a lot because some plants cannot grow in wet soil. If the soil is too heavy in texture, it needs to be amended accordingly to facilitate the growth of the plants. Paying attention to the soil's ability to retain water also ensures the nutrients present in it are not being washed away while watering the plants.

You will learn more about the different types of soil and how to create the ideal conditions for vegetable plants in the subsequent chapters. For now, let's get back to other factors that must be considered before starting a garden.

Maintenance

Maintaining and tending to the plants in your garden is needed. It's not just about sowing the seeds and waiting for them to develop into established plants. You must take into consideration their watering requirements as well. Along with this, you must also focus on regularly amending the soil so that the plants have the nutrition needed. Some vegetable plants also have specific growing requirements and need to be pruned occasionally. This not only ensures the plants' growth in a specific state, but prevents them from overtaking your garden as well. Taking these factors into consideration is needed, because it automatically determines the amount of time you will have to spend in the garden taking care of the plants. Depending on your needs and requirements, or the time you can allocate tending to the garden, you can opt for plants that require low maintenance or don't need much work.

Fencing

One aspect of a vegetable garden that is commonly overlooked is fencing. A fence might not look pretty, but it is needed to ensure the health of your plants. After all, your time and energy go toward taking care of these plants. It is surprising how quickly pests, critters, and animals can eat through all your efforts. Protecting your vegetable garden without a fence can become an endless uphill battle. Consider fencing both above and below the garden. Some animals and critters burrow under the surface and can pop up anywhere.

Plant Size

Plants come in a variety of shapes and sizes. Therefore, an important consideration you must pay attention to before selecting plants is to determine how big they will be upon maturation. This is needed to determine the area they will require to grow. For instance, vines require trellises or any other means of vertical support to grow properly. Some can also grow on the ground, but you must pay attention to the area they will need if you don't want your garden to be overrun by a single variety.

Tools Needed

Whenever you start a new activity, you need the right set of tools and equipment to do it properly—gardening is no different. There are two important stages you must focus on when it comes to a vegetable garden. The first stage is preparing the garden, and the second is taking care of the plants. Some basic tools you will need to create the garden include a trowel, tiller, and so on. Similarly, to take care of the plants, you'll need some type of irrigation system, twines and stakes, pruners, and so on. You will learn more about the basic tools every gardener requires in the subsequent chapters.

Chapter 4:

Pay Attention to the Soil

If you want to start your own vegetable garden at home, you'll need to make different decisions. You'll need to design a layout, opt for a specific type of garden, select the type of vegetables you want to grow, the tools you will need, and so on. However, before you spend any time thinking about all these things, a basic choice you need to make is about the type of soil you want to use. This decision will not only depend on the existing soil in your garden, but also on the vegetables you want to grow.

Before getting into more details, it is important to understand what soil means. It is a broad term used differently by different individuals. Usually, soil refers to an unconsolidated loose material that includes rock and covers the outer mantle of the earth's surface. Sand, lake clay, silt deposits, and so on are just a few types of terrains. When it comes to gardening, soil usually refers to the top 40 cm of the ground in which the seeds will be sowed and vegetables will be harvested. Speaking from a scientific perspective, the 1.5-2 m beneath the surface is known as soil.

When it comes to gardening, you will need to focus on topsoil. This is the crumbly material on the surface that leaves your fingers looking dirty when you touch it. It includes different particles of minerals, small stones, clay, sands, and even organic material from the compost plants.

Different Types of Soil

In this section, we will look at the most common types of soils.

Sandy Soil

Sandy soil is usually dry, light, and warm. When compared to the other types of soil, it has fewer nutrients and is usually more acidic. If you want to increase the acidity of garden soil, mixing it with sandy soil fixes the situation immediately. This is ideal for any garden where you require quick drainage of water. Since the soil is light and dry, it tends to warm up rather quickly during summer and spring. Adding compost or any other organic matter will improve the nutrient profile of sandy soil, especially in terms of water retention. This type of soil is the most prone to erosion, especially during rainfall. Because it tends to warm up quickly, it doesn't hold many nutrients. This is a relatively easy soil to cultivate, but drains and dries out quickly. Sandy soil is usually ideal for growing vegetables such as potatoes, zucchini, and carrots.

Clay Soil

Clay soil is the exact opposite of sandy soil. It's also known as heavy soil. It is usually rich in fine clay particles that account for more than 30% of its total volume. This soil can be hard to manage and even sticky to touch, but is extremely fertile. It is ideal for growing different types of vegetables, as well as grains. As the soil becomes dry or wet, the clay particles in it shrink or swell, respectively. Walking on such soil, or even digging into it, can easily damage and compress it. Clay soil also takes longer to warm up during the summer months and spring when compared to sandy soil. In a way, this soil is capable of handling drought better when compared to the other variants discussed here. This soil doesn't offer good water drainage and must be infused with compost and other organic matter to maintain its structure and drainage. It is usually hard and rocky when dry, and turns lumpy and sticky when moist. Ornamental plants, along with shrubs and perennials, thrive in clay soil.

Loam Soil

Loam soil is believed to be the ideal gardening soil for growing a variety of vegetables. This soil is usually a mixture of clay, silt, and sand in equal proportions. It is fine-textured soil, and is generally damp to the touch. Since it is usually acidic as well, you must keep infusing it with organic matter regularly to maintain an ideal nutrient profile and structure. This is the perfect soil for gardens and potted plants. This easy to cultivate soil warms up but doesn't become too hot during summers, making it ideal for an outdoor garden.

Silt Soil

As the name suggests, this type of soil is predominantly made of silt, including silt loam and sandy silt loam. It usually has a silky texture. Such soils are formed from river, marine, and glacial deposits from millennia ago deposited by wind and other environmental factors. These soils are highly fertile due to their excellent water capacity. This soil is relatively easy to cultivate, making it ideal for gardening. It has a soapy and soft texture. Silty soil is ideal for a variety of vegetables and fruit plants, along with perennials, climbers, and shrubs.

Peat Soil

These soils are rich in organic material. Peat soils are the result of decomposed plant materials that were compressed for years in anaerobic and watery conditions. These soils are usually found in bogs, and account for up to 3% of the earth's surface. Due to the anaerobic conditions in which peat soils have formed, the decomposition by microorganisms is also slowed down. This results in the accumulation of high levels of carbon dioxide. Here's a fun fact about peat soils— their ability to absorb carbon dioxide makes them an ideal player in tackling climate change! Peaty soil is ideal for legumes, root vegetables, and leafy greens—along with a variety of shrubs.

Chalky Soil

Chalky soils are also known as lime-rich soils. They are predominantly alkaline, making them a rather challenging medium for home gardens. Such soils are usually stony and shallow. Due to this, any organic materials added to improve its quality—such as compost—are decomposed extremely quickly. This, in turn, makes it challenging to maintain its nutrient profile and fertility. Opting for plants that thrive in alkaline soil is your best bet if you are starting with chalky soil. Adding humus to it is an excellent way to improve its workability. These soils are stonier and grainier than the other types discussed above. Ideal vegetables to grow in it include cabbage, corn, beets, and spinach.

Selecting the Right Soil

Since soil is the foundation for any plants you want to grow, selecting the right soil is a crucial decision. The three considerations you can use to select ideal gardening soil are as follows:

- The type of soil you opt for must be in accordance with the variety of plants you desire to grow in the garden. For instance, a vegetable garden usually requires soil that is moist and loose. This ensures the roots have sufficient flexibility to expand and grow, while also obtaining the required nutrients from the soil.

- Ensure that you do not ignore the quality of the soil. If the soil is too sandy or clayey, then it is not ideal for growing most plants. Usually, garden soil is a mixture of different types of soils that are ideal for optimal plant growth. So, ensure that you carefully identify the type of soil available in your garden by using the information given above. After this, amendments can be made to ensure the soil is of the right quality by following the suggestions given in the next section.

- Where you decide to grow is also an important factor when deciding the type of soil you will need. For instance, plants that are growing in pots and containers will require soil that is more nutrient-dense than ones directly sown in the ground. Spending some time and investing in good quality soil is a simple, yet effective, means to ensure that your garden thrives and that all your plants are healthy.

How to Improve Soil Quality

The quality of soil plays a crucial role in ensuring plant growth. If you want vigorous plants that are resistant to diseases and pests and yield a good harvest, soil quality matters. Regardless of whether you are gardening in native topsoil or starting with fresh soil, improving it is a continuous process. Soil is an amalgamation of different arts, and it is alive. It includes minerals, water, microorganisms, and even organic matter. Ensuring there is a balance between all these aspects of the soil is needed for a healthy garden. Since soil is alive, tending to it is needed. You cannot have a healthy garden without healthy garden soil.

Previously, you were introduced to different types of soil. Regardless of the soil type, ensure it is fertile enough to support the plants you wish to grow. It should also be loose enough to promote the growth of roots, air circulation, and drainage. Healthy soil includes different minerals, nutrients, and organic matter—the latter, organic matter, is crucial because it strengthens the nutrition profile of the soil and creates a biodiverse subculture within it that is needed for plant life.

No conversation about improving the quality of soil is complete without discussing the importance of organic matter. Organic matter improves the structure of the soil, promotes soil buffering, and supplies plants with desired nutrients. As mentioned, different microorganisms are present in the soil. These organisms are constantly working on breaking down the organic matter present within and converting it into humus, which is a nutrient-rich substance.

The microorganisms feed on the soil, and organic matter starts tunneling in the dirt and creates air pockets. This, in turn, promotes aeration of the soil and better drainage. If the soil is heavy or clayey, it tends to compact easily—this increases the risk of waterlogging. It also prevents the essential circulation of air, water, and nutrients to the roots. By adding organic matter to such soil, its structure improves.

On the other hand, certain types of soil are extremely light and loose. It doesn't have sufficient structure to ensure nutrients and water are adequately supplied to the roots. In such instances, adding organic matter helps hold the soil together and improves its ability to retain nutrients as well as moisture.

Now, let's look at some simple ways in which you can improve the quality of garden soil.

Using Compost

The best and most effective means to improve the quality of garden soil is to add compost—this essentially refers to decomposed organic matter. When compost is added to the soil, it not only improves its structure, but also improves its ability to retain nutrients as well. It also feeds the soil with essential nutrients needed for plant growth. Adding compost is known to promote better drainage and nutrient absorption, and keeps the soil aerated. This, in turn, improves root health and growth. Compost is also needed for maintaining a neutral pH that further enhances plant health. As mentioned, there are different microorganisms present in the soil. Compost also feeds the essential microbes and supports their life. The microbial action within soil promotes aeration and drainage. These microbes also leave their casings behind, which in turn increases soil fertility.

Start With a Soil Test

One thing you must understand is that improving the quality of the soil is a continuous process—it's not something you can do once and forget about. You will need to keep renewing the nutrient profile of the soil, because the nutrients present in it will be utilized by the plants you are growing. Every couple of years, a soil test must be conducted to determine the additional nutrients it requires to support and sustain plant growth and production. These days, DIY soil testing kits are available, and you can use them to test the quality of the soil. On the other hand, you can also send a soil sample to your local county office to obtain a better and more in-depth analysis.

Whenever you conduct a soil test, it gives you basic information, including the pH level and nutrient profile. It also offers information about the nutrients present in it and their levels. The most common nutrient levels you can obtain from a soil test include potassium, copper, sulfur, calcium, phosphorus, and magnesium. The soil test also helps determine the level of organic matter present in it, along with lead content. This information comes in handy when you need to adjust the levels of nutrients in it.

Mulching Helps

If you want the garden soil to be healthy and wish to grow strong plants, mulching cannot be overlooked. It helps stimulate essential growing conditions that are needed for plant growth. Mulching ensures that the soil can retain moisture, regulates its temperature, and prevents the growth of weeds. As the mulch starts decomposing, it automatically increases the organic matter content in the garden soil. This, in turn, improves its fertility.

Tackle Soil Compaction

If the soil is too hard or compacted, it reduces aeration and prevents the plant roots from seeking water and nutrients from the soil. When left unchecked, ultimately the soil becomes dry and barren. Remember, plants will dehydrate and starve if their roots cannot spread out and obtain the nutrients and water needed for their growth. Microbiological activity that's needed for the conversion of organic matter into essential minerals and nutrients is also hampered due to soil compaction. Clay soils are susceptible to this, especially during winters. If the soil is too wet, compaction is possible. If you start walking on the soil, this results in compaction as well. As a rule of thumb, avoid walking on the soil where you are growing plants. If you are opting for a raised garden bed, ensure that there is a sufficient place in between the beds for easy access. This is one of the reasons why you must always plan ahead before starting a garden at home.

Rotate Crops

You can prevent the depletion of soil nutrients and disrupt cycles of diseases and pests by opting for crop rotation. If you grow the same type of plants in the same spot repeatedly, the harvest will be reduced. You might have a bountiful harvest during the first growing season, but it will not be the same during the subsequent ones. For instance, the nematodes and fungi responsible for scaly patches of skin on potatoes increase in the soil within no time during a single growing season. By the end of the season, you might have a good harvest; but if you plant potatoes in the same location again, the disease-causing organism's leftover in the soil from the previous season will destroy the subsequent batch. These organisms will die if they do not have access to their preferred crop. So, crop rotation works.

A good rule you can follow when it comes to garden crops is the three-year rule. It means vegetable plants belonging to the same family must not be grown in the same place for three consecutive years. This gives the soil sufficient time to recover and ensures there are no disease-causing pathogens in it. For instance, if you are growing any crops that require plenty of nitrogen, growing legumes, or any other nitrogen-producing crops, then this is a good idea. If you are growing a specific vegetable in a spot this year, don't grow the same crop there until three years are up.

Using Cover Crops

Growing cover crops offers dual benefits to any garden. If you plant a row of cover crops close to the end of the growing season, it helps improve the health of the soil. The first benefit is it ensures that the soil (especially the fertile topsoil) is not eroded by environmental factors such as snowmelt, high-speed winds, or even heavy rainfall. The second benefit is it ensures the soil doesn't compress, and that weeds do not crop up in between the growing seasons. Ideal cover crops include kale, radish, legumes, clover, and peas.

Aged Animal Manure

Apart from adding compost and mulching, you can also add aged animal manure to improve the overall health and fertility of your garden soil. Fresh animal manure is usually too hot, and results in damaging the plants. It also contains pathogens that are harmful to human consumption. Ensure that the manure used is aged for at least a couple of months to up to a year before adding it to the garden soil. Manure made of goat, sheep, chicken, horse, rabbit, cow, and even bat droppings, is usually rich in a variety of nutrients. Using this ensures the desirable nutrients are incorporated into the garden soil. It also improves the soil structure. A word of caution while using animal manure is to ensure that it is not contaminated with homicide or pesticides. Once these elements enter the garden soil, you cannot reverse it, and they can result in herbicide injury if you aren't careful. Therefore, ensure that the animal manure you are purchasing is not just aged, but also doesn't contain any herbicides or pesticides either. Remember, what you feed the plants will ultimately make its way into your body. So, be careful!

Following the different suggestions given in this section is not a one-time process. Instead, it is a continuous process and if you stick to it, you'll have a thriving garden on your hands. This, in turn, results in better harvests.

Chapter 5:

Nutrition Requirements

Chances are you think about a diet upon hearing the words nutrition requirements. From ensuring your body gets sufficient iron and calcium, to other antioxidants, vitamins, minerals, and fiber—there is a lot to consider. Similarly, you must also carefully consider whether your plants are getting their required nutrition or not. Even a newcomer gardener knows that plants require fertilizer. Well, do you know why they need it and in what ratio? Learning about the nutrition requirements of the plants and how to cater to them is needed to ensure your garden is healthy. Depending on the stage of growth, the nutrition requirements of plants differ. So, let's learn more about all this!

Nutrients That Plants Need

When it comes to nutrients, soil and plant health aren't too different. So, what do your garden companions require to stay healthy? How can you cater to their needs? In this section, you will learn about the most common nutrients that plants require. Learning about this also makes it easier to find the desirable fertilizers, and choose the right one for your plants.

Nitrogen

The benefits associated with nitrogen for plants are the same as those associated with proteins in humans. Even the protein you consume produces nitrogen that the body uses for its growth. Similarly, nitrogen acts as a building block for plant growth and health. Whether it is the health and growth of the stalk, its immunity, or the ability to bear fruits—plants need sufficient nitrogen. They also need this essential nutrient for fruit development. The green coloring of plants is due to a pigment known as chlorophyll, and nitrogen is needed for its production.

Phosphorus

Phosphorus gives plants the strength needed to withstand any environmental stress or harsh weather conditions, especially in winter. This nutrient also strengthens the health of the root systems, promotes the creation of seeds, and increases their resistance to several diseases. Plants also require plenty of phosphorus during the flowering stages. It helps strengthen their tissues and increases the flavor profile of vegetables and other edible plants.

Potassium

Potassium is needed for the early growth of plants. Their ability to retain water is also influenced by this nutrient. Plants also require potassium for the health of the roots and the production of seeds. It is also known as potash, and increases its ability to withstand extreme temperatures. When plants have sufficient potassium, it prevents excess absorption of minerals such as calcium and magnesium.

Calcium

Calcium is needed for the growth and development of the cell walls of plants. This, in turn, reduces their susceptibility to diseases and gives them the strength to fight disease-causing pathogens. It also supports their metabolism and makes it easier to absorb nitrogen. Calcium also neutralizes any acidity present within and in the surrounding soil of a plant to improve its overall health.

Magnesium

The plant's ability to utilize and absorb phosphorus and the production of chlorophyll increase when they have sufficient magnesium. Chlorophyll is the green pigment that enables the absorption of carbon dioxide. When plants don't have sufficient magnesium, they develop an anemic look and have poor coloring as well.

Sulfur

Plants require sulfur to fight diseases and make them disease resistant, and it also contributes to the growth as well as the formation of seeds. Plants also need sulfur to produce essential amino acids, vitamins, and enzymes needed for their overall growth.

A Balanced Diet for Plants

Chances are all the nutrients that were mentioned until now sound quite familiar to you. It is because these nutrients are not solely important for plants, but for humans as well. Just like us, even our garden companions require nutrition in the right doses from different sources. Understanding the amount of nutrients they require is needed to ensure the plants get it at the right stage. Multiple foods must be included in our diet. Similarly, fertilizers and amendments must be given to plants at varying states. Their nutrient requirement also depends on the type of plant you are catering to. One thing that is similar for all plants is they require nutrients in a balanced manner. Think of it as a balanced diet for your plants.

The simplest way to ensure your plants get a balanced diet is by giving them fertilizers and using other soil amendments. Whenever you purchase a fertilizer, you will find a label that says, 'NPK,' or, 'N: P: K,' on it. The NPK ratio on packaging refers to the three important nutrients plants require—nitrogen, phosphorus, and potassium.

Understanding what this ratio means is needed to ensure your plants get the required doses of these nutrients.

The NPK ratio of most fertilizers presents three identical numbers. Regardless of whether it is 6:6:6 or any other number, do you know what it means? This essentially suggests that the fertilizer has 6 parts, or 6%, each of nitrogen, phosphorus, and potassium for their general nutrition. Some fertilizers have different ratios, too. For instance, you might come across some that have a higher ratio of nitrogen when compared to the other nutrients. Plants usually require nitrogen more than other nutrients, just like humans require more protein. You will also come across certain formulae that cater to the specific needs of the plants, and not just their general care.

For instance, plants require fertilizers that have greater levels of phosphorus for better rooting and after they are transplanted. In such cases, the ratio of NPK can be something like 6:20:6. Similarly, plants require higher levels of phosphorus for good flowering. Depending on the needs of the plant, you can find a fertilizer that caters to it. It's always important that you keep these specifications in mind to ensure you have selected the right fertilizer.

Amending the Soil

By now, you would have understood that even plants require a healthy and well-balanced diet—just like us. So, to ensure this, you will need to feed them a variety of fertilizers and other organic matter to ensure your garden thrives and stays strong. An important consideration here is to understand that we have the option or liberty to go to a different restaurant, or change our diet if something seems amiss. Unfortunately, plants are rooted—and therefore, as their primary caregiver, it is your responsibility to ensure they get their required nutrients. Without proper nutrients, your garden companions cannot thrive or grow as intended.

These days, a variety of fertilizers and other amendments are available to cater to gardening requirements. Opting for prepackaged and premixed fertilizers provides an easy option. On the other hand, if you want to, you can also opt for natural or organic soil amendments such as mulch and compost. Regardless of the option you choose, the aim is to ensure your garden thrives and the plants are healthy. Let's look at all the different options available.

Synthetic Fertilizers

Synthetic or chemical fertilizers usually contain sulfates, nitrates, phosphates, and other man-made constituents that ensure your plants get their required nourishment. They are commonly found in the form of liquids, granules, and powders. A primary benefit of opting for synthetic or chemical fertilizers is that they are extremely simple to use and fast-acting when compared to the natural options. However, on the downside, they contribute to environmental pollution. Also, you should remember that whatever chemicals you feed to your plants—especially the edible varieties—matters a lot because these pollutants ultimately make their way into your system upon consumption. This is the primary reason why organic options are gaining popularity these days.

Sodium nitrate is one of the most popular nitrogen-based fertilizers, whereas phosphate provides the phosphorus plants require. You will also come across ammonium sulfate, nitrate, or chloride that provide the plants with sufficient nitrogen. A low-cost chemical fertilizer that offers the plant sufficient nitrogen is urea.

Organic Fertilizers

Organic fertilizers are created using animal and plant by-products, such as dead or decaying plant material, fish, bone, blood meal manure, and so on. As with synthetic fertilizers, you can obtain these in the form of liquid sprays, powders, and granules. When compared to the previous ones, these are gentler on the environment but are slow-acting.

Natural Amendments

There are a variety of natural amendments to choose from which include compost, wood ash, lime, and even worm castings. These natural additives automatically enhance the nutrient profile of the soil and its bioavailability. Unlike chemical fertilizers, you cannot determine the NPK ratio of these nutrients—but they are quite helpful:

- Fish emulsion is a by-product obtained from fisheries. It offers an organic NPK ratio wherein the percentage of nitrogen is generally higher than the other nutrients.

- Blood meal and bone meal are also by-products of the animal husbandry sector. The bone meal usually has a higher amount of nitrogen and phosphorus, which is especially helpful after a plant is transplanted or for its root growth. On the other hand, blood meal has a higher level of nitrogen.

- Manure is also a natural fertilizer that is usually sourced from animals including cattle, pigs, rabbits, sheep, and even worms.

- Biofertilizers include soil bacteria that increase the natural production of nutrients within the soil, especially around the roots. This, in turn, makes it easy for the plants to obtain their required nutrients.

Apart from all of these natural amendments, you also have the option of using cover crops. These seeds can be purchased from a local gardening shop and are cultivated as temporary plants. They help increase the presence of helpful bacteria in the soil along with needed nutrients.

Compost

Compost can be made from waste materials available at home. If not, you also have the option of purchasing it from a gardening store! Don't think of compost as a fertilizer. Instead, it is a type of plant food. It is a nutrient-friendly medium that improves the nutrient profile of the soil. Adding compost to the soil also increases the activity of helpful microbes within. This, in turn, further improves the availability of nutrients, making it easier for the plants to obtain what they require. Here are a couple things you must remember while adding compost to the garden:

- You should only add fully ready compost. This means you must wait for the different nitrogenous materials present in it to fully break down. The time it takes for this to happen differs, and rushing into it is not a good idea. If the compost is too fresh, it can burn or harm the plants instead of helping them.

- Ensure the compost you opt for is rich in nutrients. As mentioned, plants need certain specific ingredients at specific times. Depending on the requirements, opt for one that fulfills them. Pay attention to the amount of compost you add as well. Adding too much compost is undesirable. Balance is needed in all aspects, and this applies to the plant's health, too. A simple rule to remember is to spread compost in a one-inch layer over the entire area.

Mulch

Mulch refers to fresh organic matter that is usually added close to the roots of the plant, or even in between rows of plants. It helps maintain moisture within the soil, prevents the growth of weeds, and reduces the chances of erosion or soil runoff. Some common ingredients that can be used to make mulch include grass clippings, untreated cardboard and newspaper, shredded leaves, dead leaves, hay, and even pine needles. Using mulch is quite similar to compost. Do not think of it as a fertilizer, instead think of it as a medium-strength soil enhancer. It increases the ability of the plants to absorb nutrients by improving their carbon uptake. Carbon is needed for breaking down nitrogen and increasing its bioavailability, too. The activity of the soil microbiome also increases when plants are nestled in a layer of mulch. You should be careful and not use too much of it, however, because excess mulch increases the level of nitrogen in the soil to an undesirable level. This, in turn, renders the soil unworthy of plants.

Wood Ash

Using wood ash helps increase the level of potassium in the soil. Adding too much wood ash can turn the soil extremely alkaline. If the plants prefer acidic soil or the soil already has a high pH and potassium, don't use too much wood ash.

Lime

Garden lime is commonly used for improving the nutrient profile of the soil and tweaking its pH level. The ideal time to use lime is only when magnesium is missing in the garden soil. The level of magnesium is generally higher in dolomitic lime when compared to calcified lime. Calcific lime increases the level of calcium in the soil. If the soil is already alkaline or the plant prefers acidity, avoid using any type of lime because it increases the pH of the soil.

Gypsum

If you want to break up clayey or compact soil and increase the level of calcium present in it, then you should add some gypsum. It also reduces the levels of sodium and salt in the soil. Don't use gypsum frequently, and the ideal time to use it is for freshly broken grounds. Even though it has a neutral pH, adding too much of it can acidify the soil to an extent that is harmful to plants.

Effect on Soil Condition

Any amendment used to alter the nutrient profile of the soil also affects the soil conditions. The most common aspect of the soil influenced by this is the pH level. The pH of the soil also influences the availability of nutrients to the plants. The bioavailability of helpful nutrients such as magnesium, potassium, and calcium are low if the soil is acidic. On the other hand, if all of these nutrients are present in excess, then the soil is highly alkaline. Regardless of the side of the spectrum, the soil extremes are not ideal for most plants.

Adding certain amendments and nutrients helps rectify any pH imbalances, but not always. Using lime or wood ash helps stabilize the pH of acidic soils and brings them to a more alkaline level. Adding gypsum, which has high levels of magnesium and calcium, can increase the acidity of the soil. If you want to improve the pH of the soil, the best option available is to opt for healthy and adequate doses of microbridge and natural compost.

Paying attention to the nutrient requirements of the plants is incredibly important. Even though plants have varying requirements, by following the general guidelines given here, you can ensure your garden's overall health.

Chapter 6:

Watering Systems for a Home

Garden

Water accounts for up to 95% of plant tissue, and is an essential nutrient for them. The seeds will not sprout and the plants will not grow if they do not get sufficient water. Water also acts as a carrier for nutrients and performs a variety of functions within the plant tissues. This is an essential ingredient for photosynthesis, which is the process through which plants create energy utilizing sunlight, carbon dioxide, and water. During this process, carbon dioxide from the air and hydrogen from water is taken up by the roots. The by-product of photosynthesis is oxygen and glucose.

Also, water evaporates on the leaves through a process known as transpiration. This ensures the plants don't overheat, even during warm climatic conditions. The rate of transpiration is affected by temperature, quality of air, and wind. So, the plants pull more water through their roots as the water evaporates from the leaves. The nutrients and sugars produced during photosynthesis are further dissolved in water. This moves from areas of high concentration to those of low concentration. It essentially describes the moving path nutrients need to take that a plant requires from its roots to blossoms, leaves, and stems for proper growth and reproduction.

Another function performed by water is to maintain the structural support of plant cells. It creates a constant pressure within the cell walls, known as turgor. This ensures the plant is strong, yet flexible. In turn, it ensures the plant can withstand winds and does not break. Leaves start curling and browning due to low moisture. If they do not get sufficient water, they will eventually die. So, watering your plants is one aspect you cannot overlook if you want a healthy garden. In this chapter, you will learn everything there is to know about different watering systems, selecting an ideal system, and tips to water your garden.

So, an important question all gardeners must consider is to decide how they want to water their plants. What is the ideal watering system? Before learning about this, let's look at the importance of a watering system.

Selecting an ideal watering system is needed, because plants cannot survive without water. Also, this is a daily chore—and ignoring it is not good for the health of your garden. Selecting the right system not only ensures that the plants are watered more efficiently, but can also save you time, money, and effort as well. You can always opt for conventional methods such as a watering can or a garden hose. However, these days a variety of irrigation systems are available. All of these systems can be effectively customized to ensure that your garden's watering needs are perfectly taken care of.

Different Watering Systems

One of the most labor-intensive aspects of gardening is to ensure that the plants get sufficient water. Tending to your garden using a hose and spending time outdoors is certainly enjoyable. However, automatic options are available as well, which reduces the manual effort involved. In this section, you'll be introduced to all the different types of watering systems to choose from.

Sprinklers

One of the most common types of water systems is a sprinkler. There are different types of sprinklers available, and they are usually classified as in-ground or above-ground systems. The obvious benefit of using a sprinkler system is there is no manual effort involved. Once a system is installed, you simply need to turn it on and that's about it. Another benefit is it ensures that all the plants in its path are perfectly soaked. On the downside, sprinklers result in loss of sprayed water. Also, any other hardscapes (including driveways or paths) in their way will be drenched, too. Water wastage is a significant problem with any sprinkler system.

An above-ground sprinkler essentially refers to the kind that is placed at the end of a garden hose. The hose needs to be moved around from one area to another to ensure that all the plants are thoroughly watered. Portable sprinklers are another type you can consider, and you will learn more about them later in this section.

Now, let's move on to the in-ground sprinkler systems. These systems have watering heads directly connected to a pipe system that's underground. The sprinklers are directly hooked into the main water supply, and are managed by a centralized unit or controller. These highly automated systems are extremely convenient. The system can be designed such that different watering zones are created as per the needs of the plants. The sprinklers can also be automated to ensure they start watering at a specific time. Some of the more sophisticated ones have rain sensors, and they automatically turn themselves off when it rains. This ensures your garden isn't watered when it isn't needed.

A sprinkler system can be customized with a variety of sprinkler heads. This ensures that the distribution of water is customized as per the watering needs of the plants that you are growing. For instance, some sprinkler heads can cover 360 degrees, whereas others stick to a 180-degree radius. You can opt for a 180-degree radius if the garden is close to the sidewalk, and you don't want to spray the hardscape. These systems also give you an option of opting for sprinkler heads that produce single or multiple streams of water. Some can also be subterranean when not in use. This ensures better and even distribution of water. Some are permanently fixed above ground and rise over the foliage. When compared to most of the other watering systems available, the initial cost of investment in them is quite high.

These are pricey to install, but automatically reduce the effort involved in gardening.

Soaker Hoses

Soaker hoses are an incredibly effective, yet affordable, watering system for any garden. These hoses are usually made of recycled tires, and have small holes in them through which the water seeps into the garden. Hook it to a faucet, or to a leader hose that's hooked to a faucet, and simply turn on the water supply. This is the only process involved. As the water flows, it starts dripping along the entire length of the hose. The hose must be placed such that it winds around the garden and covers all the plants. However, on the downside, it means the hose will also inevitably end up watering areas where there are no plants—and this can result in water wastage. There are also different options for customizing these hoses. For instance, using T connectors or elbow connectors splits the water line into multiple sublines, which can further improve water distribution. You need to install a couple of landscape staples as well to ensure that the hose stays in position and doesn't move around. Once installed, maintaining this water system is quite easy.

Drip Irrigation

The drip irrigation system is quite similar to how a soaker hose functions, at least on paper. This watering system is made of drip emitters extending from an intact hose or a tube. The drip emitters are nothing but extended tubes with small holes in them. When compared to a soaker hose, this watering system is slightly expensive, but is cheaper than the sophisticated in-ground sprinklers. A major benefit of using this system is it offers precise placement of the outlets and watering lengths. Also, you can rest easy knowing that the water directly soaks into the soil and reaches the roots. This means that water isn't splashed onto the foliage, and ensures only the important parts of the plants receive water—their roots. With sprinklers, water is usually spewed into the wind, but this problem is rectified by a drip irrigation system. Since water reaches only the roots, a damp environment is not created. This, in turn, further reduces the spread of any diseases such as root rot.

Rain Barrels

Using rain barrels is perhaps not an irrigation system per se, but it is extremely beneficial. Collecting rainwater is a great way to tend to the watering needs of your garden. Also, this is an environmentally-friendly practice. Collected rainwater from gutters or downspouts can be stored in barrels. This water can then be used for watering the garden. The barrels can be connected to a soaker hose, regular hose, or any other irrigation system of your choice for further even distribution. Apart from this, you can also water the plants by hand using the collected rainwater. Rain barrels come in a variety of shapes and sizes. Depending on the local climatic conditions, opt for one that works. For instance, if you live in a drought-prone area or your water supply is limited, then collecting and harvesting rainwater is a brilliant idea.

Buried Reservoirs

Using buried reservoirs is not a common practice, especially in modern gardening. However, this trend has been steadily gaining popularity these days. This is a tried-and-tested gardening irrigation technique that's been used by many gardeners for years. You will essentially need to bury vessels, usually made of clay, sporadically throughout the garden. These clay pots must be filled with water, and then that's about it. This is also known as clay pot irrigation. It is based on the principle of soil tension, which is the tension that exists between things that are dry and wet.

In practice, when the soil around the water-filled clay pot is dry, the water is sucked out of the container. Similarly, if the soil is still moist, no water is leached out of the clay pots! Clay pots used for this purpose are known as ollas. This technique of irrigation is believed to have originated somewhere in Northern Africa. However, a similar technique was believed to have been used in China over 4,000 years ago! This is an environmentally-conscious method of watering, and eliminates the problem of water wastage. It also ensures that only the roots of the plant are watered. Unglazed and porous pots made of clay must be used for this purpose. This technique can be used in a conventional in-soil garden, and even raised beds. While using buried reservoirs, ensure that they are buried with their necks sticking out of the ground—at least 2-3 inches of them must be above ground. This makes it easier to refill the pots when they dry out.

Portable Sprinklers

As the name suggests, these sprinkler systems are portable and can be moved from one place to another. They offer comfort and convenience. These systems have a portable mainline, along with lateral submains and a pumping unit or a plant that is portable, too. You can move it from one side to another with ease. The movement of these systems can be either manual or mechanical. When compared to the sprinkler systems you were introduced to previously, the initial investment for them is quite low but is labor-intensive. These hose-end sprinklers ensure the even distribution of water and have different types of water-distribution functionality such as pulsating, oscillating, whirling, and even sweeping sprinklers. These sprinklers can be fitted with a timer to ensure that they are turned on and off at specific times to cater to your garden's needs. This is a perfectly affordable irrigation system, especially for an outdoor garden.

Garden Hoses

A garden hose is one of the most conventional forms of watering options for any garden. All you need is a water source and a pipe. It is also known as a hosepipe or a hose. It is a flexible tube that is used for moving water from a source to the plants. A variety of attachments, such as sprinklers and sprayers, can also be attached to the end of the hose to create a sprinkler system. They are made of soft plastic, or synthetic fiber, that makes them sturdy. Use a backflow prevention

Size of the Garden

The next factor you must pay attention to is the size of the garden. This is an obvious, yet commonly overlooked, aspect of gardening. If you have a massive garden, opting for a hand watering method will become labor-intensive. Unless you have some help, choosing this watering system and managing the garden will not be possible. It will also take up the time available and increase the efforts involved. On the other hand, a watering can is ideal if you have a small patch of vegetables growing in the garden. If you just have a couple of pots of plants, even collecting rainwater and using it will suffice most of their watering requirements. Depending on the size of your garden and the number of plants you wish to grow, you'll need to choose an ideal method of watering.

Cost Involved

Another factor you need to consider is the cost involved. For instance, an in-ground sprinkler system is quite easy to maintain and use just like a drip irrigation system. However, the costs of setting it up are on the higher side. If you are not willing to spend that much, you might need to opt for a more affordable system, such as a garden hose fitted with a sprinkler head. When it comes to the source of irrigation, you should also consider if there are any water outlets present near the plants you are growing. If you have a massive vegetable garden, but a water outlet is only available on the other side of the property, you will need a method that works well. If you decide to water the plants by hand, ensure that an outlet is nearby.

Water Quality

The third factor you need to consider is the water itself. While selecting a watering system, you'll need to focus on the location of the water as well as its availability. If the availability of water is a concern, you will need to be more judicious about its utilization. Similarly, the pressure on the water supply also matters. A sprinkler system is not ideal if the water pressure is quite low. In such instances, a drip irrigation system works. You should also factor in whether the water contains any chlorine or minerals in it. Tap water is usually not treated, and such water can damage the foliage when spread on the earth. Ensure that the water you are using is filtered, to get rid of any chemicals that can ruin the growth of plants and kill them from the inside. You should also check for any traces of disease-causing pathogens in the water before using it.

Type of Plants

The final factor to be considered is the type of plants you decide to grow. This is an important decision and matters a lot, because it determines the watering system you will be using. For instance, the requirements of a leafy plant will be extremely different from that of tomatoes. The answer to this will also depend on whether you are growing vegetable beds, seedbeds, hanging planters, or are growing them in containers. If you are not careful and regularly spraying water onto the foliage, plants can contract infections.

If you want to opt for a hand-watering system, go for it. There aren't any restrictions that you must select, go with one type of watering system and stick to it. You can decide to hand water because it gives you a better chance of observing the plants, spending more time in the garden, and installing a drip irrigation system, too! The choice is yours.

Tips for Watering Plants

Regardless of whether you have a green thumb or not, learning how to water plants is a crucial aspect of gardening. Yes, you read it right, because there *are* incorrect techniques for watering plants. When done improperly, it increases a plant's susceptibility to diseases and infestations. If you aren't careful while watering, you might unknowingly kill a healthy plant as well. So, here are some do's and don'ts of watering plants.

Water in the Morning

As much as possible, always water plants early in the morning. Avoid watering them at noon or when the sun is at full mast. Do it right before the temperature heats up. During the early hours of the day, the soil is cool, and this makes it easier for the water to seep in. In turn, it gives the roots a better chance of obtaining the desired supply of water. Also, if you water when the sun is out and bright, the chances of water being evaporated even before reaching the roots is high. If the plants don't have sufficient water or moisture in the soil, they will wilt and die, especially when it is hot outside. Another benefit of watering early in the day is it reduces the time spent under the harsh sun. This is especially important if you opt for any handheld methods of watering your garden.

Don't Be Too Frequent

The frequency of watering the plants is crucial. If you water them constantly or provide too little water, the garden will not be healthy. When it is hot outside, the temptation to regularly water the plants increases. Do not do this though, because if the ground is unnecessarily damp, it will kill the plants. Similarly, shallow watering the foliage is also a bad idea. Unless the water seeps into the soil, the roots cannot absorb it. So, the best practice is to ensure that you opt for a watering routine that is less frequent, but thoroughly saturates the ground. Even if the surface appears dry, there can be film moisture within that caters to the plant's requirements. A general rule you can follow when it comes to watering plants is to ensure they get an inch of water per week. If the summers are extremely hot and dry, they will need up to 2 inches of water per week.

Water at Soil Level

Whenever you are watering, ensure the stream of water is directed close to the base of the plant. This offers the needed hydration while ensuring it is delivered to the right part of the plant, especially where it is needed—the roots. An ideal way to ensure that the garden bed is thoroughly soaked is by using a soaker hose. While hand watering, ensure you do it at the base level and no higher.

Avoid Soaking the Leaves

One practice we must avoid while watering plants is to water the foliage. If the leaves are soaked, it creates a moist environment that is an ideal breeding ground for several disease-causing pathogens, including fungal diseases. So, avoiding a broad sprayer or sprinkler head is a good idea. Not only are such systems usually expensive to install, but they do not serve the purpose. Unless you have a lawn, a broadcast sprinkler is not the ideal choice for a vegetable garden. Another problem with such sprinklers is that most of the water that shoots up from their head is lost to the elements due to exposure to wind and sun. This means the roots of the plant do not get the water they need. Less water reaches the base of the plant, and most of it is lost.

Watering Container Plants

One thing you cannot forget is watering your container plants. Just because they are growing in containers and don't require much space, this doesn't mean they don't need much water. These plants must be watered at least once a day. Depending on the size of the container, the frequency of watering will increase. The smaller the container, the more water it will need. So, you will need to keep watering them repeatedly. Ensure that the soil within the container is soaked in the morning. If the top layer feels dry to the touch, water it again sometime around the afternoon or early evening. However, ensure that you are watering the plants only close to their base and not the foliage.

Avoid Jet-Type Spray Nozzles

Regardless of whether it is an in-ground garden or container plants, ensure that you avoid using jet-type spray nozzles. Such nozzles are usually designed to deliver water at incredibly high speeds. It probably looks like you'll get the job done, but it will end up damaging the plants. Such pressurized nozzles are usually an ideal choice for washing sidewalks and driveways. However, the tender foliage of plants will be severely damaged when that spray is directed at them. It also disrupts the roots of the plant when targeted at the soil. Instead, opt for a watering nozzle that slowly produces a gentle spray, unlike a jet-type spray nozzle.

Check the Moisture

If the soil in the garden dries out, then the plants will suffer. On the other hand, if the roots are soaked in water or are sitting in it for too long, they will not get sufficient oxygen. The soil surface can appear dry, especially when it is hot and windy outside. However, the earth under it can still be moist. Therefore, always perform a quick check to ensure that you are not overwatering the plants. A simple way to check whether they need water is by inserting your finger into the ground. Another option is to use a wooden dowel. Insert the dowel a couple of inches into the garden soil and remove it. If the soil is moist, then it will stick to the dowel. If the dowel comes out dry, it is a sign to water the plants!

Plants Need More Than Rain

As mentioned previously, plants—regardless of whether they are vegetables, flowers, or shrubs—require up to an inch of water per week. Therefore, do not simply rely on rain to water your garden. Rain isn't always sufficient, especially if you want a thriving full-fledged garden. If you are living in an area that receives regular rainfall, you'll still need to check whether the moisture in the soil is sufficient to support the plant growth or not. To do this, follow the suggestion mentioned in the previous point.

Avoid Treated or Softened Water

Avoid using treated or soft water. Water softening usually adds sodium to the tap water. Initially, it might not make much of a difference to the plant growth, but ultimately it affects the mineral composition of the soil itself. So, ensure that the water is filtered out of unnecessary chemicals and other mineral additions.

Selecting the Right Soil

Selecting the soil is extremely important if you want to improve the overall health of your garden. This is an even more important factor, especially if you are growing plants indoors. Avoid using outdoor garden soil for indoor pots. This is because the outdoor soil can contain insects, pathogens, and other critters, which can result in an infestation when transferred indoors. These days, a variety of soilless houseplant mixtures are also available that are made of vermiculite, perlite, and peat moss.

Avoid Highly Water-Retentive Potting Mix

If you are using the potting mix for your garden, ensure that you do not opt for one that is highly water-retentive. If the water or the potting mix stays soggy for hours or even days after a session of watering, the plants will die. As mentioned previously, opt for a potting mixture that contains perlite, coconut coir, or vermiculite that promotes better drainage. If you are looking for a potting mix, ensure that it contains one part of peat moss and no more.

Invest in a Soil Moisture Gauge

Investing in a soil moisture gauge is a wonderful idea. These are inexpensive and cost less than $20. You simply need to insert the gauge into the soil to determine whether it is wet, dry, or moist. Using a moisture gauge is ideal, because it ensures that you are watering the soil only when it is needed instead of doing it on a schedule even when the plants don't need it. Using it initially will give you a better idea of the regular watering schedule of the plants you are growing.

Containers Must Have Drainage Holes

If you are growing plants in containers or pots, ensure holes are drilled into the pot. If not, the house plants will not have well-drained soil. The drainage holes ensure that excess water is eliminated from the pot and the roots are not subject to excess water. If the containers don't have any drainage holes, drill a few into them.

Watering in Winter and Spring

The watering schedule and requirements of the plants will also depend upon the weather conditions. For instance, plants will need more water during spring than in winter. This is true for plants that are growing outdoors as well as indoors. The days are shorter during winter, and the sunlight the plants receive will reduce. Due to this, photosynthesis slows down, and the plants move on to a resting phase. During this, their water requirement reduces. On the other hand, the days are longer during spring, and thus plants are exposed to sunlight for longer periods of time. Therefore, their watering needs to also be increased.

As briefly previously mentioned, also remember not to overwater your plants. Regardless of whether you have in-soil garden or house plants, overwatering is extremely harmful. When you overwater, it increases the risk of root rot and other plant diseases.

Chapter 7:

Gardening Tools and Requirements

Before you can learn about the different types of plants that can be grown in your garden or how to start gardening, it's important to gather a few basic tools. It is easy to go overboard while purchasing any landscaping or gardening tools, so stay focused on only the basics— because these tools can be pretty expensive and take up plenty of your valuable space, too. Always opt for quality tools within a budget and maintain them properly. This is the best way to make the most of your investment. Also, having the right set of gardening tools makes the entire process easier and hassle-free. So, here are some basic tools all gardeners need.

Gloves

Gardening is a wonderful hobby, but while dealing with splinters and thorns, it can become downright painful. Therefore, you will need a good pair of gloves. You will need gloves that are not only durable but also sturdy, without being too bulky. This comes in handy while handling seeds or transplanting delicate seedlings. Also, ensure that they fit you properly. If the gloves are too big or too small, it increases the risk of blisters or accidents caused by the gloves coming off. Apart from this, ensure that the fabric is breathable, comfortable, and water-resistant. This is the only way with which you can properly work in the garden without hurting yourself. While opting for gloves, look for ones that have slightly longer cuffs to keep your wrists protected while dealing with plants. Longer cuffs also ensure that soil doesn't get in and irritate the skin.

Pruning Shears

Pruning shears, or secateurs, are also known as hand pruners. These tools come in handy when you need to reign in plants that are getting a little out of control or are taking over your garden. You have two different types of pruners to choose from, and these are: bypass pruners and anvil-style pruners.

A bypass pruner has a sharp blade that passes by another sharp-edged and flat surface. They are quite similar to a sharp pair of scissors. On the other hand, an anvil-style pruner has a sharp blade that meets a flat surface. This is quite similar to a sharp knife working on a cutting board. Investing in both these types of pruners is a good idea, because they perform different functions.

For pruning live plants or green woods, you will need bypass pruners. On the other hand, anvil pruners come in handy when dealing with deadwood. When you use them on living plants, it can injure their green stems, leaves, and branches. The pruners you opt for should be easy to handle, and the ideal size is such that it fits in the palm of your hand. Ensure that you sharpen these pruners regularly to keep their blades sharp and for cleaner cuts. It also reduces any risk of accidentally injuring the plant.

Loppers

A lopper is a long-handled pruner used for trimming areas that are hard to reach, and for cutting thick branches. This is another cutting tool worth investing in. Cutting through branches that are mature and tough takes extra strength, and the long handle of the lopper provides the required leverage. Just like a regular pruner, anvil and bypass loppers are available as well. The handles can be anywhere between 16 to 36 inches long. If you want to make a cut in a precise location, then you will need a bypass lopper. Depending on what you will be cutting or how far you'll need to reach, select an appropriate lopper handle length. As the length of the handle increases, the weight of the lopper increases, too. Therefore, be careful here. These days, you also have handles that are made of lightweight aluminum or carbon composite. These are lighter and easier to use. The lopper blades must be kept in good condition and sharpened regularly if you want them to function effectively and efficiently.

Garden Fork

An incredibly efficient tool that's needed to turn garden soil is a garden fork. When compared to a spade, these are easy to use—especially while digging into dense soil. They have a slight curve to the spine that makes it easier to scoop mulch or even turn compost piles. It works pretty much like a pitchfork. If the soil is compacted clay or rocky, then the straight tines come in handy. The square tines on a garden fork are stronger and more durable, especially when they hit a rock or a root of the plant.

Hand Trowel

This is one of the most essential tools every gardener should have. A hand trowel comes in handy while transplanting seedlings into the soil, taking care of planting containers, and even removing weeds. While selecting a trowel, opt for a broad blade so it's easier to move soil along. If the blade is narrower, you can use it for digging through rocky soil or removing weeds. Ideally, the hand trowel should comfortably fit in your hand and shouldn't be too heavy. Opting for a stainless steel trowel or a trowel with a stainless steel head is better, because they are more durable.

Spade

Spades are short-handled shovels that are square-shaped. This is an essential garden workhorse, because they perform a variety of functions. From digging holes for planting, to edging and lifting leaves and moving small amounts of dirt from one path to another, you can do a lot with it. Even if they are slightly expensive, this is an incredible investment—especially if you want to be a gardener. While selecting a spade, look for one that has tines on the top of the blade. This makes them easier to use, and also gives sufficient foot surface required for an extra push. The most durable variants have ash wood handles that absorb shock as well as vibration. You can select one that has a long or short handle, depending on the leverage you will need. Select one that has a stainless steel head, because it's not just durable, but rust-free as well.

Rake

You will need a garden rake when autumn comes around. Rakes help get rid of leaves, as well as plant debris, during the fall. So, opt for a sturdy rake. They are available in different styles and sizes, but to get started, a regular leaf rake is sufficient. If you have an adjustable rake, you can reach into narrow areas or even gather a large pile of leaves in one go. You can either opt for a rake that has plastic or metal tines. That said, steel tines are harsher on delicate lawns or plants.

Hoe

Depending on the type of garden you have, the hoe you need will differ. You will need a sturdy and wide hoe if you have a vegetable garden. A delicate and thinner one will be needed if you have a perennial garden. From preparing the garden bed to cutting down weeds, a hoe does a lot. Ensure that the hoe you select has a comfortable handle that offers a long reach. The blade must be easy to use, and it should be sharp.

Garden Hose

In the previous chapter, you were introduced to one of the most basic methods of watering plants—a hose. You will need a garden hose, especially one that comes with an adjustable nozzle. The hose should be long enough so that it reaches every area of the garden. The basic diameters of the hose to choose from are 1/2 inch, 5/8th inch, and 3/4th inch. The water pressure, as well as the radius of the spray, can be regulated by selecting an adjustable nozzle. It is better to estimate the length or the area of the garden to be covered before you purchase a hose. The length also affects the water pressure. Therefore, the pressure is lower if the hose is longer. When compared to rubber hoses, vinyl ones are lighter and less expensive. However, the vinyl hoses kink easily and the rubber ones are sturdier and long-lasting. Ensure that the hose is always coiled up and kept away from sunlight. Weak spots will be created if you use a hose with a kink in it.

Watering Can

Apart from a garden hose, you'll also need a watering can as well. Watering cans are made of plastic or metal. They come in different sizes, colors, and styles. They also have different nozzle options. A plastic can is obviously lighter than metal, but it isn't as long-lasting. If you are purchasing a metal watering can, get it galvanized to reduce the risk of rusting. The size of the can you opt for must be directly proportional to your strength. If you want something lightweight, opt for a plastic one.

Wheelbarrow

A final piece of equipment that all gardeners must have is a wheelbarrow. You can use it to move around extra soil or compost. It can also be used for any other heavy lifting. Regardless of whether you need to move or hold something, a wheelbarrow comes in handy. A single-wheel conventional dual-handle wheelbarrow is slightly trickier to balance, especially while moving heavy loads. You can also opt for a single-handle two-wheel wheelbarrow. Such models are easier to navigate, and can be used for pulling or pushing on uneven terrain even with limited strength. Ensure that you store it properly, and always keep it clean and dry, because this reduces the risk of rusting. For easier movement, ensure its wheels are properly inflated.

Chapter 8:

Basics of Planting and Growing

Until now, you were introduced to different aspects of creating a thriving garden. Now, it is time to design your garden layout and plan for the growing seasoning. In this chapter, you will be introduced to the basics of planting and growing.

How to Design a Garden Layout?

Before you learn to design a garden layout, let's see why you need to do this. It can be quite tempting to try to grow all the plants you want at once. However, not only is this impractical, but it can also make things harder than needed. While designing a garden layout, you can easily calculate how many plants you need. Overplanting is a common cause of different pests and plant diseases. The risk of all this can be reduced once you have a layout in mind. It gives you an opportunity for proper recordkeeping. While designing the garden, keep a sketch of the layout with you. This gives you a better idea of where each plant is located. Since most plants have varying needs, a sketch of the layout ensures you can cater to the same. Another benefit is that you can have a garden that not only looks aesthetically pleasing, but is more productive as well. Optimal space utilization becomes an achievable goal if you plan the garden design and layout. You can take this opportunity to make the most of the vertical and horizontal space available. Apart from all of this, designing your garden can be a stressbuster, too!

Well, if you want to reap all these benefits, it is time to start planning. As with any other aspect of life, failing to plan is planning to fail.

To design the layout of your vegetable garden, you will need a few sheets of paper, a pencil, an eraser, and a ruler. Once you have these supplies ready, follow the steps given here:

1. The first step is to make a list of the vegetables you want to grow. Go through the different categories of plants and types of vegetables discussed in the second part of this book. Make a note of the ones you want to grow. Once you have a list in front of you, it becomes easier to determine the space needed to grow everything.

   After this, it's time to sketch the basic outline of the vegetable garden. Outline the plot on a piece of paper. It doesn't have to be a professional outline, it simply needs to be a general structure of the space available. Now, add any existing hardscapes to this sketch. Whether it is a fence, path, arbor, or even raised beds, add it here. If there aren't any, you can move on to the next step.

2. The second step is to draw the beds and the path for your garden. It's not just about simply growing plants. You will also need to tend to them and take care of their maintenance requirements. To do this, you'll need easy access. There is no point in completely filling the space available without leaving any walking room. If you cannot reach your plants, how can you take care of them? This is why you need to decide where you want to plant and where the walking path will be.

   While doing this, ensure that the path between each bed or growing area is at least 2 feet, in order to offer sufficient movement space. Another consideration is that if any vegetables tend to sprawl, they will need plenty of room to grow. If the plants are overcrowded, it doesn't mean a better yield. Instead, it will harm the health of all the plants you are growing and reduce the yield, too.

3. The third step is to add the plants you want to grow to within the sketch. Think about the plants you want to grow and how to group them. You simply need to make a note of where you want to grow the different plants. While doing this, you should also take into consideration their sunlight requirements or ideal weather conditions. For instance, some plants require plenty of sunlight, while others don't. So, if such plants are planted under shade-giving ones, it will be detrimental to their health.

4. The fourth step is to review the design you have made so far. Take a couple of moments to sit back and visualize how the layout will look in reality. Consider whether the plants have sufficient room to grow. Also, check whether there is sufficient room for you to move around while tending to the plants. It is better to make any changes during this stage than later. Be impartial here. If you think it is better to skip a couple of plants now, you can get to them later.

Seeds or Transplants?

A dilemma all gardeners face before they get started is to decide whether they want to start with seeds or transplants. Understanding the benefits each offers will make it easier to decide.

The three simple reasons to start your own seeds indoors include diversity, cost-saving benefits, and satisfaction. When you purchase transplants For instance, your choices will be restricted only to the plants available at a local nursery or garden center. When you purchase seeds and start them yourself, the options available are wider than any other means. You can grow whatever you want if you opt for seeds. The time taken for seeds to turn into mature plants until they are ready for harvest is longer than transplants. That said, the entire process is deeply satisfying. Knowing that you managed to grow the vegetables on your own is rewarding. The experience of seeing the seedlings sprout and slowly turn into full-grown plants is irreplaceable. And finally, starting plants from seeds is cheaper than purchasing transplants or fully-grown plants!

If you're still confused, use the following questions to determine whether you should opt for direct seeding or transplanting seedlings:

- Is it easier for the vegetables to germinate from seeds?

- Is the growing season long enough for the seeds to turn into fully matured vegetables?

- Do the vegetables require special care if you grow them from seeds?

- Can the vegetables be transplanted without any problems?

The answers to these questions will help understand how you plant in the garden. To a certain degree, your regional climatic conditions play a significant role here. For instance, the growing season usually extends from February to November in the southern states; whereas in the northern regions, the growing season is restricted to just five months. If you want to grow tomatoes and peppers from seeds in the southern states, it's perfectly fine, but this might not be the case in the northern regions.

Keeping the climatic conditions aside, some plants benefit when you start the seeds indoors or opt for transplants. Some seeds are highly susceptible to fungal diseases that might exist in the garden soil, of which you are unaware. This is one of the reasons why the soil must be thoroughly tested before you decide to start a garden. Carefully check the information given on the seed packets to understand what would be better. Basic information, such as the time for maturity and sowing time, will be mentioned on the seed packets. For instance, if the time for maturity on the packet is 75 days, understand that you will get a harvest only after this period—and seldom before it. The seed packets will also give you information about when to sow the seeds. Don't get overwhelmed looking at all these factors that you need to consider.

Instead, rest easy because all the information you need to grow different vegetables is discussed in detail in the next part of this book.

Some plants fare better when started from seeds. For instance, vegetables that have long taproots—such as carrots and legumes—are not ideal for transplantation. In such instances, sowing them directly in the garden is a better idea. Even quick-growing crops such as summer squash and peas are better off when directly sowed in soil, instead of starting them indoors.

Some common vegetables that are ideal for direct seeding are:

- beans
- cucumber
- lettuce
- corn
- peas
- garlic
- beets
- squash
- radishes
- pumpkins
- turnips
- zucchini

You can pretty much grow any vegetable from seeds, but some slow-growing vegetables are better started from seedlings. Vegetables that are usually transplanted as seedlings include:

- cabbage

- artichokes

- basil

- broccoli

- cauliflower

- collard greens

- eggplant

- tomatoes

Some vegetables can neither be started from seedlings or transplants. However, they are started from roots or bulbs. Some common examples belonging to this category are asparagus, onions, potatoes, sweet potatoes, and horseradish.

Regardless of whether you are opting for transplants or direct seeding, decide the strategy you want to use before the growing season.

Steps to Follow

Now, let's get to the most interesting part of gardening—planting and growing. These are the basic steps you'll need for any plant you decide to grow.

The Location

As with real estate, location is of primary importance in gardening, too. Select a prime spot, and you can improve your chances of success as a gardener. The location that you opt for must receive sufficient sunlight daily, should be close to a water source, and have sufficient space available to grow the plants you want. Ensure that the area is leveled instead of a sloping surface, to prevent soil erosion. Once you have the right spot in place, things become easier. The location also determines the type of garden for which you can opt to have.

Select the Plants

Once you have chosen a specific spot for your vegetable garden, the next step is to decide the vegetables you want to grow. The choices are truly endless when it comes to the list of vegetables you can grow at home. However, the growing requirements differ greatly. Take some time and think about the plants you want to grow and the reasons for this. Some of the best plants that are ideal for beginners are carrots, peppers, cucumbers, lettuce, and beans.

Prep the Soil

Once you are aware of the plants you want to grow, you cannot immediately sow the seeds in the soil. Instead, the soil must be prepared properly first. Preparing the soil promotes better plant growth and health. Natural fertilizers mixed into the garden soil (along with compost and manure) will improve its arability and water retention. Ensure that the pH of the soil is also ideal for the plants you are growing. If not, soil amendments will be needed. The information about this was discussed in the previous chapters.

Check the Dates

The growing conditions, along with the maturity cycles, vary from one plant to another. You should also consider the climatic conditions before you decide to start a garden. A little planning and preparation go a long way when it comes to a healthy and thriving garden. You will be introduced to the growing conditions needed for different vegetables in the subsequent chapters.

Sowing Seeds

Now it is time to start sowing seeds. Depending on the plants you want to grow, the sowing requirements will differ. Usually, it's better not to sow seeds too deeply in the soil. If they are in too deep, most of their energy and nutrients available will be exerted for the sapling to make its way out. This reduces the health of the plant, increases its susceptibility to pests and insects, and results in poorer yields. The sowing depth and spacing requirements for different vegetable plants will be discussed in detail in the next part of this book.

Add Water

Don't forget to gently spray the garden with water to ensure that the soil stays evenly moist throughout the growing season. You were introduced to different watering systems in the previous chapters. Depending on the size of the garden you are growing, the quality of soil, and the watering requirements of the plants, select one that fits your needs and requirements. Regardless of the watering system you opt for, ensure that the foliage is not soaked and only the roots receive water. Avoid overwatering or underwatering the plants. Overwatering or underwatering the seeds, seedlings, or young plants—and even the mature ones—will quickly destroy them.

Remove Weeds

Ensure that you keep the weeds out of your garden at all times. Regardless of whether it's a vegetable patch, raised bed, or a full-fledged in-soil garden, weeds do not belong in a healthy garden. Weeds not only leech essential nutrients from the soil that your vegetable plants need, but they also attract harmful insects and pests, too. The best way to prevent the growth of weeds is by adding a layer of mulch to the soil. A 2-to-4-inch-thick layer of organic mulch on the soil surface ensures that weeds do not overtake your crops. Be vigilant and don't hesitate to remove weeds as and when they appear. Sharply yank the weeds to ensure they are completely uprooted. If not, new weeds will appear in the same spot again.

Provide Sufficient Space

If the seedlings are overcrowded, or it looks like your garden is overcrowded, then you will need to thin it out. If not, you will not have a healthy harvest—or even a healthy garden, for that matter. Plants require sufficient space to grow. If there are too many plants in close quarters, they will fight with each other for the nutrients available in the soil. This results in a poor harvest. Instead, it's better to thin the seedlings.

Fertilize the Plants

Ensure that you fertilize the plants depending on their state of growth and needs. Till the soil lightly with your hands and add the fertilizer. You can purchase ready-to-use fertilizer from a gardening supplies store, or make your own at home. A simple recipe for homemade fertilizer includes Epsom salt, kitchen compost, water from a fish tank, and eggshells. Mix all of these ingredients together and simply add them to the plants. Ensure that you do not overfertilize the plants.

Time to Reap What You Sow

Once you have followed all the steps mentioned until now and have taken care of your plants, it's time to harvest. Ensure that you are harvesting vegetables when they're still young and tender. Such vegetables are tastier than the mature ones. Also, ensure that you are harvesting them only when needed, or plan to preserve them in one way or another. The root crops can be pulled out as soon as they reach their edible size, whereas the leaf crops can be harvested by simply cutting them close to the base.

Don't forget to share your labor of love with others to make the harvest even more memorable!

Part 2:

Time to Start Growing

Now that you are armed with the basic information and knowledge needed about gardening, let's get to the most interesting part of this book—growing veggies. In this part, you will be introduced to different categories of vegetables you can grow, along with step-by-step instructions to grow them.

Chapter 9:

A List of Vegetables for Your Garden

Vegetables are not only among the healthiest foods, but they also come in a variety of shapes, sizes, and colors. They are versatile, and depending on the type they can be cooked in different ways. As per the Mansfield Encyclopedia of Agricultural and Horticultural Plants, 1,097 vegetables are grown across the world. Vegetables are of different types and are classified according to their edible parts. Despite the extreme diversity known, it is believed that we are barely aware of a small percentage of all the species of vegetables.

Before learning about the different vegetables that can be grown in your garden, it is important to understand the classifications. Vegetables are categorized as follows.

Leafy Vegetables

These are also known as vegetable greens or salad greens. Leafy vegetables are a powerhouse of essential nutrients the body requires. They can be consumed either raw or in cooked form. As the name suggests, those belonging to this category are primarily grown for their edible leafy parts. The different types of leafy vegetables you will learn to grow are:

- spinach

- kale

- collard greens

- watercress

- mustard greens

- red chard

- iceberg lettuce

- red leaf lettuce

- romaine lettuce

- dandelion greens

- amaranth

- arugula

- bok choy

- Rapini

Fruit Vegetables

Some vegetables are botanically classified as fruits, but in the culinary world they are referred to as vegetables. Such vegetables belong to the category of fruit vegetables. For instance, most think tomatoes are vegetables—but they are, in fact, fruits. The different types of vegetables belonging to this category you will learn to grow are:

- tomatoes

- peppers

- pumpkins

- cucumbers

- peas

- string beans

- eggplant

- okra

- olives

- avocado

- corn

- zucchini

- beans

- chickpeas

Flower Vegetables

Plants that produce flowers used for culinary purposes are known as flower vegetables. Usually, they are seasonal and are grown for their flower heads. Even though they have roots, stems, and leaves, the flowers are the only edible parts. The different types of vegetables belonging to this category you will learn to grow are:

- artichoke

- broccoli

- cauliflower

- courgetti flowers

- squash blossoms

Bulbs

These vegetables grow underground and produce edible bulbs. Bulb vegetables are aromatic and have multiple layers on them. Depending on the type, most varieties can be consumed both raw and in cooked forms. The different types of vegetables belonging to this category you will learn to grow are:

- chives

- shallots

- fennel

- leek

- garlic

- onion

- spring onion

Roots and Tubers

The vegetables that are grown underground are known as root vegetables. As the name suggests, the roots are the edible parts of the plant. Root vegetables are a source of sugar, starch, carbs, and a variety of other essential nutrients. These vegetables can be long or round, and usually have a fleshy texture. Another category of vegetables is known as tubers. There is a difference between root vegetables and tubers. Even though tubers grow underground as well, they grow on the root of the plant. For instance, carrots are a root vegetable, whereas potatoes are a tuberous one. As with root vegetables, even tubers are rich in starch and used as a staple in cuisines across the world. The different types of vegetables belonging to this category you will learn to grow are:

- beetroots

- turnips

- parsnips

- celeriac

- carrots

- potatoes

- sweet potatoes

- yuca

- daikon radish

- salsify

- fennel

Stems

Some vegetables are grown only for their edible stems that grow above ground. The different types of vegetables belonging to this category you will learn to grow are:

- asparagus

- bamboo shoots

- kohlrabi

- celery

- rhubarb

- Florence fennel

Pods and Seed Vegetables

These vegetables are also known as legumes. They are known so because the edible part of the plant are seeds present in a pod. These vegetables are rich in different minerals, and are an excellent source of dietary fiber and protein. The different types of vegetables belonging to this category you will learn to grow are:

- black beans

- chickpeas

- black-eyed peas

- fava beans

- green peas

- groundnuts

- lima beans

- soybeans

- runner beans

Chapter 10:

Leafy Vegetables

In this chapter, you will be introduced to different leafy vegetables, their benefits, and simple steps to growing them!

Spinach

The botanical name of spinach is Spinacia oleracea. It is a popular and hardy leafy green that's usually planted quite early in spring. In some regions, it can be grown during fall and winter as well. This extremely nutritious leafy vegetable is versatile, and can be consumed in both raw and cooked forms. It is a powerhouse of calcium, iron, and vitamins A, B, and C. Spinach thrives when exposed to full sunlight, but grows well in light shade as well. Before planting, prepare the soil by mixing compost in it and leaving it for a week. After this, the soil is ready to get started!

Spinach prefers cool weather, and it requires around 6 weeks until it is ready for harvest from planting. The seeds can be directly sown in the garden soil as soon as the ground is around 40° F. If you want to speed up this process, then cover the soil with a sheet of black plastic and leave it until you are ready to grow spinach. These seeds can be started indoors, but it is not a recommended method, because the seedlings are tricky to transplant.

In the northern climate, spinach can be harvested in early spring. If you want to do this, ensure the seeds are sown before cold weather sets in. To protect the young plants from the cold, a layer of thick mulch can be used—and this can be removed as soon as the soil temperature is around 40° F. If you want to harvest spinach in the fall, then the seeds can be sown during mid-august. Spinach prefers soil of neutral pH, or anywhere between 6.5 and 8 on the pH scale.

Planting and Growing

Once the soil is prepared, the next step is to sow the seeds. Sow the seeds such that they are 2 inches apart and ½ inch in the soil. Cover this with ½ inch of soil. You can plant them in rows, and the rows must be 12-18 inches apart. Alternatively, you can sprinkle them over a bed or a patch in the garden. For a continuous harvest, resow every couple of weeks during the growing season.

Ensure the soil is moist for a healthy harvest of spinach. Row covers can be used to regulate the soil temperature and to keep pests away. Once the seedlings are about 2 inches tall, thin them out such that they are 3-4 inches apart. The uprooted seedlings can be consumed. Apart from thinning, nothing else is needed. Be careful while handling young plants, because their roots are extremely delicate and can be easily damaged.

Water the plants daily, and ensure they get up to an inch of water per week. Mulch regularly to help the soil retain moisture. Once the plants are about 1/3 of their mature growth, use a high-nitrogen fertilizer. If you notice the growth is stunted and distorted or the leaves turn pale yellow or green, then it is a sign of a nutrient deficiency. Other signs to watch out for include bronzing of the leaves and early dropping of the leaves.

Spinach is a hardy vegetable and can tolerate a temperature as low as 15° F. However, the young plants are tender and cannot withstand such drastic temperatures. Using row covers helps insulate them from harsh weather.

Harvesting

Once the leaves have reached the desired size, harvest the outer leaves first. This promotes the growth of inner leaves. Alternatively, the entire plant can be harvested, too. To do this, cut the stem close to the base. Don't wait for larger leaves, and do not wait too long to harvest. As the leaves mature, they turn bitter, and the tender leaves usually taste better. Spinach can bolt if the plant is exposed to over 14 hours of sunlight daily or the temperature is too high. When it bolts, the stalks become big, and the leaves start to narrow. Also, it will taste bitter at this stage. If you notice that it is bolting, then uproot the entire plant and harvest the leaves. To slow down bolting, remove the flower or seed heads. Providing shade and keeping the soil moist will also help slow the bolting.

Kale

The botanical name of kale is Brassica oleracea var. acephala. Kale is a superfood and is extremely popular in the world of fitness and nutrition. It is packed with different vitamins and helpful antioxidants. It aids digestion, is rich in iron, contains powerful antioxidants, and has several other helpful nutrients.

What's more? It tastes really good! Whether you add it to salads or turn it into healthy chips, it is versatile. Kale is a resilient plant and is a cold-hardy green leafy vegetable belonging to the brassica family. It is a biennial plant—this means leaves are produced by it during its first year, whereas flower stalks are developed during the second year. The stalks then produce flowers that house seeds. The plant dies as the seeds start maturing. Kale is not just restricted to the varieties you see in the local grocery store. If you decide to grow it from seed, you have the option of selecting the variety you want to grow. Some are mild, while some have a slight sweetness to them—and all varieties are perfectly ideal for salads. This is not only an extremely nutritious vegetable, but it looks quite good as well. You can improve the aesthetic appeal of your garden by adding a couple of these plants. The different varieties of kale range from bright green to dark purple. It is also extremely simple to grow once you know what to do.

Planting and Growing

Kale requires well-drained and neutral to alkaline soil. Apart from this, they need plenty of exposure to sunlight. They can also tolerate partial shade, too. If the soil isn't essentially rich, ensure that you add sufficient compost to amend the nutritional profile and structure. Using nitrogen-rich amendments such as cotton seed meal, composted manure, or blood meal also helps. Do this at least a week before you want to start planting.

Kale tastes best when it is harvested right before the summer sets in, or after the fall frost. During such periods, the climatic conditions are perfect, and kale thrives. Also, kale's growth is quite speedy during such periods. As mentioned, the plants are cold and hardy—but if it gets too hot, the leaves turn bitter.

Kale can be started from seeds as well as starter plants. It is entirely up to you. However, direct seeding is simple and cost-effective, too. You can grow it during spring, fall, or even winter. If you want to grow kale for spring, then directly sow the seeds into the soil 4-6 weeks before the last spring frost. Since it is a cold-hardy plant, its seeds can germinate even if the soil temperature is around 40° F. If you want to harvest them early in the season or don't want to wait too long, then opt for the early maturing varieties and sow the seeds at least 3 months before the first frost date of the fall. If you reside in an especially hot area, then wait until the temperature cools off to start planting. As mentioned, the flavor of the leaves is affected by the temperature it is exposed to. If it is extremely hot outdoors, then the leaves aren't as tender or sweet. The sweet leaves with a nutty flavor that kale is predominantly known for grow well when it is cold outdoors.

You can also grow it during the winter, but remember to grow it under row cover. If the winters are mild, then you can certainly try growing kale. Usually, this practice will give you a harvest all winter long.

Prepare the soil before you sow the seeds. Add fertilizer such that it is mixed properly into the top 3-4 inches of the soil. If you are using compost, a simple rule to remember is that 100 square feet of your garden area require an inch of well-composted organic matter. Sow the seeds such that they are 1/2 inch deep in the soil and 1 inch apart. Ensure the rows are 18-30 inches apart. If you are using young plants or transplants, they should be planted at the same depth at which they were growing in a container or a tray. Ensure that the plants are 12 inches apart and there are 18-30 inches between each row as well. Regularly water the plants once they are planted.

If you started with seeds, the seedlings would have to be thinned out after 2 weeks, so that they are 8-12 inches apart. Ensure that the seedlings are well watered, and the soil is properly fertilized. They require 1-1.5 inches of water per week. Using nitrogen-rich fertilizer helps improve scale growth. To keep the weeds away and retain moisture, since kale prefers cold temperatures, mulch the soil regularly. After the first hard freeze, mulch heavily to ensure a regular supply of mature leaves throughout the winter.

Harvesting

Once the kale leaves are as big as your hands, it is ready for harvest. Simply pluck a fistful of the outer leaves. Ensure that you are not harvesting more than 1/3 of the plant at any point. Do not pick the terminal bud that is at the center of the plant, since this is what is necessary for plant productivity. As long as the temperatures do not drop below 20° F, kale will grow. If you want to extend the harvest, using tops or row covers helps.

Collard Greens

Collard greens are among the most nutritious vegetables you can grow in the garden. They are high in minerals, vitamins, and proteins and are extremely low in calories. Collard greens belong to the same family as cabbage, but they do not form any heads. These are also harvested for their leaves. Collards are hardy plants and are equally tolerant to heat and cold. They are extremely simple to grow, and are ideal for both small and large gardens. Even though they survive in heat, they thrive in cool weather and require plenty of sunlight.

Planting and Growing

Before you start planting, the soil must be well-drained and prepared. The roots of these plants can easily grow up to 2 feet long, or even more. So, the soil must be tilled at least 10 inches deep in order to loosen properly. This, in turn, ensures the tiny feeder roots have sufficient space to grow out. Remove any large stones or rocks from the soil, and amend them with plant material or compost. Give it at least a week before you start sowing. Don't forget to add organic matter if the soil is predominantly clayey or sandy. Usually, adding a layer of oranges to compost does the trick. The compost must be evenly spread over the planting area before you start digging. Additionally, use a 10-10-10 garden fertilizer to further improve the soil quality in the area you want to grow. You will need 2-3 lbs of fertilizer for 100 square feet.

You can either directly sow the seeds in the soil, or even use transplants. Transplants are ideal if you want a spring crop. Transplants, in this case, help prolong the growing season by 4-5 weeks by giving you a head start. You can also grow them indoors until the weather outdoors is ideal for collards. They require a soil temperature of around 45° F to sprout.

Sow the seeds such that they are ½ inch deep in the soil. Make a shallow furrow of the same depth in the center of the growing area. After this, simply scatter the seeds. Cover the seeds with 1/4 inch of topsoil and compost, then sprinkle the area with some water. Within 6-12 days, you will see seedlings. The rate at which the seeds sprout is dependent on the soil temperature. So, as the soil cools down, the germination process slows down, too. If you are using transplants, then the ideal time to grow collards is as soon as spring starts. The transplants must be planted at the same depth at which they were growing in containers. Space them such that the rows are 18-24 inches apart. Don't forget to water them after this. If you want a fall crop, the right time to start seeds is 80 days before the first frost. Always seed heavily, because you can thin them later. This increases the chances of their survival, too.

Once the seedlings appear, let the young plants grow until they are 4-6 inches tall. If they seem too crowded in the row, it is time to start thinning. The plants must be 18 inches apart, and the same space must be maintained between the rows, too. If the plants are too crowded, the leaves will be smaller and paler than they are supposed to be. You can either transplant the extra plants to another area, or consume them.

Collards need about a teaspoon of fertilizer per plant. Always mix the fertilizer with water and soil instead of adding it directly to the plants—this is known as side-dressing. Ideally, repeating this process once every 4-6 weeks guarantees a good harvest. More fertilizer might be needed if the plants thinned after the final spacing and turned pale green, or if their growth is stunted. These plants require nitrogen for producing dark green leaves, and need an inch of water per week.

Harvesting

If the small plants require thinning, then the entire plant can be cut close to the ground such that only 4 inches of it are visible. Usually, the lower parts of the plant are harvested. If you do this regularly, you will have a continuous supply of collard greens. Do not harvest more than 1/3 of the plant at any point. Harvest the young leaves instead of waiting for them to grow as big as they can. The younger leaves taste better than the older ones. These plants can withstand temperatures of as low as 20° F, and even lower in some cases. In fact, they taste sweeter after a mild frost.

Watercress

The botanical name of the watercress is Nasturtium officinale, and it is a perennial plant. It is an underrated leafy vegetable, and a powerhouse of nutrients. It consists of small and round leaves along with edible stems, and has a slightly peppery and spicy flavor. It belongs to the brassica family. During the early 1800s, it was considered to be a weed, but now is grown across the world. It is rich in vitamin K, helpful antioxidants and polyphenols, vitamin A, vitamin C, vitamin E, calcium, and manganese. It is extremely low in carbs, too. Regular consumption of watercress reduces the risk of chronic health conditions and is good for improving heart health.

A common reason why most gardeners avoid planting watercress is that it usually thrives in clear and slow-moving water. That said, this is an incredibly adaptable plant, and you can grow it in your garden in no time. Usually, it is found in moderately equal climatic regions and is partially submerged in running water. That said, it grows well in wet soil as well. The ideal pH is between 6.5 and 7.5, and it thrives in full sun. Before you can grow watercress, the first step is to ensure that the soil is amended with peat moss or any other compost to improve its water retention.

Planting and Growing

You can grow it from seeds, cuttings, and transplants. There are different varieties of watercress to choose from. Regardless of the variety, they require similar care.

For planting watercress, the location you should opt for is sunny and the soil must be amended with 4-6 inches of composted organic matter. The seeds are quite tiny, so simply sprinkle them over the desired area. The ideal time to start sowing the seeds is three weeks before the last frost so that they enjoy plenty of sunlight to grow. It germinates best in cold plantations, and the ideal temperature is 50° F-60° F. It likes a cold climate, but not frigid conditions. The soil must be moist, but should not be covered in water. Within five days the seedlings will appear. Ensure that the plants are about 8 inches apart once the seedlings start to appear. If not, thinning is needed.

Watercress plants should have consistent moisture in the soil—they need way more than the usual 1 inch of water per week. They do not have any special requirements for nutrients, but the common deficiencies these plants form are potassium, phosphorus, and iron. Therefore, utilizing soluble fertilizer helps mitigate these issues before they crop. Ensure that you regularly mulch the area and keep it free of weeds to promote water retention in the soil. The most common insects and pests that watercress attracts include snails, whiteflies, and spider mites. So, ensure that you keep an eye on the plants.

Harvesting

During the cool months, watercress is the most flavorful. The flavor is further reduced when the plant blossoms. As soon as the plant reaches the 3-week mark from its emergence, you can start harvesting. Regularly cutting and pruning the plants promotes a thicker growth. Always harvest around 4 inches of the plant, and no more. Don't forget to thoroughly wash the cuttings before consumption.

Mustard Greens

The botanical name of mustard greens is Brassica juncea, and it belongs to the brassica family. The mustard plant is quite popular for its tiny yellow-tinged seeds. It is used for producing one of the most popular condiments across the globe—mustard. However, even the leaves of this plant are perfectly edible and offer a variety of benefits. Their leaves are a rich source of vitamins A and C. They promote kidney functioning and help detoxify the blood. Mustard greens are an age-old remedy to treat sore throat and cough. They also have antiseptic and disinfectant properties, and helpful antioxidants that strengthen the functioning of the immune system. Their leaves can be consumed either raw or in cooked form.

Mustard greens are not usually the go-to plant for most gardeners. In fact, most are unfamiliar with it. However, it is incredibly easy to grow these spicy greens, and you can do it quickly as well. The ideal soil for mustard greens must have a pH of 6 to 6.8. They thrive in well-drained and loamy soil. Ensure the soil is amended with compost before planting. These plants require plenty of sunlight, but grow well in partial shade, too.

Planting and Growing

You can grow mustard greens from seeds as well as seedlings. Growing it from seeds is extremely simple, and also the most popular method. Sow the seeds in the garden soil three weeks before the last frost. If you want a regular harvest, then replant seeds every three weeks. Even though they need plenty of sunlight, they don't grow too well in the summer. So, don't plant the seeds toward the end of spring. Instead, you can start replanting from midsummer to harvest the greens in the fall; the seeds must be sown shallowly and should be 1/2 inch apart. Once the seedlings are about 3 inches tall, thinning is needed. Ensure the seedlings are 3-5 inches apart for best results.

These hardy plants barely require any extra care. As long as they get plenty of sunlight, their growth will be rapid. Using a balanced fertilizer is sufficient, but they don't need it if the garden soil is properly amended before planting. These plants require 2 inches of water per week. Ensure there are no weeds around them, especially when they are quite young, to promote their growth.

Harvesting

Harvest the mustard greens when they are young and tender. The leaves not only become tough as they mature, but they become extremely bitter, too. If you notice any yellow leaves, discard them immediately. You can either pick individual leaves or let the plant grow. Alternatively, the entire plant can be cut down and all its leaves can be harvested at once.

Red Chard

The botanical name of red chard is Beta vulgaris subsp. vulgaris, and it belongs to the amaranth family. Red chard (or Swiss chard) is an extremely nutritious leafy vegetable. In fact, consuming just a cup of it offers three times the required daily quota of vitamin K. It is also known as silverbeet, or spinach beet. Red chard contains high levels of nitrates that reduce blood pressure, vitamin A, vitamin C, calcium, iron, phosphorus, magnesium, and folate. It also contains traces of other helpful antioxidants.

Red chard (or just chard) grows well in both warm and cool climates. This incredibly nutritious superfood comes in a variety of colors as well. It prefers slightly acidic to neutral soil, and the right time to grow it is in summer and fall. It's usually grown as a cool-season crop, because it matures quickly during colder temperatures prevalent around fall and spring. It is tolerant of warmer climates as well. However, its growth is slower in warmer climates when compared to cool seasons. Apart from all of the different nutritional benefits it offers, chard is a lovely edible ornament plant as well. It will definitely add a dash of color to your garden. Ensure that the growing area allocated for chard gets sufficient sunlight daily. Well-drained soil with a pH between 6 to 7 is ideal for it. Therefore, to improve soil fertility, amending it with compost or aged manure will do the trick.

Planting and Growing

The ideal time to grow chard during spring is to sow the seed 2-3 weeks before the last frost date. If you want to harvest during the fall, the ideal time to sow the seeds is 40 days before the first frost date. If you want to quicken the germination process, ensure the seeds are soaked in water for 24 hours before sowing in the soil. Use 5-10-10 fertilizer to boost the soil quality before planting. It must be sown 1 to 1/2 inch deep in the soil, and must be 2 to 6 inches apart. Make sure that the rows are 18 inches apart for the best growth. You can keep planting the seeds at 10-day intervals for an entire month for a continuous harvest later.

As soon as the young plants are 3-4 inches tall, it is time to thin out the patch. The plants must be 4-6 inches apart, or up to 12 inches apart, if they are taller than 4 inches. For thinning, use a sharp pair of scissors to avoid disturbing the roots of the nearby plants. Usually, these plants don't require any additional fertilizer provided the soil was amended before planting. However, if it looks like the plants are consistently smaller, applying a balanced fertilizer halfway through the growing season does the trick. Don't forget to water the plants evenly for consistent growth and better development. Suppress the growth of weeds and promote moisture retention in the soil by carefully mulching around the plants. To encourage the growth of tender leaves, snip back or prune the plant once it is a foot tall. The leaves become less flavorful if the plants are overgrown. So, regularly pruning mature plants is needed for better growth and harvest.

Harvesting

When the plant is about 6-8 inches tall, you can start harvesting—or wait until the leaves are of the desired size. The outer leaves must be cut 1 1/2 inches above the ground using a sharp knife. Ensure that you do not damage the center of the plant, because this is what keeps producing leaves. If you want the plant to produce continually, then you will have to harvest regularly. Start by harvesting the oldest in the larger leaves while allowing the younger ones to grow. The ideal temperature for these plants to keep growing is 50° F. If the temperature becomes colder than this, you can prolong the harvesting season by transferring the plants into a container and placing them in a greenhouse.

Iceberg Lettuce

The botanical name of iceberg lettuce is Lactuca sativa var capitata, and it belongs to the Asteraceae family. This is the same family that sunflowers, asters, and daisies belong to. Iceberg lettuce is also popularly known as crispy head lettuce. It grows in cabbage-like bulbs and has pale green leaves. It's an extremely popular type of lettuce, with a crisp and crunchy texture. It has a mildly sweet flavor, making it ideal for different salads. Regular consumption of iceberg lettuce is known to prevent blood clotting and improve eye health. It is low in calories and contains plenty of sodium, dietary fiber, and protein— along with vitamins A, C, and K, calcium, folate, iron, and manganese.

Iceberg lettuce is the most popular type of lettuce, and is stable for different salads as well as sandwiches. With its crunchy and sweet-tasting leaves, it is quite popular across the world. These plants prefer cold weather, but usually require a long growing season. If you plant properly, the lettuce will start maturing as the warm weather sets in. However, if the weather becomes extremely warm, it results in bolting or rotting of the head. You can either plant the seeds directly in the garden or start them indoors. The ideal pH of the soil is 7-7. Once you take care of these factors, growing lettuce becomes easier.

Planting and Growing

Ideally, start the lettuce seeds indoors to ensure that the head is mature before warm weather begins. To start it indoors, sow the seeds in a seed tray and cover it lightly using fine starter soil. Ensure that the soil stays moist for germination. The seedlings will appear within 10 days of seeding. For a continuous harvest, reseed every week or so. If you are directly sowing in the garden, then ensure the seedlings are 12 inches apart for best results. If the seedlings appear too crowded, then thinning is needed. The rows must be 18 inches apart. These plants require full sun and well-draining, fertile soil.

So, you must keep feeding the plants plenty of water and fertilizer for quick growth and development. A nitrogen-rich fertilizer is well-suited for iceberg lettuce.

Harvesting

Iceberg lettuce is usually ready for harvest within 80-90 days. This is the period within which the plant reaches full maturity. If you have a big crop, you can start harvesting the lettuce as soon as its head forms. The outer leaves are also edible. However, the inner leaves are sweeter than the outer ones. As soon as the heads look big and tightly packed, it is ready for harvest. If you don't harvest quickly at this stage, lettuce will start bolting within a few days.

Red Leaf Lettuce

The botanical name of red leaf lettuce is Lactuca sativa, and it belongs to the daisy family. Even though it looks like romaine lettuce, the distinguishing feature is that it has red- or purple-tinted tips. This extremely colorful leafy vegetable is rich in vitamins A, C, K, E, and B6, iron, folate, magnesium, manganese, potassium, and riboflavin. It is extremely hydrating, is loaded with antioxidants, and is known to improve heart health.

Red leaf lettuce is a loose-leaf lettuce, and it does not form a compact head. It is grown for its tender and delicate leaves that crop up from a central stalk. Usually, these plants reach full maturity 45-50 days after seeding. The larger leaves can be collected regularly throughout the growth cycle. They are sensitive to excess light and heat—therefore, ensure that there is some shade for their growth. If they're exposed to extreme heat, this results in wilting and bolting. The ideal temperature for germination and growth is between 40° F to 85° F, and they prefer well-drained soil. The ideal pH of the soil should be between 6.2 and 6.8. It is tolerant to a variety of soils, but it prefers cool, loose, and well-drained soil with plenty of moisture retention. Before planting, amend the soil using organic compost.

Planting and Growing

The right time to start the seeds is 4 weeks before the last frost. If you are transplanting the seedlings outdoors, then move them outdoors in late spring. Select a partially shaded location that receives sufficient sunlight if you are growing this lettuce in summer. Since it is sensitive to low pH, carefully amend the soil before you directly sow the seeds. If you want to get an early start in the growing season, the beds must be prepared in the previous fall by adding compost or manure to them. The seeds require sufficient light to germinate, and therefore, they must be sown at a shallow depth. Ensure that they are covered with a thin layer of topsoil. They need to be sown no more than 1 inch in the soil, and the rows must be 12-18 inches apart. As soon as the young plants have 2 or 3 true leaves, thin out the seedlings. They need around 6 and 10 inches between them.

Don't hesitate to use row covers if you are growing them quite early in the season, especially to prevent them from catching a cold. This also protects the young plants from pests and insects. Succession plantings made every week or two offer a continuous supply throughout the growing season. Bolting occurs if the plants are exposed to high moisture and temperatures, especially at night. Opting for bolt-resistant varieties is always a better idea. They have a shallow root system, and therefore, the soil must be moist for their growth. Regular mulching helps retain moisture while suppressing the growth of weeds. You can also obtain a quicker growth by opting for natural fertilizers, such as fish emulsion, throughout the growing season. However, ensure that the fertilizer is not too rich in nitrogen, because the leaves turn bitter due to it.

Harvesting

The joy of harvesting any type of leaf lettuce, such as red leaf lettuce, is that it acts as an invitation to the plant to grow more foliage. All you require is a sterilized pair of pruning shears or scissors, and gloves. The outer leaves must be snipped before the inner ones; this is how the plant keeps growing. Gently snip the outer leaves as close to the base as you possibly can until you have the required amount of lettuce. Alternatively, you can simply grab a handful of the leaves you need and tip them outward away from the crown. After this, snip the entire clump together.

Romaine Lettuce

Romaine lettuce belongs to the Asteraceae family, and its botanical name is Lactuca sativa var. longifolia. If you have eaten a Caesar salad, wedge salad, or chopped salad, then you have eaten romaine lettuce. Unlike other varieties of lettuce, romaine leaves are green at the top and gradually fade to a white stock. They have a neutral flavor, with a slight bitterness close to the bottom. This crispy salad green is rich in calcium, dietary fiber, magnesium, potassium, phosphorus, folate, sodium, beta-carotene, and vitamins A, C, and K. Romaine lettuce is known to support the health of the cardiovascular system and eyes.

This is a common salad vegetable to plant within the United States. It grows well in cool weather, and is simple to grow. It is an annual vegetable, but it is usually considered to be a spring or fall crop. Usually, they mature within 30-45 days, but you can harvest them earlier in the form of microgreens as well. By successive sowing every 10 days or so, you'll have a continuous supply throughout the growing season. The ideal pH of the soil is between 6 and 7. Apart from this, the ideal temperature for germination is between 40° F to 85° F. Lettuce thrives in soil that is well-drained, loose, and cool. If the pH is not within the recommended range, lettuce will not grow properly because it is sensitive to low pH.

Planting and Growing

Since lettuce loves cold weather, you can start planting as soon as the soil is amended in spring. As mentioned, for an extended harvest, successive plantings are needed every 10 days or so. Plant a month before the warming temperature of the summer sets in to prevent summer bolting. Planting in late summer is ideal for fall lettuce, because it quickly reaches its maturity once the air turns cold. A preferable area for growing lettuce is a spot that receives sufficient sunlight daily. This is around 6 hours of direct sunlight per day. If you want to grow during summer or in a warm area, ensure that they have a little shade so that bolting doesn't occur.

Growing lettuce from seed is quite easy. The seeds are extremely small, and should not be sown more than 1/2 inch deep in the soil. If you are growing different types of lettuce, try growing them in alternating rows for a better aesthetic look. Ensure that the seeds are sown such that there are no more than 10 seeds per foot, and the rows are 12-18 inches apart. Once the seedlings are about 14 inches tall, thinning is needed if they are placed close together. Ensure there is a space of at least 6-8 inches between each plant. Deep root growth is not needed for this plant—and in fact, leaf growth must be encouraged over rooting. Also, light watering is sufficient. However, you must be consistent and frequent while watering because the soil must be moist. If you water too often, though, it results in stunted growth of the plant and increases the risk of root rot as well.

Harvesting

This is one of the simplest vegetables you can harvest, and you don't have to worry about how to pick lettuce leaves. Usually, you can start harvesting 30-70 days after planting is complete. The harvest essentially depends on the varieties of lettuce you are using. The timing is also entirely up to you. As soon as the leaves are the size you want, it is time to harvest. Usually, do this early in the morning because they are the most flavorful at that time. You can either cut the entire clump close to the base, or remove a couple of leaves at a time. If you harvest the outer leaves and leave the inner ones, the plant will produce more, and you will have a continuous harvest. However, ensure at least 1/3 of the plant is left behind while harvesting.

Dandelion Greens

Most consider dandelion to be a weed, but technically it is an herb. The botanical name of the dandelion is Taraxacum, and it belongs to the Asteraceae family. It was initially native to Eurasia, but now grows across North America. These greens are rich in vitamins K, C, E, and A, dietary fiber, calcium, magnesium, iron, folate, and potassium. They are filled with powerful antioxidants that fight inflammation, promote cardiovascular health, assist in weight loss, and regulate blood pressure. They also stabilize blood sugar and cholesterol levels.

Dandelion is a hardy-flowering perennial herb that produces pretty yellow flowers. These yellow flowers open up into white puffballs. Dandelion leaves can be added to salads and stir-fries. You can also brew tea from the leaves as well as its roots. Growing dandelions is incredibly simple, and they germinate within 10-14 days. Ensure that the soil is well-drained, loose, and fertile if you want the plants to thrive. They require a sunny spot, but partial shade is better—especially if you plan on eating the leaves. Shade slows their growth and ensures the leaves do not turn bitter. The ideal pH of the soil for dandelions is between 4.2 to 8.3. So, a little amendment is needed as long as the soil is fertile and well-drained. These low-maintenance plants are incredibly simple to grow.

Planting and Growing

From early spring to late summer or even early fall, these seeds can be sown at any time. These plants will grow even if the soil temperature is as low as 50° F. However, they do prefer a warmer climate. These plants are self-seeding, and if you wait for too long to harvest, the seed heads will be produced and the seeds will be scattered all throughout the garden. The right time to pick the leaves is when they are tender and young. The longer you wait, the more bitter they will taste.

To get started, the seeds must be directly sown into the soil 6 weeks before the last frost. Ensure that the soil temperature is at least 50° F. Don't plant these seeds too deeply, just 1/4 inch below the surface does the trick. Lightly cover them with topsoil to ensure they receive sufficient sunlight for germination. While planting in rows, the seeds must be sown a couple of inches apart to give them the space required for growth. These plants can be around 6 inches tall, and grow in clusters. Once the dandelion seedlings have sprouted, thinning might be needed to ensure there is at least 6 inches of space between the plants. These are self-pollinators, and hardly require any additional maintenance. If you want to get rid of them permanently after a growing season, however, you will have to uproot them thoroughly.

These plants prefer moist soil, and therefore, you must water them regularly. The top 2 inches of the soil must be watered to ensure that the roots get sufficient moisture. They need at least 6 hours of sunlight while growing; once they are fully established, though, they don't need as much. Another great way to prevent weeds while promoting their germination and growth is to mulch regularly.

Harvesting

As mentioned before, as the leaves mature, they become bitter. A simple way to avoid this is by covering the area with dark fabric for a few days before you want to harvest. This helps block out additional sunlight, and slows down the maturation process. Simply snip the leaves and flowers as and when you need them. Always use a clean pair of scissors, and leave a bit of the stem so that the plant keeps growing. If you want to harvest the roots as well as the leaves, simply remove the entire plant from the soil. Do not harshly tug or pull it out of the ground; instead, use a trowel to loosen the soil around it. This is the best way to harvest without snapping the roots. If you want the plants to keep growing, always leave a little bit of its root behind.

Amaranth

Amaranth's botanical name is Amaranthaceae. The leaves of this plant are not only delicious, but are also rich in a variety of nutrients. The seeds produced by this plant are healthy, too. Amaranth contains phytonutrients and antioxidants that reduce inflammation; they are low in calories and filled with dietary fiber. It is a good source of vitamins A, C, K, and B, potassium, calcium, and protein. They help regulate blood pressure levels and promote digestive health, too.

A surprising thing about amaranth is that it is usually grown as a decorative flower in Europe, as well as in Northern America. However, it is an excellent food crop grown across the world, and is a leafy plant and grain as well. It develops flowers that can be trailing or upright depending on the variety of amaranth you are growing. The flowers then produce grains. The leaves can be used just like any other greens. The ideal temperature for germination is around 60° F to 70° F. They require around 6-8 hours of exposure to sunlight daily. The soil must be amended with aged manure or compost before you start showing. These plants require more nitrogen, and using a nitrogen-rich fertilizer or blood meal during the growing season does the trick. However, excess nitrogen results in bolting and thin growth of the plants. These quick-growing plants usually germinate between 7-14 days. They grow well in average quality soil, but extremely dense clay soil is unsuitable for its growth. It is a warm-season crop, so you will need to wait until after the final frost to start growing it outdoors. The ideal pH of the soil is between 6 to 7. Let's see how to grow this low-maintenance crop.

Planting and Growing

As soon as the last frost has ended, it's time to get started. Sow the seeds 1/4 inch deep in the soil and lightly cover them with a layer of soil. They require plenty of sunlight for germination. The roots are not too deep, so they need to be carefully watered. Ensure that there is 6-18 inches of space between the plants, and around 12-18 inches of space between the rows. While starting, you can sow plenty of seeds to promote germination. However, thinning will be needed at a later stage. Once the seedlings are a couple of inches tall, you can start thinning them. They can be up to 5 feet high when fully mature. You don't need any other fertilizer or amendment once the amaranth plants are established.

Harvesting

As with any other green leafy vegetables, you can start harvesting Amaranth whenever the need arises. Just wait until the leaves are of ideal size. Also, it is better to pluck the leaves when they are young and tender, because they taste the best at this point. The larger leaves have a more developed flavor. Ideally, start harvesting the leaves before the plant flowers. Even though you can keep harvesting the leaves of a flowering plant, their taste varies. Simply snip the leaves whenever you need them. You can also cut the plant such that only a couple of inches of it are left behind to promote better growth. Alternatively, you can uproot the entire plant once it starts flowering, provided you don't want more amaranth plants to grow.

Arugula

The botanical name of arugula is Eruca vesicaria. Arugula is believed to have originated in the Mediterranean region. It belongs to the brassica family, and is also known as Italian cress, salad rocket, and rucola. It has a slightly peppery flavor that makes it quite easy to recognize, and is an incredibly delicious green and nutrient-dense food. It is rich in dietary fiber and low in calories, and contains plenty of calcium and vitamins A, C, and K.

These plants thrive when exposed to sufficient sunlight. They prefer slightly acidic to neutral soil, and the bloom time is spring, summer, and fall. Their mustard-flavored leaves are incredibly easy to grow. Young leaves can be harvested during early spring within 6-8 weeks of planting. The seeds germinate when the soil is cool, and the seedlings are hard enough to tolerate light frost. However, using row covers is recommended if you are starting when the season has slightly begun. They require well-drained and nutrient-rich soil, but are not too choosy about the growing conditions. However, the soil pH must be between 6 and 7.

This plant must receive 6 hours of direct sunlight daily, and it does not do well when grown in shade. Ensure that these plants are not planted where other members of the brassica family were recently planted. These seeds will germinate even if the soil temperature is as low as 40° F. Work the soil in spring and check the local frost date before getting started. If you want to harvest in fall or winter, you will need to start sowing late in summer or even early fall.

Planting and Growing

The seeds must be sown 1/4 inch deep in the soil. There must be at least 1 inch between each plant, and the rows must be 10 inches apart for best growth. The seeds will start germinating within a week, or might take a little longer if the soil is colder than the required temperature. To quicken the germination process, soak the seeds before you sow them. After every 2 or 3 weeks, sow the seeds for a continuous harvest throughout the growing season. Ensure that the soil is evenly moist, especially if the weather is warm—if not, bolting occurs. Once the seedlings are around 3 inches tall, thinning will be needed if they are too close together. Even though they can be sown close together, there must be at least 6 inches between each plant. If you are planting during warm seasons, to reduce heat stress and bolting, you will need to provide them with some form of shade.

Harvesting

Harvest the arugula leaves when they are young and tender. Their flavor is altered as they mature. Also, the older leaves are tougher to eat than the young ones. The leaves are ready for harvest as soon as they are about 2-3 inches in length. You can either snip the individual leaves, or uproot the entire plant and harvest accordingly. If the plant sports any white flowers, these can be consumed as well.

Bok Choy

The botanical name of bok choy is Brassica rapa subsp. chinensis, and it belongs to the brassica family. It is also known as Chinese cabbage or pak choi. Even though it belongs to the brassica family, it doesn't form a typical head like cabbage. Instead, it has thick and crunchy white stems with broad leaves. This plant is native to China, and has been cultivated in North America for over 100 years. It is packed full of vitamins A, C, K, and B complex vitamins. It contains calcium, potassium, phosphorus, selenium, zinc, copper, and magnesium.

This is a cool-season and fast-growing biennial plant, and can be harvested within the first year of its growth. It has crispy stalks and tender leaves. The flavor is somewhere in between that of chard and cabbage. The ideal time to get started is early spring—you can also start late in the summer for a fall harvest. Succession planting every 3 weeks or so will help prolong the growing season. These plants require plenty of sunlight, but thrive in partial shade as well. They need well-drained soil with a pH between 6.5 to 7.

Planting and Growing

This is a quick-growing plant, and the seeds can be directly sown in the soil. As soon as the last frost has passed, get started. You can also start the seeds indoors and transplant the seedlings later, but you needn't go through this hassle. However, weather plays a significant role in its growth and maturity. If it's too warm, this results in bolting. On the other hand, the young plants will bolt if the temperature is any lower than 50° F. They need around 5 hours of sunlight daily. Once you are happy with the chosen location, it's time to get started.

Sow the seeds such that they are ¼ inch in the ground. Cover them with a light layer of garden soil. The seeds must be sown ½ inch apart for best results. Thinning of the seedlings will be needed later to ensure there are 6-12 inches between each plant for quick growth. The rows must be 18-30 inches apart. If you want a continuous harvest of bok choy, then sow the seeds after every 2-3 weeks during the growing season.

They prefer moist soil, but overwatering isn't recommended. If the soil is too moist, this results in root rot. Alternatively, if it is too dry, this results in bolting. They usually require 1 inch of water every week. Since they are heavy feeders, consider adding organic manure or fertilizer a couple of times during the growing period.

Harvesting

Depending on the variety and the climatic conditions, bok choy can be harvested within 45-60 days of seeding. Always harvest the outer leaves to promote plant growth—this will give you a continuous harvest of fresh bok choy whenever you need it. If all the leaves are harvested, then leave the plant such that only 1 inch of its stem is left above ground. This gives it a chance to resprout. You can also propagate the stems in water for resprouting. If the young and tender seedlings were thinned, they can be added to stir-fries and salads as well.

Rapini

The botanical name of rapini is Brassica ruvo—it is also known as broccoli raab or rabe, broccoletti, and ruvo kale. Turnip and bok choy are believed to be their subspecies. This is a spicy and zesty leafy vegetable commonly featured in Mediterranean cooking. Unlike a full head of broccoli, it features small flowering heads and turnip-like jagged leaves. Rapini is loaded with vitamins A, K, C, and E, helpful minerals such as calcium and iron, dietary fiber, folate, and electrolytes. It is also filled with helpful antioxidants.

This plant has tiny, spiked leaves surrounding a central green bud. They look like small heads of broccoli, and the stem, leaves, and buds are edible. In fact, it is considered to be a culinary delight in Europe. The yellow flowers produced by this plant are edible, too. It has a nutty and slightly pungent flavor similar to a combination of turnips and broccoli. It is usually said that the longer rapini takes to mature, the better its flavor profile. Since it is a member of the cabbage family, avoid planting rapini in the same soil for at least three years after the first harvest. Following this practice of crop rotation is good for the overall health of your garden and soil.

This plant prefers full exposure to the sun, and the ideal pH of the soil is 6.5. If the soil is too acidic, you can add lime to create the ideal pH. These plants are moderate feeders and prefer soil that is deep and loosely cultivated. Before sowing, prepare the soil by mixing it with plenty of compost and an all-purpose fertilizer such as fish meal or bone meal.

Planting and Growing

Rapini can be grown both indoors as well as outdoors. Wait until the frost has passed before you start sowing seeds outdoors. Sow seeds such that they are 1 inch deep in the soil, and in rows that are about 24 inches apart. Initially, you can sow 10-12 seeds every 12 inches or so.

You can always thin it out later, but the first step is to ensure there are sufficient seedlings. To protect the seeds, use row covers—or even add a thin layer of mulch. The soil must be moist without becoming too soggy, lest the seeds will not germinate. Alternatively, you can start the seeds early in the season if it is too cold outdoors. Ensure that the medium used for starting seeds is of good quality.

As soon as the seeds sprout, move the container with the seedlings to an area that receives plenty of sunlight. Once the growing conditions are ideal, the seedlings grown indoors can be transplanted. The seedlings must have sufficient space around them for further growth. If the patch is too cluttered, then start thinning the seedlings. Do this only after the seedlings are about 4 inches tall. Ensure that any infested or infected plants are immediately uprooted.

Harvesting

Once the buds are formed, you can harvest rapini. The buds will quickly turn into flowers if the weather is hot. Even after flowering, rapini is edible, but the leaves become bitter, extremely peppery, and tough to eat. Cut the main stem of the rapini plant to 4 inches or so above the lower leaves. The lower leaves are coarser and don't taste as good as the tender ones. While harvesting, leave a couple of leaf nodes on the stem to promote the growth of the next set of leaves. You can also pick individual buds from the plant.

Chapter 11:

Fruit Vegetables

In this chapter, you will be introduced to different types of fruit vegetables that are ideal for your garden. You will learn in detail about their ideal growing conditions, how to plant them, and the harvest techniques!

Tomatoes

The botanical name of tomatoes is Solanum lycopersicum. Growing tomatoes at home is incredibly simple. They prefer acidic to slightly acidic and neutral soil, and thrive when fully exposed to the sun for 6-8 hours daily. The bright red color of tomatoes is associated with a substance known as lycopene—this substance also protects the tomatoes from damage caused by the ultraviolet rays of the sun. Similarly, consuming tomatoes also helps protect your body from the inside. They are loaded with vitamins C and B, potassium, and other nutrients. Regular consumption of tomatoes strengthens the functioning of the immune system, reduces the risk of cardiovascular diseases, and improves eye health. They also reduce inflammation, promote blood circulation, regulate cholesterol levels, improve lung functioning, improve skin health, and even support oral health.

The ideal bloom time for tomatoes is in the summer. This warm-season crop is quite tender, loves sunlight, and cannot deal with frost. You must wait for the right time before planting. If you get started too early, the temperature of the soil will not be warm enough to sustain its growth. Depending on the variety of tomatoes you are opting for, their maturity date ranges from 60-100 days from seeding until harvest.

When compared to other plants, they have a relatively long growing season. Also, the planting date is quite late in the year. This is one of the reasons why most gardeners usually opt for transplants or starter plants instead of starting with seeds, especially once the weather has warmed up. If you choose not to start from seeds, transplants can be purchased from a local nursery or garden center.

When it comes to transplants, ensure that you are purchasing them from a reputable garden center or nursery, and that the plants are healthy. This means they shouldn't have any spots on the leaves, yellow leaves, or any other damage. Similarly, they shouldn't have any fruit or flowers already in progress. Instead, they must be short and stocky with straight and short stumps under green-colored foliage. Alternatively, purchase good quality seeds should you choose this route.

Planting and Growing

Tomatoes grow when exposed to at least 8 hours of sunlight daily, and are red and bright. So, ensure that the site you opt for offers plenty of sun exposure. However, if the climatic conditions become extremely hot, then using row covers does the trick. Before sowing the seeds or transferring the transplants to the garden, you must provide the right soil structure. Simply till the soil and mix it with compost or aged manure. Let it sit for two weeks to promote the organic breakdown of the compounds present in it, and start planting. Also, do not make the mistake of planting the seeds or transplants in an area where other members of this family have previously grown (potatoes, eggplants, and peppers) in the last couple of years.

These plants require a longer growing time, and they love warm weather. Since they cannot tolerate frost, timing plays an important factor here. The seeds can be sown indoors around 6 weeks before the last date of expected spring frost. If you are doing this, you will need small trays that are at least 2 inches deep. Fill them with soil and sow the seeds such that they are ½ inch deep. The seedlings should appear within 2 weeks, and they can be transplanted outdoors. The ideal time to transplant the seedlings to the garden is when the temperature is around 50° F during the day and night.

On the other hand, you can directly sow in the garden, especially if the growing season is long enough for their maturity. As mentioned, simply sow the seeds directly in the garden soil such that they are ½ inch deep. Do not plant them any deeper, because tomatoes have extremely fine roots, and the idea is to not stress them initially. Ensure that the soil temperature is around 50° F, and no less. The perfect soil temperature for optimum germination within a week of seeding is 70° F.

If you are purchasing starter plants or growing the seeds indoors, hardening the seedlings is needed before transplantation. This essentially means that you will slowly need to get them accustomed to the natural growing conditions outdoors instead of the environment indoors. Place the tray with the seedlings in shade for a couple of hours on the first day. After this, slowly increase the time they spend exposed to direct sunlight. Within a week, they will be strong enough and you can transform them into the garden soil.

Do not transplant the seedlings until all signs of frost have passed. The soil must be close to 60° F to ensure your seedlings do not die. Whenever you are transplanting, ensure that the soil is properly amended. The simplest way to do this is by adding a little bone meal or any other organic tomato fertilizer to the soil. Such fertilizers are usually an excellent source of phosphorus. Ensure that you are not using fertilizers rich in nitrogen, because it increases the growth of foliage, but also reduces the chances of flowering and fruiting. Since this is undesirable, opt for phosphorus-rich fertilizer.

The ideal time to water the plants is early in the morning so that they have sufficient moisture to make it through a warm day. They require around 2 inches of water per week, and therefore, deep watering is needed. Never water the foliage or water the plants during the afternoon, because it increases the risk of plant diseases. After every 5 weeks, don't forget to mulch around the plant. Around 2-4 inches of organic mulch is sufficient for this purpose.

Harvesting

Leave the tomatoes on the plant for as long as you possibly can, and harvest them at the very end. The ideal time to harvest tomatoes is when they are firm and have taken on the right color. Simply pluck the fruit close to the stem using a twist and pull method. Do this gently and don't give the plant a sudden jerk.

Bell Peppers

The botanical name of bell peppers is Capsicum annuum. These plants thrive during the warmer months and come in a variety of colors, sizes, and shapes. Also, they are usually resistant to a variety of garden pests and insects. They prefer slightly acidic to neutral soil. Bell peppers are excellent sources of vitamins A and C, and contain trace amounts of several other helpful minerals. They can not only be consumed in raw form, but can be cooked as well. Whether it is a snap, salad, or stir-fry, bell peppers are versatile veggies. They are low in calories and are a rich source of vitamins A, C, B6, and E, beta-carotene, potassium, and folate. The different nutrients present in them are known to lower and regulate blood pressure levels, reduce the risk of cardiovascular disorders, promote digestive health, and reduce the risk of diabetes.

The growing time required for most types of peppers is between 60-90 days. Therefore, it is surprising that gardeners usually opt for starter plants or transplants instead of starting with seeds at home. That said, as with tomatoes, even bell pepper seeds can be started indoors provided you start a little early. This will not only give you a head start, but also reduces their growing time in the garden—even if the weather conditions are not ideal.

Before you start planting, don't forget to amend the soil. To do this, mix compost or aged manure into the soil such that it is well-mixed within a depth of10 inches. Also, rake the soil a couple of times to break up any large chunks of soil as well. Another tip that can be used to ensure that the soil has reached the right temperature is by covering it with a dark plastic sheet, or a layer of mulch, for 1 week or 10 days before sowing. This increases the chances of their survival.

Planting and Growing

The spot that you choose for growing peppers must not only receive plenty of sunlight daily, but should also have well-draining soil as well. The ideal soil for these plants is a combination of sandy and loamy— this promotes water drainage while creating the ideal growing temperature. Before you start planting, ensure that you work compost or any other organic matter into the soil, especially if it is heavy or rich in clay. Working in compost improves the fertility and nutritional profile of the soil, along with its structure. Make sure that the area where you want to grow bell peppers was not recently home to any other plants belonging to the nightshade family such as eggplants, tomatoes, or potatoes.

If you want to start the seeds indoors, the ideal time is around 6-8 weeks before the last frost has passed. Once the soil temperature is around 65° F, then you can shift the seedlings to the garden outdoors. Usually, you need to wait until 2-3 weeks after the final threat of frost has passed by to do this. If not, the plants will die.

If you are starting the seeds indoors, then you will need a tray lined with potting mix. Sow the seeds ¼ inch deep in the soil. For a quicker germination, the ideal temperature of the soil should be around 70° F. If sufficient light or the temperature cannot be maintained naturally at this stage, you can use grow lights. If the conditions are ideal, then the seedlings will appear within 2 weeks of sowing. However, some varieties can take up to 5 weeks for germination. So, do not give up on your plants and instead, be patient. The ideal time to transfer the seedlings outdoors is once they have around 8-10 leaves and the soil temperature rises. Ensure that you harden the transplants before making the move, because they are extremely sensitive to cool temperatures.

If you are purchasing starter plants, ensure that the ones you opt for have a couple of leaves and no blooms or flowers. Instead, they should have straight and sturdy stems with dark green foliage. Start by hardening the plants indoors to improve their chances of survival. To harden them, place them in sunlight and gradually increase their time spent outdoors daily. Once the temperature in the area is around 65° F, they are ready to be transplanted. Alternatively, the seeds can also be started in the ground provided the above-mentioned temperatures can be reached. As long as you are living in a warm area, you don't have to opt for the starter plants, and can directly sow the seeds in the garden.

If the growing patch looks too crowded, you will need to thin the plants. Make sure there are 12-18 inches between each plant and the rows are 2-3 feet apart. While moving the transplants to the garden, ensure that you are extremely careful because the roots are delicate. So, move them as gently as you possibly can and ensure that you do not hurt their roots. Make small 3-4-inch-deep holes in the garden soil, and place the transplants in these. Then, cover them gently with soil. Follow the above-mentioned spacing requirements. Also, to increase the chances of success for the young plants, feed them a low-nitrogen and phosphorus-rich fertilizer. You can also use organic manure or liquid fertilizer for this purpose.

Bell pepper plants require around 1-2 inches of water per week, depending on the general climatic conditions. Avoid shallow watering the plants, and ensure their roots receive the desired moisture. Also, avoid watering the foliage and only water the plants once the soil has almost dried out. Slow and deep watering keeps their roots strong. Inconsistent watering at this stage can cause the plants to wilt and increase the risk of blossom-end rot, too. Daily watering will be needed if the general climatic conditions are too dry or warm.

Even though they thrive in warm weather, they are heat-sensitive after a certain point. If the daytime temperature is above 85° F, then the blossoms will droop and the plants start wilting. This also occurs if the nighttime temperature is below 60° F. So, ensure that you avoid exposing the young bell pepper plants to such extreme climatic conditions to increase the chances of a good harvest. Also, if it is too hot, then the peppers produced will have blisters on them—their flavor will also be compromised. To retain the required moisture in the ground, don't forget to regularly mulch and remove weeds.

Harvesting

As the fruit starts appearing on the plants, you can start harvesting. This encourages the plants to produce more fruit. However, the longer the fruit stays on the plant, the sweeter its taste. It's entirely up to you as to when you want to harvest them. For better produce, regular harvesting is needed. As soon as the fruits have reached the desired color and size, go ahead and pluck them. Cleanly cut the peppers away from the plant by using a pair of sharp scissors or a garden knife. Ensure that you do not jerk the plant or tug the peppers. Doing so can damage not just the stems, but also the underground root system as well.

Pumpkins

Pumpkin is a fruit vegetable and includes different varieties of squash that belong to the Cucurbitaceae family. The most common botanical names of pumpkins grown in gardens include Cucurbita maxima, C. Moschata, and C. Argyrosperma. These plants thrive in full sun, and the ideal bloom time is the summer. Regardless of whether you are growing them for culinary purposes or to carve jack-o'-lanterns during Halloween, growing pumpkins is simple. Pumpkins are an excellent source of beta-carotene, vitamins C and E, iron, folate, and potassium, and are also rich in dietary fiber. Adding pumpkins to your diet will help improve your eyesight, reduce the risk of certain types of cancer, improve immune functioning, reduce the risk of hypertension, promote bone density, and improve your ability to sleep through the night as well.

Pumpkins have been grown for approximately 5,000 years in Northern America. The 2 primary requirements to grow this native vegetable include a prolonged growing season and plenty of space. Usually, they need anywhere between 75-100 frost-free days for proper growth and maturation. They are also heavy feeders, but easy to maintain. These plants require around 10-50 square feet per plant. If you are running low on space, then you can plant them toward the edge of the garden and encourage them to directly vine across the path or the lawn. The vines will be a slight inconvenience for a couple of weeks. Depending on the variety, you can also grow pumpkins in 10-, 12-, or 15-gallon buckets. Since they are heavy feeders, aged compost or manure must be thoroughly mixed into the soil before planting.

Planting and Growing

The ideal time to plant pumpkins is when the soil temperature is between 65° F and 95° F. Since they are sensitive to cold, do not directly sow the seeds in the garden until the danger of frost has passed completely. The seedlings usually emerge between 5-10 days after seeding if the soil temperature is around 70° F. If the growing season is rather short in the area you reside, then start sowing the seeds indoors 2-4 weeks before the last spring frost.

You can plant pumpkins in rows or on hills. Ensure that the rows are 6-10 feet apart, whereas the hills require a spacing of 4-8 feet. A hill doesn't necessarily mean that the soil is mounded. Instead, it refers to a spot that contains multiple groups of plants or seeds. By making a hill, it improves the soil temperature, which promotes quicker germination. It also aids with pest control and drainage. To create a hill, dig 12-15 inches deep in the soil, and then mix it with plenty of compost or aged manure of your choice. After this, add between 4-6 seeds per hill. The seeds must be sown 1 inch deep in the soil, and no more. If directly growing them in rows, sow them 6-12 inches apart.

Regardless of whether it is a hill or a row, thinning will be needed once the seedlings appear. As soon as the seedlings are 2-3 inches tall, space the plants such that they are 18-36 inches apart. You simply need to snip out the unwanted plants, and that's about it.

If you are planting rather early in the season, then using row covers helps prevent any potential damage caused by insects and pests. However, to promote pollination these covers will need to be removed later. Do not use any insecticides or fungicides that end up killing bees and other essential insects. If you have to use fertilizer, the ideal time is sometime late in the afternoon or early in the evening. As a rule of thumb, ensure the plants get 1 inch of water per week, and make sure that you deeply water the plants—especially if the weather is quite hot and the fruit has set in. Do not water the foliage or the fruit unless it is exceptionally sunny outside. If there is any moisture dampness, it simply attracts more diseases. Always be careful, because the roots of pumpkin plants are quite shallow and get damaged easily. Do not damage the delicate vines, because they are responsible for bearing the fruits later.

You will need to fertilize the plants later in the season, especially right before flowering and fruiting, to promote better growth. Before the vines start running or the plant is about a foot tall, use a nitrogen-rich fertilizer. After this, side-dress them with a phosphorus-rich fertilizer as soon as they start blooming. It's quite normal if the first bunch of flowers don't form fruit. This is because both the female and the male blossoms must be open—only then will the pumpkins be formed.

After the vines or plants have produced a few pumpkins, it is time to stop the vine growth. To do this, the fuzzy ends of the vines must be pinched off. This encourages the plant to refocus its available nutrients and energy to grow and develop the pumpkins. Regular pruning is needed, too. The three types of veins a pumpkin plant has are primary, secondary, and tertiary veins. The central, or the mainframe, that sprouts from the ground is the primary vein. All veins growing from this are the secondary veins, and the ones growing from the secondary veins are the tertiary veins. As soon as the plant develops fruits, prune the primary and secondary veins to within 10-15 feet—the tertiary veins must be removed altogether.

Harvesting

The right time to harvest pumpkins is once they're fully matured, and not before this point. Even if the pumpkin has reached your desired size, leave it on the vine for a while longer and it might grow even bigger. Harvest the pumpkins when their skin has turned hard, and the plants die back. The skin of a ripened pumpkin takes on a deep and solid orange color for most varieties, whereas the stem becomes quite hard. When you thump the pumpkin with your finger, it should produce a hollow sound. If it does this, the pumpkin is ripe for picking. Similarly, another test you can perform is to press your fingernail into the skin of the pumpkin. If there is any resistance, it means it is ripe. Ensure that you do not tear the fruit of the vine, and instead use a sharp knife or a set of pruners to cut it. Do not cut too close to the pumpkin, and keep at least 3-4 inches of the stem attached to prolong its shelf life.

Cucumbers

The botanical name of the cucumber is Cucumis sativus. These green garden vegetables are technically fruits, and belong to the same family as pumpkins and watermelons. Around 90% of a cucumber is water, and therefore, they're quite hydrating. They have several phytonutrients, vitamins A and K, magnesium, manganese, and potassium. Consuming them regularly is known to aid in weight loss, improve antioxidant levels, promote hydration, and regulate blood sugar levels.

Cucumbers are extremely easy to care for. These low-maintenance vegetables love water as well as sunlight. If these two conditions are met, they grow quickly. The ideal pH of the soil is slightly acidic to neutral. These plants usually bloom during the summer. Cucumbers are of two types: vining cucumbers and bush cucumbers. Vining cucumbers are the most common varieties, and they grow on vigorous vines. These quick-growing vines offer a significant yield if you take care of them properly. When trained up a fence or a trellis, they thrive. On the other hand, bush cucumbers grow at ground level and are ideal for small gardens.

The ideal time to start planting cucumbers outdoors is 2 weeks after the last frost has passed. These sun-loving plants are susceptible to cold and frost. The ideal soil temperature for germination is 70° F. If you want to extend the growing season or get a head start, then you can sow the seeds indoors 3 weeks before the date you want to shift them to the garden outside. When it comes to cucumbers, starting too quickly is not a good idea. Unless the ideal climatic conditions are present, the plants will not grow. You can make successive plantings every two weeks or so for a continuous harvest throughout the growing season. Regardless of the variety of cucumber you opt for, they usually mature within 6 weeks and are ready for harvest.

As mentioned, these plants prefer plenty of sunlight, so opt for an area that receives lots of sunlight. They prefer fertile soil, so working on the soil is needed if it is not fertilized. Adding around 2 inches of compost or aged manure and working it into the soil does the trick. They require well-drained soil, but it shouldn't be too soggy, lest the seeds will not germinate. They prefer slightly acidic to neutral soil with a pH between 6.5 to 7. If the soil is clayey or too compact, organic matter will help loosen it. Adding rotted manure or compost also does the trick. They prefer sandy and light soils.

Planting and Growing

Once you have taken care of all the growth requirements, it's time to get started. While sowing the seeds, don't place them any deeper than 1 inch in the ground. You can also plant them in hills or mounds. If you are doing this, ensure the mounds are 2 feet apart. You can add 2-4 seeds per mound. Alternatively, if you want to train the vines on a trellis or fence, they must be 1 foot apart for best results. The rows must be 3-5 feet apart for best results.

Thinning will be needed to ensure the plants grow properly. Once the plants are around 4 inches high, ensure there is just 1 plant per mound, and no more. If you reside in any cold climatic region, then warming the soil before sowing is needed. To do this, simply cover the required area with a black plastic sheet and wait until it is warm enough. Once you have planted, it's time to mulch the area around the mound. You can use organic mulch, chopped leaves, or any other material of your choice to improve their resistance to diseases and pests. It is better to train the vines, especially if you have a space crunch in the garden. Place 1 stake per mound, and encourage them to wrap around the stake as they grow.

Water regularly and consistently once the seedlings emerge. The primary requirement for cucumbers is a good watering schedule. They require 1 inch of water per week, and even more if the climate is too dry and hot. The fruit will be bitter if the plants aren't watered consistently. The ideal time to water the plants is early in the afternoon, or in the morning. Ensure that you do not dampen the foliage, because this increases the risk of diseases and attracts unnecessary insects. Using a soaker hose or irrigation system is the best idea for cucumber plants. To retain soil moisture, don't forget to mulch around the plants.

If the organic matter was worked into the soil before planting, a little side-dressing will be needed with compost or aged manure later in the growing season. Using a 5-10-10 fertilizer is also a good idea. Fertilizer must be applied 1 week before the plant blooms, and every 3 weeks after that. The fertilizer must be directly added to the soil around the plant. However, do not overfertilize, because this results in stunted growth of fruits.

Harvesting

Harvesting cucumbers is not only fun, but quite a rewarding experience as well. One thing you must remember is to pick them at the right time. If you wait until they become too large, the fruit will be bitter. Once they reach the peak harvesting time, cucumbers must be picked every couple of days—this increases further growth. Slice the fruit off the vine when they are around 6-8 inches long. It is best to consume them when they are tender and young, because overly mature ones have hardened seeds. The skins also become too tough when left on the vine or bush for too long—this also reduces the plant's productivity. Always use clippers or a sharp knife to cut the cucumber off the vine. Avoid tugging or pulling the fruit, because it can damage the vine and even its stems and roots.

Peas

The botanical name of peas is Pisum sativum, and they belong to a food group known as legumes. They thrive in slightly acidic to neutral soil, and prefer exposure to full sun. That said, they grow well in partial shade, too. The bloom time of these plants is in the spring and fall. Peas grown in the garden will be sweeter than any purchased from grocery stores. Peas are packed full of antioxidants, vitamins, and nutrients such as vitamins A, B, C, and E, and zinc. Consuming them regularly helps regulate blood sugar levels, improve cardiovascular functioning, and strengthen immune functioning.

Even though peas are relatively easy to grow, their growing period is limited—therefore, you must be quick to act. A simple trick to ensure that you obtain a sufficient harvest is to plant early in the spring, so that they can be harvested when it is cold. Don't forget to enjoy peas immediately after harvesting, because they do not stay fresh for long. The three common varieties of peas that are suited for most gardens as well as culinary purposes include: sweet peas, snow peas, and snap peas. Sweet peas are also known as English peas or garden peas. They have inedible pods with edible seeds. Snow peas, on the other hand, are edible and flat stringless pods that contain small peas inside. Snap peas also produce thick inedible pods that contain large seeds. Peas can be planted along with other vegetables such as turnips, kale, cucumber, carrot, and beans. Companion planting is an excellent idea if you want a good harvest.

Even though they require a relatively colder climate to grow, you will need to opt for a sunny location. The soil must be well-draining and of a neutral pH so that the peas will thrive. You can grow them in shade, but the harvest and flavor of the ones grown in full sun are always better. The ideal time to prepare the soil is during the fall for a spring harvest. Mix some compost or aged manure into the soil to improve its water retention and structure.

You can start sowing the seeds 4-6 weeks before the last frost date. Around this time, the soil is neither too hot nor cold. Instead, it is of the desired temperature. If the temperature of the soil is around 40° F, the germination process will be quite slow. So, for quicker germination, ensure the soil temperature is around 60° F but no more than 85° F. If the first set of peas doesn't make it, you'll have to replant. It is perfectly okay to do this. For a continuous harvest or a fall harvest, planting late in the summer or early in the fall is a good idea. If you are planting in a specific area during one cycle of growth, then avoid replanting in the space spot for the next 3-4 years. They are ideal for companion planting just like all other legumes, because they enhance the nitrogen levels in the soil.

Planting and Growing

Once you have chosen the right spot for growing peas, it is time to get started. Directly sowing the seeds in the soil is the best method available, because they have incredibly delicate root systems and do not like any disturbance. If you want to opt for transplantation, then ensure that the seeds are started only in biodegradable pots. If not, you will be compromising the health of the plant. To quicken the germination process, soaking the seeds in water overnight before planting is a great idea.

Sow the seeds such that they are 1 inch deep in the soil, and 1 inch deeper if the soil seems a little dry. The seeds must be around 2 inches apart, and you do not have to thin them later. As mentioned, the roots do not like being disturbed. The rows must be 7 inches apart. Pay extra attention to how you sow them, because the plants must not be disturbed later in the growing cycle. A potassium and phosphorus fertilizer later in the season is good for their growth. However, if there is too much nitrogen, then it increases the growth of the foliage instead of flowers and peas.

Unless it looks like the plants are wilting, they do not need more than 1 inch of water per week. Overwatering results in root rot. That said, ensure the plants do not dry out, because this will hamper the production of the pods. If you notice any insects, gently remove them by hand without disturbing the peas around them. A common reason for the leaves turning yellow is the stress caused by hot weather. If that's the case, offering partial shade does the trick.

Harvesting

Most varieties of peas are ready for harvest within 70 days of planting. These plants mature rather quickly. As soon as the peapod shows signs of mature seeds within, it is ready for harvest. Before the pods take on a waxy look, harvest them. The ideal time to harvest is right after the morning dew has dried—this is when they taste the best and are at their crispiest. Keep harvesting them regularly to improve the plant's productivity. Hold the vine with one hand and gently pluck the pod off it using the other. If the pods harden or look dry, then they've become overmature, and their flavor will be compromised.

String Beans

The botanical name of string beans is Phaseolus vulgaris. String beans are a source of essential vitamins and minerals including calcium, potassium, iron, zinc, magnesium phosphorus, folate, niacin, and vitamins A, C, and K. They are also an excellent source of protein and dietary fiber. These helpful nutrients are known to support heart health and digestive functioning, aid in healthy pregnancy, and improve bone health. Apart from all this, they are also known to tackle anemia.

Regardless of the space available, green beans can be easily added to your garden and they are so easy to grow. Green beans are also known as snap beans or string beans. These tender annuals prefer slightly acidic to neutral soil, and they bloom during the summer. Beans are usually classified as bush beans or pole beans. Bush beans grow to be compact, as their name suggests, and can grow up to 2 feet tall. However, they don't need any additional support. On the other hand, pole beans are vines that can grow up to 10-15 feet tall. They require staking, or training on a trellis. The maintenance needed for bush beans is lower than that of pole beans. That said, pole beans produce a greater yield and are usually disease-resistant. The maturity period of bush beans is up to 55 days, whereas pole means can take up to 65 days.

Staggered planting once every 2 weeks or so ensures that you have a continuous harvest during the growing season. They prefer soil that is of medium fertility, but it must be well-draining. The soil pH ideal for growth is between 6 and 7. They don't require any additional fertilizer, because they fix the nitrogen present in the soil by themselves. However, if the soil is of particularly poor quality, then amending it with compost or manure is needed. Do this during the fall, or at least 1 week before you decide to plant in the spring. Beans also don't like their roots being disturbed, just like peas. So, if you are growing pole beans, ensure the stakes or trellis are in place before planting.

The ideal time to plant beans outdoors is after the last spring frost. The soil must be around 48 °F to 50 °F for germination. If you plant too early and the soil isn't warm enough, they won't germinate. If the soil is too cold or moist, it causes the seeds to rot. If you want to get a head start on planting, then cover the desired area with black plastic to warm the soil. It is not ideal to start the seeds indoors, because they have extremely fragile root systems that cannot withstand transplantation. They are quick growers, so you don't have to worry about getting a head start here.

Planting and Growing

Once the ideal growing conditions and requirements for the beans are in place, the next step is to start planting. If you are planting bush beans, sow them 1 inch deep in the soil. There must be at least 2 inches between each seed, and the rows must be 15-18 inches apart. On the other hand, you will need support structures in place before planting pole beans. Once you have the support structures, sow the seeds 1 inch deep in the soil. An important thing you must remember is that if the soil is predominantly sandy, then you will need to sow them ½ inch to 1 inch deeper.

If you want a continuous harvest throughout the growing season, the seeds must be resown once every 2 weeks. To ensure that there is no buildup of diseases or pests in a single spot, practice crop rotation.

Make sure moisture is retained in the soil by mulching around the plants. The soil needs to be well-drained without becoming too moist. Since they have shallow roots, mulching ensures the temperature is ideal. Beans require a little more water than other plants. Unlike the typical 1 inch of water per week practice, these plants need up to 2 inches of water per week. If the plants are not watered well, they will not flower. To encourage the formation of pods after a heavy bloom, using fertilizer is a good idea. However, you don't need a nitrogen-rich fertilizer, or you will end up with extremely lush foliage and no beans. Side-dress them after flowering by using a fertilizer made of aged compost or manure. Doing this halfway through the growing season is also a good idea.

Don't forget to carefully weed the patch where you were growing beans. While doing this, be extra careful because the roots are delicate, and the idea is not to disturb them. As soon as the pole beans reach the top of the support structure in place, it's time to pinch their tops off. This encourages them to redirect the energy available for the growth of pods instead of the foliage. If the temperature rises dramatically, use row covers to shield the young plants.

Harvesting

The ideal time to harvest beans is early in the morning—this is when they are the sweetest. Ensure that green beans are picked every day to encourage the plant to grow more. Harvest beans when they are young and tender, right before the peas have fully developed within. To harvest, simply snap or cut off the pod from the plant with a sharp knife. Ensure that you do not tear it away from the plant or jerk the plant. If the beans are fresh and young, they will snap easily. Also, harvest young because their flavor reduces as they mature.

Eggplant

The botanical name of eggplant is Solanum melongena. Eggplants are also known as brinjal or aubergine, and they come in a variety of shapes, sizes, and even colors. Though dark purple is a color that's commonly associated with them, they can be green, black, white, pink, streaked with purple, and white as well. Eggplants are a rich source of vitamin C and calcium, phosphorus, magnesium, and potassium. This vegetable has been used in the traditional system of Ayurvedic medicine for thousands of years. It was used to treat diabetes, while the roots were used as a treatment for asthma. It's also rich in a variety of antioxidants that protect the cells and organs from inflammation and oxidative damage. Polyphenols help regulate blood sugar levels, and therefore are an effective means to combat diabetes. It is believed to reduce the risk of cardiovascular diseases, assist in weight loss, and also has certain cancer-fighting benefits.

These are warm-weather-loving plants, and the ideal time to harvest them is mid-to-late summer. Growing and harvesting eggplants is quite easy. It is a perennial plant that grows in the wild in South Asia, but is cultivated as annuals in most of Northern America. They require relatively higher temperatures than other plants due to their subtropical and tropical heritage. Just like tomatoes and peppers, these vegetables also belong to the nightshade family. Their growth slows down as the weather cools down, and they grow quickly when the temperature is between 70° F and 85° F. These plants can grow up to 2 feet tall, and just like bell peppers and tomatoes, even the fully-formed eggplants hang from the branches.

These plants prefer warm soil. You can start the seeds indoors, directly sow them in the garden, or even purchase a transplant. If you want to purchase transplants, always opt for ones that are 6-8 weeks old. This will give you a head start during the growing season. These plants come in a variety of shapes and sizes, too.

The ideal time to get started with them is 6-8 weeks before the last date of the spring frost. As mentioned, the soil must be warm. While starting the seeds, ensure that the soil is well-drained and loamy. If the soil is fairly rich in organic matter, these plants will thrive. To improve the overall soil fertility, amend it with some well-rotted manure or compost. Alternatively, a 5-10-5 general fertilizer also works. Mix it through the soil and let it rest for at least 1 week before you want to start planting. The optimal range of pH for their growth is 5.8 to 6.5.

Planting and Growing

If you are starting the seeds indoors, you will need peat pots or flat trays. Fill the pots or trays with amended soil and sow the seeds at a depth of ¼ inch. Water the seeds regularly, and within a couple of days the seedlings will appear. After this, it is time to transplant them outdoors. Do this only after the last spring frost has gone by. The daytime temperature must be around 70° F to 75° F, whereas the nighttime temperature should not be any lower than 60° F. In the garden soil, the seedlings must be transplanted such that they are set in rows that are 3 feet apart. The space between each seedling must be 24-30 inches. If the soil temperature isn't warm enough, do not be in a hurry. Instead, increase the temperature by covering the growing area with a sheet of black plastic for 1 week before the intended transplant. Patience is needed if you want to grow eggplants.

As soon as the seedlings appear, it's time to give them a little support. To do this, you will need to set stakes that are 1-2 inches away from each plant. The stakes can be up to 24 inches high. They will offer the required support, especially during the fruiting stage. After this, start watering well. An additional layer of mulch will prohibit the growth of weeds, while helping the soil to retain water.

You will need to water such that the top 6 inches of the soil is moist without becoming soggy. Therefore, consistent watering is ideal. The critical period for moisture retention is when the fruiting period approaches, and later for its development. If the plants don't get sufficient water or are watered inconsistently, this results in a lack of fruit or misshapen fruit. Adding a balanced fertilizer every fortnight is also a good idea. However, you should not be using one that's rich in nitrogen—especially during the fruiting stage, because it promotes the growth of foliage instead of the fruit.

These vegetables are extremely susceptible to any fluctuations in temperatures. Fruiting can slow down or even be completely absent if the days are extremely hot and the nights are cold. If the temperature at night is less than 55° F, and the temperature during the day is over 95° F, the harvest will be reduced.

Harvesting

Depending on the variety of eggplants you are growing, they are usually ready for harvest within 80 days of transplantation. If you are starting from seed, the maturity period can be anywhere between 100-120 days. Harvest eggplants when they are young and tender, because this is when they taste the best. Also, if you harvest regularly, energy in the plant will be directed toward facilitating the growth of newer eggplants. If you want to check whether the fruit is ready for harvest or not, simply press on its skin. If the skin doesn't rebound when pressure is applied, they are ripe. If the fruits are underripe or overripe, they will taste bitter. Instead, look for eggplants that are evenly colored and have a glossy appearance. Avoid pulling the fruit when you are harvesting it, because it will not come out. Instead, simply cut it close to the stem using a sharp knife. Certain types of eggplants can have prickly stems, therefore, consider using gloves while handling the plants.

Okra

The botanical name of okra is Abelmoschus esculentus. This vegetable is quite popular and widely cultivated in the warm and tropical climates of South Asia and Africa. It usually comes in two colors—red and green. Okra is rich in a variety of nutrients such as magnesium, dietary fiber, folate, and vitamins A, B6, C, and K. It is believed to contain plenty of beneficial antioxidants that tackle inflammation and fight aging. It reduces the risk of cardiovascular disorders, has anti-cancer properties, helps regulate blood sugar levels, and is especially beneficial for pregnant women.

These plants thrive in warm weather, and are commonly grown in the southern states of the U.S. They are easy to grow and harvest, and prefer plenty of sunlight and soil that's slightly acidic to neutral. Okra produces small white or yellow flowers. The flowers look quite similar to hibiscus. This is because okra belongs to the hibiscus family.

If you want to grow okra, then ensure that the weather is hot and the evening temperature is no less than 60° F. The ideal soil for growing okra must be well-drained and fertile, with a pH between 6.5 and 7. Before you get started, it's important to amend the garden soil by mixing some compost or well-aged manure into it. After this, simply leave the soil to settle for 1 week, and then you can start planting. The right time to start planting okra is 3-4 weeks before the last spring frost. If you start planting at this time, you will need to use a cold frame (or even a grow tunnel) to keep the soil warm and let it stay in place until the weather warms up. Alternatively, you can also wait until the soil temperature is between 60° F and 75° F to start planting in the garden without any additional requirements.

Planting and Growing

Okra seeds are quite small, so they are slightly tricky to sow. To quicken the germination process, it's recommended to soak the seeds overnight in some water to get started. The seeds mustn't be planted too deep in the soil. Ensure that there are 12-18 inches between each row. If you are using okra seedlings or transplants, make sure that they are 1-2 feet apart to give them sufficient room to grow. Remember, these plants can grow quite tall, and therefore, the rows must be 3-4 feet apart if you are using transplants.

A balanced liquid fertilizer can be used. If not, you can also use aged manure or side-dress the plants with a 10-10-10 fertilizer. Ensure that you do not opt for a fertilizer with too much nitrogen—especially as the plants start blooming—or the fruit will not develop.

The next step is to start thinning the seedlings. As soon as the plants are 3-4 inches tall, there must be sufficient space between each plant and the rows as well. During the summer months, the plants must be properly watered. They require up to 1 inch of water per week, and a little more if the climate is extremely arid or hot. High heat slows down the growth of these plants. Don't forget to carefully prune the top of the plants as soon as they are 5-6 feet tall. This increases their growth rate and encourages the plants to produce more fruit.

Harvesting

You might be quite eager to pluck the fruit off the plant with your hands, but avoid doing this. Instead, use gardening gloves when harvesting okra. This is because they have hairy leaves and tiny spikes on the pods, and touching them can cause skin irritation. The ideal time to harvest okra is when they are around 4 inches long. Usually, they are ready for harvest within 2 months of planting. Use a sharp knife and cut it close to the stem to harvest. If the stem seems too hard to cut, it means the pod is also quite old and will be tough to eat. The more tender the pods, the more flavorful they are. You will need to harvest okra as often as you can, and just like you do with any other fruits and vegetables. The more you harvest, the more the plant will produce.

Olives

The botanical name of olive is Olea Europaea. Olives are a powerhouse of nutrients. They are rich in vitamin E, calcium, sodium, iron, copper, a variety of antioxidants, and healthy fats and fibers. Olives are an incredible source of omega-3 fatty acids that are needed for improving the heart's health, promoting cognitive functioning, and tackling inflammation. All the antioxidant compounds in it also do the same. Regardless of whether they are black or green, olives are known to improve cardiovascular health, strengthen bones, and reduce the risk of certain types of cancer.

Olives are native to the Mediterranean region, but if the right climatic conditions can be maintained, you can grow them anywhere. If the summers are hot and long while the humidity is low, these plants will thrive. They are rather easy to grow and care for once they take root. Olives come in different sizes, shapes, and flavors, and there are around a dozen varieties of olives to choose from. They cannot be consumed in raw form, because they're quite bitter. This is the reason why they are usually cured before serving. Another culinary utilization of olives is to extract olive oil from the ripe fruits. You might have come across either green or black olives. Their color isn't the only difference between them; the difference is also when they are plucked from the tree. Black olives are harvested when the fruit is fully ripe, while green olives are the unripe ones. When cured, they both have a tangy and salty taste.

The plants require a little winter chill to produce flowers, and the right temperature for flower growth is between 40° F and 50° F. That said, they can withstand temperatures as low as 12° F, but no lower. They require plenty of sunlight for proper growth. The ideal pH of the soil is between 5.5 and 8.5, and they prefer well-drained, sandy and loamy soil. However, these hardy plants can adapt themselves to different soil conditions. Before you start planting, select a spot for growing olives that is not directly in the way of strong winds or rains—this is because cold air or wind can easily damage the crop. Unlike the other vegetables you were introduced to until now, these require plenty of space to grow. These trees can grow up to 30 feet tall, and are quite massive. You can train and prune them to grow to a smaller size, but they still require a lot of space. The ideal space between olive trees must be at least 20 feet. Also, instead of starting with seeds, it is recommended to opt for transplants.

Planting and Growing

The ideal time to plant olives is either in the fall or spring—avoid planting them when the weather is too hot or dry. To get started, select a planting site that receives plenty of sunlight, but is sheltered from high-speed winds or gales. Well-aged manure or compost must be worked into the soil to create the right growing conditions. Now, it is time to start planting. To do this, dig holes that are half as deep and twice as wide as the roots of the olive tree. After this, add an all-purpose fertilizer to the bottom of the holes. Drive a tree stake into the soil close to the hole, and 2 feet deep in the soil.

Now, place the tree in the hole while ensuring its roots are evenly spread out. Use the native soil to refill the hole. Firm in the soil to remove any air pockets and to make sure the roots are grounded, then water the soil. After this, secure the tree to the stake using tree ties. The final step is to fertilize it using a fertilizer rich in phosphorus. Until the roots of the trees are stabilized, you will need to water the plants regularly. Mature trees can go for a couple of days without water, but it's better to water them regularly and consistently. You will also need to fertilize the plants annually to promote better growth and development. The established trees will need to be pruned regularly to maintain their shape, and to ensure they don't grow too tall. Any disease from damaged deadwood must be removed, and the congested wood should also be thinned to ensure that sufficient sunlight and air reach the plant.

Harvesting

Harvesting olives is a truly rewarding experience, but it is a long-term process. You will need to wait for around 5 years before you can pluck olives. These trees are alternate bearing, which means that under the right circumstances, they produce a heavy crop one year and a relatively light one the following year. You can either wait until the fruit is fully ripe and harvest then, or pluck them young—this will give you black and green olives, respectively. Ensure that you handpick the olives if you want them for table use. On the other hand, if the primary purpose is to extract oil, they can also be knocked from the tree by hitting the branches with a pole.

Corn

The botanical name of corn is Zea mays. This is one of the most popular cereal grains across the world. Whether it is cornbread, tortilla, or even polenta—different products are made from it. Corn has plenty of dietary fiber and is a decent source of protein, potassium, antioxidant vitamins, and minerals. It is also a gluten-free grain and is known to reduce inflammation. Regular consumption of corn promotes eye and digestive health.

Corn is said to be one of the three sisters, and has been cultivated for thousands of years. The three sisters refer to corn, squash, and beans. Companion planting these three together is a brilliant idea, because they sustain and support each other's growth and development. Even though corn is native to Northern America, it's believed to have been domesticated somewhere in central Mexico for the first time, and spread to North and South America from there. These days, corn is grown on an industrial scale and is one of the most popular foods across the globe. It's fascinating that corn belongs to the grass family of Poaceae.

This is an annual crop that thrives in full sun, and the ears produced by it can be white, yellow, or even bicolor. They prefer a frost-free and long growing season. The ideal soil to grow corn in must be slightly acidic to neutral. Depending on the level of sucrose present, the flavor and texture of the corn varies. Before you start planting, ensure that the spot you opt for receives around 6-8 hours of sunlight daily. Corn prefers well-drained, consistently moist soil. These plants also require plenty of water. Working aged manure or compost into the soil before planting is a good idea. Do this during the fall so that you will have fertile and well-drained soil by the spring. If not, simply mix in some aged compost a week before you want to start planting.

Another thing you must remember is to plant them in blocks instead of singular rows—this is needed to ensure sufficient pollination takes place. The blocks of corn must have at least 4 rows for best results. Unlike a lot of other plants, the flowers of corn are pollinated by wind instead of honeybees. When you plant them in blocks, this increases the chances of them producing fuller ears.

It's not recommended to start the seeds indoors; instead, it's better to directly sow them in the garden because the roots do not like being disturbed. Also, the roots are extremely sensitive to any change in the usual environment. The right time to start the seeds outdoors is around 2 weeks after the last spring frost. You will need to plant early in the season, because they need longer to mature. Also, they require warm weather to mature. If you reside in an area that doesn't cater to these requirements, it's better to opt for quick-maturing varieties of corn. As mentioned, these plants are quite sensitive to general growing conditions. The ideal temperature for germination of corn must be between 60° F and 65° F, and no less. If you want, place a layer of black plastic over the growing area, and leave it in place for 1 week before planting. This helps create the right soil temperature for germination. Within a couple of weeks of the first round of corn, you can start the second batch. This will give you a continuous harvest throughout the growing season.

Planting and Growing

Now that you are aware of the growing conditions needed along with the basic requirements to grow corn, it is time to get started. For quicker germination, moisten the seeds. To do this, place them on moist paper towels and keep them wrapped in them. Place the paper towels containing the seeds in a plastic bag for up to 1 day. Leave it undisturbed, and then get started.

The seeds must be planted so that they are up to 2 inches deep in the soil, and they are 4-6 inches apart. The space between the rows must be 13-36 inches. Use a balanced 10-10-10 fertilizer to ensure the plants get the required nutrients. You can skip this step if you believe the soil is thoroughly amended and fertile enough to support corn. While planting, don't forget to sufficiently water as well.

Thinning the plants is needed as soon as they are 3-4 inches tall. Do this such that they are 8-12 inches apart in each row. Be extremely careful while thinning so that you do not disturb the roots of the plants you want to retain. The same precaution must be followed even when you're weeding around these plants.

They have shallow roots, and are extremely sensitive to drought. Therefore, the plants must be well watered. They require around 2 inches of water per week, and a little more if the soil is extremely sandy or the weather has turned hot. Side-dressing the plants using a fertilizer high in nitrogen is needed once the plants are about 8 inches tall—this process has to be repeated once they are around 18 inches tall. Regularly mulch around the plants to improve moisture retention in the soil.

Harvesting

The maturity of corn depends on climatic conditions. So, if you want the corn to mature quickly, then it will need plenty of warmth. Corn is usually ripe for harvest within 23 days of silking, and even sooner if it is warmer. If 2 ears are growing on a cornstalk, the lower ones will mature a day or two after the upper ones. While harvesting, ensure that the corn ears are blunt or well-rounded—they should not be pointy. Their silky tassels must be slightly brown and golden. When the corn looks like this, it means the kernels are ready and ripe. To test whether the corn is ripe or not, simply pull down the husk and use your fingernail to pierce a kernel. If you notice any white substance leaking out, this means it's ready for harvest. Simply pull the ear downward using a twisting motion to separate it from the stalk.

Zucchini

The botanical name of zucchini is Cucurbita pepo. Zucchini contains a variety of vitamins, nutrients, and helpful plant compounds. It is quite low in calories and contains vitamins A, B6, C, and K, manganese, copper, phosphorus, and magnesium. It also contains a little bit of calcium, zinc, and iron, and is rich in different antioxidants that protect the body from damage caused by free radicals. It's known to promote healthy digestion, regulate blood sugar levels, and improve cardiovascular functioning. It can also strengthen your vision and assist in weight loss. Other potential benefits of zucchini include improved bone health, better thyroid function, and a healthier prostate.

Zucchini thrives when exposed to plenty of sunlight, and its bloom time is in the summer. It prefers slightly acidic to neutral soil. Zucchini is a type of summer squash, and squash is usually divided into summer and winter squash. Summer squash, as the name suggests, is harvested during the summer; and winter variants are harvested in the fall. The skin of the summer squash is edible, unlike the winter variant.

These plants are vigorous growers, and offer good produce during the peak season. Before you get started, ensure that the location you opt for receives plenty of sunlight—it should also shelter the plants from wind. The soil must be well-draining and moist without being too soggy. If well-fed, the harvest will be quite good. Mix compost or aged manure into the soil before you start planting. Depending on your preference, the seeds can be either directly planted in the garden soil or started indoors. The ideal time to start it in an outdoor garden is when the soil temperature is at a minimum of 60° F. If you want to start the seeds indoors, the right time is 2-4 weeks before the last frost. However, it's important to remember that their roots are quite delicate, and they do not usually transplant well. Therefore, be extra careful when dealing with zucchini plants. If the soil temperature isn't warm enough, cover the growing area with a sheet of black plastic for at least 1 week before planting.

Planting and Growing

Once you have taken care of the growing conditions and requirements, it is time to get started. The seeds can be directly sown in the soil. Plant them such that they are 1 inch deep and 2-3 inches apart. You can also create small hills and sow 3-4 seeds per hill. The rows must be 3-6 feet apart, because they require plenty of growing space. You can use row covers or a cold frame to ensure the young plants are protected from harsh climatic conditions. To lock in the soil moisture, using a layer of mulch is also a good idea. Similarly, mulching regularly discourages the growth of weeds and protects the shallow roots of zucchini plants.

They thrive in moist soil, but it shouldn't be too soggy. This means they require around 1 inch of water per week. The watering schedule must be consistent and regular throughout the growing cycle. Side-dressing the plant is needed once the blooms appear—a well-balanced fertilizer will do the trick at this stage. If the flowers are not pollinated, the fruit will not appear. Male and female flowers are produced by most squash plants when the pollen from the male flowers is transferred to the female ones either by bees or by the gardeners. Without this, you will not have squash to harvest.

Harvesting

The ideal time to harvest zucchini is when they are immature and tender. Pluck zucchini once they are 6-8 inches long. Oversized squash might look good, but its flavor is usually poorer than the tender ones. The maturity period for most varieties is around 60 days from planting. The squash must be ready for harvest within 1 week of flowering. To harvest, do not break the fruit from the vine. Instead, use a sharp knife to cut it off. By doing this, you reduce the risk of a shock to the stem. Leave around 1 inch of the stem attached to the fruit to prolong its shelf life.

Chickpeas

The botanical name of chickpeas is Cicer arietinum. Chickpeas are also known as garbanzo beans. They are quite popular in Mediterranean cuisine, and have been consumed in that region for thousands of years. They have a grainy texture and a nutty taste that makes them an ideal combination for a variety of foods. Chickpeas are packed full of nutrients that the body requires. They are an excellent source of plant-based protein and dietary fiber. In addition, they contain significant levels of manganese, copper, iron, phosphorus, zinc, magnesium, selenium, potassium, and vitamin B_6. This legume is an incredible source of different nutrients your body requires for overall health and well-being. The fiber and protein content of chickpeas acts as a natural appetite suppressant and assists in weight loss. The protein they have is needed for strengthening muscles, improving bone health, and weight management. They also help regulate blood sugar levels and digestion, and reduce the risk of several chronic disorders such as type 2 diabetes and heart diseases. They can also promote brain health and reduce the risk of iron deficiency.

Chickpeas usually mature within 100 days from planting. They are a cool-season annual plant. Even though they are known as beans, botanically they are classified as a legume. They require plenty of sunlight, but grow well in partial shade as well. However, if they are not exposed to sunlight properly, the harvest will be reduced. They require well-drained and loose soil that is rich in organic matter. So, before planting, it is better to make some compost or use aged manure and mix it into the soil. Though they are a cool-season crop, the nighttime temperature shouldn't be lower than 65° F. The ideal daytime temperature is between 70° F to 80° F. You can start planting chickpeas in the garden 2-3 weeks before the last frost. These plants prefer slightly acidic to neutral soil, and the pH range must be between 6.3 and 7.4. Some plants that go well planted near chickpeas are potatoes, corn, celery, and cucumbers.

Planting and Growing

Once you have taken care of the planting and growing requirements, it's time to get started. Ensure that the soil doesn't have too much nitrogen. because this will promote the growth of the foliage instead of the seeds. If needed, amend the soil further with phosphorus and potassium. While planting the seeds, ensure that they are up to 2 inches deep in the soil and that there are 3-6 inches between each seed. The rows must be 18-24 inches apart for best growth. Once the plants are around 6 inches tall, you will have to start thinning them away. Cut the plants at the soil level using sharp scissors and do not disturb the roots. Do not overwater the seeds, because this can result in them cracking open instead of germinating.

You will need to keep the bed evenly moist until the seedlings have appeared. Regular watering is also needed during the flower and pod formation stages. Overhead watering is not recommended, because it not only harms the foliage, but can also result in the rotting of flowers and pods. If the weather is too warm, to retain soil moisture, mulching is needed. Side-dress the plants using compost halfway through the growing season. Do not use any nitrogen-rich fertilizer at this stage. To improve the soil structure and fertility, keep rotating chickpeas and other legumes.

Harvesting

Within 100 days of planting, chickpeas will be ready for harvest. The right time to pick them is when the pods are fresh, green, and immature. At this stage, the entire pod can be eaten just like snap beans. If you want dried chickpeas, harvest the entire plant, and place it on a flat or warm surface to let the pods dry out. As soon as the pods split open, you can collect the seeds.

Chapter 12:

Flower Vegetables

In this chapter, you will be introduced to different types of flower vegetables and their benefits. You will also learn about the simple steps to be followed to plant, grow, and harvest these vegetables.

Artichoke

The botanical name of the artichoke is Cynara cardunculus var. scolymus. Artichoke is believed to have originated somewhere in the Mediterranean region. Humans have been using artichokes for centuries for the different medicinal benefits they offer. This vegetable is a nutrient powerhouse. It contains plenty of dietary fiber, vitamins C, B6, and K, zinc, iron, magnesium, calcium, phosphorus, potassium, and riboflavin. They also contain a specifically high proportion of potent and helpful antioxidants. Regular consumption of artichokes is believed to stabilize cholesterol and blood pressure levels, improve liver health and strength, and improve digestive functioning. It also reduces any symptoms associated with irritable bowel syndrome. Artichokes and their leaf extracts help regulate blood sugar levels as well.

The artichoke is a perennial plant belonging to the thistle family. The long and lobed silver-green leaves of this plant make it look like a giant fern. The buds of this plant are the edible artichokes, and it produces thistle-like, violet-colored flowers. The bloom time is in summer, and it thrives when exposed to the sun. It prefers soil that is slightly acidic to neutral. When fully mature, the plant can grow anywhere between 3 to 5 feet tall. They prefer mild winters and humid, cool summers. If the weather conditions are ideal, this can be an annual plant as well. A single plant can produce multiple artichokes.

You can grow these plants in three ways: the first option is to start from seeds, the second is to grow them from rooted shoots obtained from growing plants, and the third option is to use propagated roots. The ideal time to start the seeds indoors is in early spring or in late winter. You will need to start the seeds 8-10 weeks before you decide to plant them outdoors. Before sowing the seeds, ensure that you soak them in warm water to quicken the germination process. Don't forget to ensure the soil stays moist while the grow trays or pots receive plenty of sunlight. The right time to transplant the seedlings or shoots to the outdoor garden is after the spring frost has passed. Ensure that the growing area opted for artichokes receives plenty of sunlight. These are heavy feeders, and therefore, the soil must be fertile. To improve the fertility of the soil, mix aged manure or compost into it at least 1 week before planting.

Planting and Growing

Once you have taken care of the growing conditions of this plant, the next step is to get started. The plants must be placed such that they are 3-4 feet apart from each other. The rows must be 4-5 feet apart. If you are using shoots or dormant roots, ensure that they are planted 6 inches deep in the soil. Only their tops must be visible at ground level. Don't forget to deeply water the plant at this stage.

The soil must be moist without being too damp. These plants require plenty of water, and they usually need around 1 inch of water per week. They might need more if the weather is exceptionally hot. Carefully mulch around the plants to improve the moisture retention in the soil. During the growing season, a balanced organic fertilizer must be applied once every month to promote better growth. As soon as the buds appear, remove the mulch and cover the soil with compost around the plant.

If the weather is too hot, these plants will go dormant. So, don't worry if the plants seem to have slowed down during summer. As the temperature reduces, during late summer and fall, the plant growth will restart. If you were growing these plants during the cold months, an additional layer of straw might be needed to insulate the ground and ensure the ideal temperature is maintained.

Harvesting

Artichokes are ready for harvest as soon as you notice tightly grown buds. Don't pluck the buds, because this can harm the plant. Instead, use a sharp knife to cut across the stem. Leave at least 1-2 inches of the stem on the bud to prolong its shelf life.

Broccoli

The botanical name of broccoli is Brassica oleracea var. italica. Broccoli is a superfood, and this green leafy vegetable resembles a miniature tree. It's associated with the family that includes cauliflower, Brussels sprouts, and kale. It is a nutritional powerhouse rich in a variety of antioxidants, vitamins, and fibers, and contains plenty of vitamins A, B, C, and K, folate, potassium, selenium, and phosphorus. This vegetable can be consumed either in cooked or raw form. It is rich in different antioxidants that reduce inflammation and promote the functioning of the immune system, and has certain cancer-protecting benefits as well. The antioxidants and fiber in broccoli help regulate blood sugar levels and promote heart health. Regular consumption of broccoli also reduces constipation, while promoting healthy digestion and cognitive functioning.

Broccoli is usually considered to be a cool-season vegetable, and the right time to start planting it is in the spring. The most common type of broccoli that's usually seen in grocery stores is known as Calabria broccoli, and is named after the Calabria region in Italy. It produces green heads growing on thick, green stalks, and is truly considered to be a superfood due to all the above-mentioned benefits. However, growing broccoli takes plenty of patience, because it takes quite some time to mature. Even after harvesting the big or main head of the plant, it will produce smaller side shoots that can be harvested later in the season.

These sun-loving plants require 6-8 hours of sunlight per day. If they don't get sufficient sunlight, the heads will be subpar, and the plants will be leggy. They require fertile, well-draining soil. Before you start planting, ensure that you work manure or rich compost into the soil. You must do this at least 1 week before planting. The ideal soil pH must be between 6.0 and 7.0. As mentioned, this is a cool-season crop, and the ideal time to get started for a summer crop is early to mid-spring. You can also start it mid-to-late summer if you want a fall crop. If the temperature is quite high, this affects the development of the broccoli head. So, the goal is to ensure that the plant is fully mature before the temperature starts soaring.

The ideal soil temperature for germination of the seeds shouldn't be lower than 40° F. Any lower, and the plant will go dormant. If you want to raise the soil temperature before planting, cover the desired grow area with a sheet of black plastic and leave it for 1 week. If you want to, you can also start the seeds indoors and move them outdoors—especially for spring planting. Ensure that you're doing this a couple of weeks before the last spring frost. Start the seeds indoors 6-8 weeks before the last frost. If you want to sow them outdoors, you can do this 2-3 weeks before the last spring frost. If you want to grow them during the fall, the seeds must be planted outdoors 80-100 days before the first frost of the fall. This is when the soil temperature is ideal.

Planting and Growing

Once you have taken care of the soil composition as well as the growing area, the next step is to get started. If you are starting the seeds outdoors, ensure that you have amended the soil. The seeds must be planted ½ inch deep in the soil, and there must be at least 3 inches between each seed. Thinning will be needed once the seedlings appear. If the plants are too crowded, you will not have fully-formed broccoli heads later. As soon as the seedlings are 2-3 inches tall, start thinning such that there is at least 12-20 inches of space between each plant. The rows also must be 3 feet apart for best results. Alternatively, if you have started the seeds indoors, then transplant them as soon as they are a couple of inches tall or have 4-5 leaves. Follow the same spacing guidelines that were mentioned above. At the time of planting, don't forget to thoroughly water them.

When the temperature is between 65° F and 70° F, these plants thrive. Don't forget to fertilize these plants 3 weeks after the seedlings appear. A 5-10-10 fertilizer, or any other low-nitrogen fertilizer, is ideal for their growth at this stage. Regularly water the plants to ensure the soil has sufficient moisture. Usually, broccoli requires between 1 and ½ inches of water per week—especially if the weather is a little warm. Never water the developing heads of broccoli plants, or their growth will be discouraged. Since their roots are incredibly shallow, be careful while mulching around them or while adding fertilizer. The roots don't like being disturbed. A consistent feeding and watering schedule must be followed, especially after the first head is harvested, to promote the growth of secondary shoots.

Harvesting

The ideal time to harvest broccoli is early in the morning. This is when the flower heads taste their best. Also, the heads must be formed and tightly packed. If any yellow petals are present, harvest them immediately. If not, it will slow down the growth of the rest of the plant. Harvest the bud such that you remove around 6 inches of the stem along with the head. Cut the flower head at an angle to promote better growth later. Until the weather becomes too hot, these plants will keep producing side shoots.

Cauliflower

The botanical name of cauliflower is Brassica oleracea var. botrytis. This is an extremely healthy vegetable, and a source of a variety of nutrients the body requires—it also offers weight loss benefits. The primary nutrients present in cauliflower are vitamins C, B6, and K, phosphorus, potassium, pantothenic acid, magnesium, and manganese. It is rich in dietary fiber, which is known to reduce inflammation while improving digestive health. It also reduces the risk of different types of cancer, regulates blood sugar levels, promotes a healthy heart, and strengthens cognitive functioning.

As with broccoli, cauliflower is a cool-season plant that loves sunlight. This annual plant also belongs to the brassica family. The name of this vegetable is a combination of two Latin words—*caulis* and *floris*—which mean cabbage on flower, respectively. After all, this plant is a descendant of the wild cabbage plant. As with broccoli, this plant too produces tightly-bunched florets that are connected to a thick core with light green leaves around it. A fascinating thing about cauliflower is that, even though they are predominantly white, some come in different colors such as orange, purple, and even yellow. However, they all have a slightly sweet and nutty taste. This is a rather challenging plant to grow, especially for new gardeners, because it requires a constant temperature of 60° F.

They prefer well-draining soil rich in organic matter. So, prepare the site by mixing compost or aged manure. You can also use a mild fertilizer such as 5-10-10 one right before planting. If the soil isn't fertile enough, this results in the buttoning of the heads. Buttoning refers to the formation of small and button-sized heads, instead of a large and single-flowering head.

Even though it's usually considered to be a fall crop, you can grow it during the spring as well. Instead of starting them from seeds (though you certainly can), it is better to opt for seedlings. The ideal time for spring planting is 4-5 weeks before the last spring frost. On the other hand, for fall planting, you need to start the seeds 6-8 weeks before the first frost.

Planting and Growing

The seeds must be planted such that they are 3-6 inches apart. They must be ½ inch deep in the soil and covered with a top layer of soil. If you are planting transplants in your garden, ensure that there is at least 18-24 inches between each plant and 30 inches between each row. Also, don't forget to protect them from harsh cold or frost by using row covers. If needed, the plants might have to be shaded from extremely harsh sun during summers. Don't forget to consistently water the plants throughout their life cycle. To conserve moisture in the soil, mulching is a good idea.

These plants are quite sensitive to any change in terms of temperature, soil nutrition, or even moisture. Any interruption in their growing conditions results in the premature formation of heads, or the lack of flowering altogether. These plants require around 2 inches of water per week, and even a little more if it is extremely hot. Side-dressing the plants using a fertilizer that's rich in nitrogen is needed after transplantation, or after the seedlings have grown. Side-dress the plant once every 3-4 weeks for best results. Initially, it will start as a loose head that slowly takes the required form.

Harvesting

Within 85 days of the seedlings appearing, cauliflower will be ready for harvest. A quick way to speed up maturation is by blanching. The white head of the flower is known as the curd. As soon as it is 2-3 inches wide, blanch it by tying the outer leaves over this head and securing it with a rubber band. You can also use twine or tape to ensure the light stays out. Usually, within 12 days of blanching, cauliflower heads will be ready for harvest. The ideal time to harvest them is when they are 6-8 inches wide. The head must be compact, firm, and white. Use a large knife to cut the head away from the plant. However, do not just take the flower head, and instead keep a couple of leaves around to prolong its shelf life. If you notice that the heads are small or are opening up, harvest them immediately because they will not grow into tighter heads later.

Courgetti Flowers

The botanical name of the courgette is Cucurbita pepo. Courgetti flowers are edible flowers that come from zucchini plants. Zucchini is commonly known as a courgette in Europe, and even the flowers produced by this plant are edible. In fact, they are considered to be quite a delicacy across the world. These flowers are a rich source of vitamins A, C, and K. They also contain different minerals such as copper, magnesium, potassium, and calcium. Consuming these edible flowers is known to regulate blood pressure levels and improve heart health. These low-calorie flowers are an excellent addition to any weight-loss diet.

If you want to grow these flowers, the first step is to grow zucchini plants. Whether it is winter or summer squash, the plants can produce edible flowers. Growing zucchini is extremely simple, and they produce a significant harvest provided you cater to their growing needs and requirements. These plants require plenty of exposure to sunlight and need well-draining, moist soil. Ensure that the soil is not too soggy, or the seeds will never produce any seedlings. So, before you start planting, it is recommended to mix some aged manure or compost into the soil. Ideally, do this 1 week before you start planting.

To grow these flowers, you can either start planting outdoors or start the seeds indoors. If you are starting the seeds indoors, do this 2-4 weeks before the last spring frost. However, it is important to remember that these plants do not transplant well, because their root systems are rather sensitive and do not do well when disturbed. So, it would be better to wait until the climatic conditions are ideal and directly sow them in the garden outdoors. The ideal time to start planting is when the frost has passed, and the temperature of the soil is around 60° F. If the soil is not warm enough, cover the area with a sheet of black plastic and leave it exposed to sunlight for a week. This should help raise the soil temperature. Avoid rushing in and planting too early if you want good produce later.

Planting and Growing

Plant the seeds in the garden soil at least 1 inch deep—the seeds must be 2-3 inches apart. Alternatively, you can also plant 3-4 seeds per hill if you want, but ensure the hills are 2 inches apart. Thinning the plants later will be needed. For now, ensure that there are at least 3-6 feet between each row. If you believe it is too windy or the climatic conditions are not yet optimal, don't hesitate to use row covers. This protects the young seedlings and ensures insects and pests do not feast on them. Water thoroughly at this stage, and you can also add a layer of mulch to lock in the moisture within the soil. This also reduces the chances of any weeds growing around your plants. Even when you are removing weeds, be extremely careful. The goal is to not disturb the existing zucchini plants.

These plants will require at least 1 inch of water per week. If they do not get sufficient water, they will shrivel and die. Excess water also results in root rot, so be mindful. Side-dressing will be needed to promote flowering.

Harvesting

These plants produce both male and female flowers, and zucchinis are created as a result of pollination between these two flowers. That said, you could also harvest the flowers. Learning to harvest the flowers properly will allow you to encourage the plants to grow more squash as well. A few male flowers will be needed so that the female ones can be pollinated and turn into zucchinis. So, you can harvest most of the male flowers.

To differentiate between the male and female flowers, examine the base of the flowers. The right time to do this is early in the morning, when the flowers have not yet opened or bloomed. The male flowers usually open first and have narrower stems than the female ones. The female flower stems are swollen, and resemble a mini version of the squash itself.

Harvest the male flowers by using a sharp pair of scissors or garden shears. Cut the flowers such that 1 inch of the stem is still attached to them, and only opt for blossoms that look healthy. Leave a few male blossoms on the plant, especially once the female ones open up. This will give you a healthy harvest of zucchinis later. If you want to limit the production of squash, then harvest a couple of female flowers too using the above-mentioned method.

Cabbage

The botanical name of cabbage is Brassica oleracea var. capitata. Cabbage is an extremely nutritious vegetable, but it is often overlooked. It looks a lot like lettuce, but belongs to the brassica family that includes cauliflower, broccoli, and kale. It comes in different shapes as well as colors. The leaves can be either smooth or wrinkled, depending on the variety. This vegetable has been consumed for thousands of years. Cabbage is rich in vitamins A and K, folate, manganese, potassium, calcium, and magnesium. It also contains small amounts of iron, riboflavin, and vitamin A. It helps reduce and regulate inflammation, promotes better blood circulation, supports healthy bones, and improves the functioning of the immune system. It also eases digestion due to its rich dietary fiber content, improves cardiovascular health, and is known to regulate blood pressure and cholesterol levels.

As with most members of the brassica family, even cabbage is a cool-season vegetable. However, you can grow it during the fall as well as the spring. This is a hardy vegetable and is a brilliant addition to any garden. Unless the right conditions are maintained, though, it is rather tricky to grow cabbage. It only thrives in cool temperatures, and is also a magnet for different types of garden pests and diseases. This plant prefers neutral soil and full exposure to sunlight, which means the growing site must receive around 6-8 hours of sunlight daily. These plants are also heavy feeders—they will quickly deplete nutrients present in the soil. They require a steady supply of nutrients and water for their growth. Therefore, you should prepare the soil before planting. To do this, mix aged manure or compost into the soil at least 1 week before planting. Once again, the soil must be well-draining without being too moist. If the roots stand in water for too long, this results in root rot, and the seedlings will not appear.

If you want a summer harvest, the seeds can be started indoors 6-8 weeks before the last frost of the spring. On the other hand, if you want a fall harvest, directly sow the seeds outdoors during late or midsummer. If you believe the area is rather hot, then wait until late summer to get started. The young plants shouldn't be exposed to high temperatures, or they will not grow properly.

Planting and Growing

Once you have taken care of the growing conditions, it is time to get started. The seeds must be planted ½ inch deep in the soil. If you are starting them indoors, the same requirement is to be followed. However, the seedlings must be hardened off before you transplant them outdoors. To harden the seedlings, gradually expose them to prolonged periods of sunlight daily. Do this for a week, and then move them outdoors. Wait until 2-3 weeks before the last spring frost to transplant the seedlings outdoors. While sowing the seeds, ensure they are at least 2 inches apart in rows.

The seedlings must be thinned out later to ensure the desired space between them. Again, the seedlings must be 2 inches apart, and the rows must be at least 12-24 inches apart depending on the size of the heads you have in mind. If you space them any closer, the heads will be smaller. As soon as the seedlings are 5 inches tall, you can start thinning the plants if they're too close together. These plants require at least 2 inches of water per week, and a little more if it is too hot. To retain moisture and regulate the soil temperature, it is better to mulch around the growing area. The ideal soil temperature for their growth is 60° F to 65° F—they can also withstand temperatures as low as 45° F. If the temperature is any lower, it will cause the heads to bolt, and can also result in the formation of loose heads.

To ensure that you have a full head of cabbage at the end of the growing season, fertilize them 2 weeks after the seedlings have sprouted. A balanced fertilizer such as 10-10-10 will be helpful at this stage. To promote growth during the early stages, mulching is needed. Ensure that you practice crop rotation as well to reduce the buildup of soil-borne plant diseases.

Harvesting

Most varieties of cabbage are usually ready for harvest within 70 days from planting. Ideally, wait until the head has reached the desired size and is firm to touch. If you leave it for too long, the heads can split on the stems. Most varieties usually produce heads that are between 1-3 pounds. Simply cut the head close to the base using a sharp knife to harvest. If there are any yellow leaves, get rid of them. Alternatively, you can uproot the entire plant and then harvest the head whenever you need it. If you want to get 2 crops from the same plant, then leave the outer leaves and harvest only the center part of it. The outer leaves, along with the roots, will result in the creation of new heads. However, the subsequent head will not be as big as the previous one. To prevent soil-borne diseases, it's recommended to uproot the entire plant—along with its root system—after harvest.

Chapter 13:

Bulbs

In this chapter, you will learn about the common bulb vegetables that can be grown in a garden. From learning about all the different benefits they offer to their growing requirements and harvesting tips, all the information you need is covered in this chapter.

Chives

The botanical name of chives is Allium schoenoprasum. Chives are filled with vitamins A, C, and K, potassium, and calcium. They have certain anti-cancer properties, improve sleep and mood, promote bone health and blood clotting, strengthen eye health, improve cardiovascular health and cognitive functioning, and tackle inflammation.

These sun-loving perennial plants belong to the onion family. They sport bright and colorful flowers. The stalks and flowers of these plants are also edible. These wonderful plants are perfect for companion planting. They deter certain pests and insects, while attracting helpful ones—such as butterflies. Growing chives is incredibly easy.

These are cool-season plants that can tolerate cold, to a certain extent. The ideal time to get started is early to mid-spring for a harvest early in the summer. Ensure that you pay attention to where you plant. Even though these plants are plentiful, if you aren't careful, they can quickly overrun the growing space. As soon as the flowers develop, the seeds are scattered by the wind and the plants grow. An ideal combination of plants chives can be grown with are celery, peas, tomatoes, and lettuce.

Chives are of two types: common chives and garlic chives. The common chives consist of thin and tubular leaves that are 10-15 inches tall, and grow from small and slender bulbs. The edible flowers produced by this plant can be white, purple, pink, or even red. On the other hand, garlic chives produce leaves that are greener and flatter than common chives. Also, these plants can grow up to 20 inches tall. Garlic chives are also known as Chinese chives. As the name suggests, they have a mild garlic-like flavor, and the bulbs are also more intense in taste. Unlike common chives, garlic chives only produce white-colored flowers in large and dense clusters.

These plants prefer plenty of sunlight, but tolerate a little shade as well. The soil must be fertile, well-draining, and moist without being extremely wet. Before you get started, it is better to incorporate a couple of inches of organic matter or compost into the soil. It must be such that the first 6-8 inches of the soil are thoroughly nourished. The roots of these plants do not grow too deep, and therefore, it's only the top layers that need to be replenished. Since they're cool-season crops, the right time to grow them is in the spring and the fall. If the summer temperature is harsh, the seeds will stay dormant until the ideal climatic conditions arrive. If you want to get a head start, especially if you reside in a colder region, it is better to start chive seeds indoors around 8 weeks before the last spring frost.

On the other hand, if you want to directly start the seeds in the garden, wait until spring. These seeds can take a couple of weeks to germinate, and therefore, you must be patient and not panic. The ideal temperature of the soil must be between 60° F and 70° F for germination. These plants prefer slightly acidic to neutral soil, and as long as you follow the steps mentioned until now, you can get started with planting.

Planting and Growing

Plant such that the seeds are ¼ inch deep in the soil, and at least 2 inches apart. Use a thin layer of soil to cover the seeds. Ensure that you do not plant them any deeper, because the seedlings will struggle to germinate. Thinning is needed as the seedlings appear, and when they are 2 inches tall. Thin the plants so that they are 4-6 inches apart. The rows must also be 4-6 inches apart for best results.

Taking care of these plants, especially ones that are properly established, is incredibly simple. They are low-maintenance, and drought-tolerant as well. However, watering them consistently will offer significant yield throughout the growing season. While watering, don't water their foliage and ensure you are watering them close to their roots. The small bulb grows quite close to the surface, and to improve moisture in the soil while preventing the growth of weeds, mulching is needed. Top dressing the plants with a nitrogen-heavy fertilizer early in the fall or late in the spring does the trick. This will be needed if the soil is not rich in the required nutrients.

If you do not want these plants to overtake your garden or spread everywhere, don't forget to remove the flowers when they appear. These plants thrive when planted in small groups. Ideally, opt for 10 plants per patch and you will have a significant yield.

Harvesting

If you want to harvest the leaves, you can do it within 60 days after seeding. If you want to harvest the bulb, simply uproot the entire plant. While harvesting the leaves, always cut close to the base and leave it 2 inches above the ground. Late spring or early summer is the right time to harvest the flowers. Harvest them when they look bright and full.

Shallots

The botanical name of shallots is Allium cepa. These small and elongated onion-like bulbs grow in clusters. They are loaded with helpful nutrients, as well as plant compounds, and contain calcium, phosphorus, magnesium, iron, zinc, potassium, and folate. They also include trace amounts of B complex vitamins and copper. Regular consumption of shallots is known to reduce damage caused by oxidative stress. This vegetable tackles inflammation, reduces the risk of several chronic illnesses, and reduces symptoms of different allergies due to its natural antihistamine properties. The antimicrobial compounds present in shallots strengthen immune functioning. It is known to promote cardiovascular health and blood circulation in general, and also regulates blood sugar levels.

Shallots belong to the onion family, and they are hard biennial plants. They also grow as annuals in certain regions. Unlike onions, shallots are less pungent and have a mild and slightly sweet taste. The outer leaves of these plants can be used just like chives. Shallots are cool-season crops, and usually grow from cloves instead of seeds. A fully-grown shallot can be up to 8 inches tall and has narrow green leaves. The bulb itself is quite small, and is usually ½ inch wide once mature.

The growing temperature for shallots is between 30° F and 50° F, and the ideal soil temperature can be between 32° F and 90° F. These plants prefer well-drained soil rich in organic matter with a pH between 5 and 6.8, and require up to 8 hours of sunlight daily. To cater to these growing requirements, it is better to mix aged compost or manure into the soil 2 days before planting. If the ideal conditions cannot be maintained, then the bulbs will not be as flavorful. The right time to start the cloves in the garden is 4-6 weeks before the last spring frost. These cloves take a while to sprout seedlings, so don't worry because—in most cases—the cloves stay dormant for a month or so.

Planting and Growing

To get started, the broad end of the shallot clove must be placed facing downward in the soil. Do not plant it too deep in the soil, usually ½ inch of depth will do. Cover it with another layer of soil. The cloves must be spaced 6-8 inches apart, and the rows must be 12 inches apart for best results. A shallot bulb usually contains 3-4 cloves that are protected by a thin layer of brown and papery skin. The individual clove must be planted instead of the entire bulb. The ideal plants that shallots can be grown along with include lettuce, beets, and tomatoes—avoid planting them with peas or beans. If the weather becomes too warm, the growth of these plants will suffer. Similarly, take care of their watering and feeding requirements as well. Never let the soil dry out completely; instead, keep it evenly moist. Right before you plant, add some aged manure or compost and work it into the soil. Side-dressing will be needed halfway through the growing season for better growth.

If you want the shallots to grow into a thicker bush, then 3-4 weeks after planting the cloves, you will need to lodge or bend the stalks. Do this once the stalks are around 16 inches tall, or even taller. If you previously planted garlic bulbs in the same area, avoid planting shallots there.

Harvesting

Shallots will be ready for harvest within 120 days of planting, or even sooner in some cases. If you want the leaves, you can harvest them throughout the growing season. They can be used as a seasoning, just like chives or spring onion leaves. Ensure that you do not cut the central stem, because there will be no new growth after this. If you want to harvest the bulbs, then wait until the leaves fall over or turn yellow.

Fennel

The botanical name of fennel is Foeniculum vulgare. This is not just a culinary herb, but a medicinal plant as well. This mild licorice-like tasting plant is packed full of vitamins—it includes vitamin C, dietary fiber, magnesium, calcium, potassium, iron, and manganese. It is also low in calories. The compounds present in fennel reduce oxidative damage and tackle inflammation; this vegetable also helps suppress appetite, and is a great addition to any weight-loss diet. It supports cardiovascular health and functioning, has cancer-fighting properties, and improves mental health. In women, it is known to reduce menopausal symptoms and improve milk production while breastfeeding.

Fennel is now cultivated across the world, but initially, it was native only to the Mediterranean region. It is an extremely aromatic perennial plant that can grow up to 5 feet tall when fully mature, and has dark green and feathery, oval-shaped leaves. It also sports small yellow flowers. The stalks and foliage of this plant are at times confused with those of celery, and the leaves and seeds can be used for culinary purposes. Their taste and aroma are quite similar to that of licorice, or star anise. Fennel is believed to be one of the oldest cultivated plants by humans, and is related to the caraway family. In fact, it was a prized possession in ancient Rome. Warriors regularly consumed fennel to maintain their health. Romans also used it as a weight-loss remedy. In Anglo-Saxon tradition, this is considered to be one of the nine sacred herbs. The Greek name of this plant is *marathon*, which translates to, "to grow thin."

This plant requires plenty of exposure to the sun. and needs to receive at least 6-8 hours of sunlight daily. They require deep and rich soil that is well-draining. The right way to get started is to directly sow the seeds in the garden, and germination usually occurs within 12-18 days. The plants are fully mature and ready for harvest within 100 days of seeding. Before you get started, amend the soil using a general-purpose fertilizer, aged manure, or compost. Work it into the soil and let it rest for 1 week before you get started for the best results.

Planting and Growing

Sow the seeds such that they are 1 inch deep in the soil, and no more. There must be 12 inches of space between each seed, and the rows must be 3 feet apart—this is because once mature, the plants grow to be quite tall and wide. These plants require 1 inch of water per week. If you reside in a windy location, staking the final plants is needed as soon as they are 18 inches tall. When fully mature, some plants can be 3-4 feet tall. Mulch carefully around the plants to protect their roots and retain moisture in the soil.

Harvesting

You don't have to worry about side-dressing or adding any additional fertilizer to the soil later in the growing season. Another benefit of growing fennel is they are self-seeding. The leaves, as mentioned, are ready for harvest within 100 days of planting—or as soon as they reach the desired size. Always use a sharp knife or a pair of garden shears to harvest. Cut the stalks and the leaves, while leaving 2 inches of foliage at the top of the bulb. The stalks and leaves are edible, and therefore, you do not have to discard them. Be careful while uprooting the plant—loosen the soil using your hands or a small garden trowel. Once the soil is loose enough, the bulb will come out. Don't forget to cut off the roots at this stage.

Leeks

The botanical name of leeks is Allium ampeloprasum. These plants belong to the same family that includes garlic, shallots, chives, and onions. Even though they resemble a giant green onion, they have a milder texture and a sweeter flavor. Leeks are low in calories, and are nutrient-dense veggies. They contain vitamins A, C, and K. They are also a great source of magnesium, and contain trace amounts of helpful nutrients such as iron. The beneficial plant compounds and antioxidants present in them reduce inflammation, and protect against different types of cancer. They promote cardiovascular health, and reduce the risk of heart diseases. Leeks are also known to promote weight loss, healthy digestion, regulate blood sugar levels, fight infections, and improve cognitive functioning.

These plants produce long and narrow leaves that are fairly flat. They have a cylindrical white shaft close to the base, but they don't form a specific bulb-like structure—unlike onions. The usual profile of the plant makes them look like green onions, but they are larger. Their growth rate is moderate, and the right time to plant them is during the early spring. In some areas, they can also be planted during the fall. A fully mature plant can be up to 3 feet tall and 12 inches wide. These sun-loving plants thrive in loamy and well-drained soil, with a neutral to acidic pH. The usual bloom time is during the spring—wait until the last spring frost to get started with planting leeks. The seedlings and young plants cannot withstand extreme cold, but can survive a light frost. However, the mature ones are hardier. To get a jump-start on the growing season, the seeds can be started indoors 10-12 weeks before the last spring frost.

As mentioned, they prefer well-drained soil. Therefore, mixing compost or aged manure into the soil before planting is an excellent idea. These are shallow-rooted plants, so be careful while transplanting them. Also, wait until the right conditions and directly sow the seeds in the garden for the best results. The ideal temperature for good growth is above 45° F, and these plants thrive in general temperatures between 55° F and 75° F.

Planting and Growing

Ensure that the growing area you opt for receives at least 6 hours of sunlight daily. If not, the foliage will be floppy and weak. Plant the seeds ¼ inch deep in the soil. They must be 6-8 inches apart, and the rows must be at least 1 foot apart for best results. These plants require at least 1 inch of water per week for the best growth. They have shallow root systems, so you will need to be extra careful while watering them. You must also remember this while mulching. Even though mulching is beneficial, if you are not careful, you might end up hurting its delicate root system.

You don't have to worry about side-dressing the plants if the soil is nutrient-dense to begin with, because they are not heavy feeders. As long as you regularly water them and take care of the sunlight requirements, you'll have a good harvest.

Harvesting

Unlike onions, the foliage of leeks does not die back to signal its maturity. As soon as the stalk is of the desired width, go ahead and harvest it as needed. Usually, you should wait until it is firm to the touch. To harvest leeks, remove them from the soil by gently twisting and pulling them by their roots until they come away from the ground. If you want to prolong their harvest during the cold season, adding a thick layer of mulch around the plants does the trick.

Garlic

The botanical name of garlic is Allium sativum. Garlic is not only a flavorful herb that instantly elevates any dish you cook, but it offers a variety of benefits as well. Garlic has several potent medicinal properties and applications. Ancient Egyptians, Greeks, Babylonians, Chinese, and even Romans used garlic for its medicinal properties. It contains plenty of manganese, vitamin C, and selenium. It also contains a trace amount of several vital nutrients. Garlic is known to strengthen immune functioning, reduce blood sugar and cholesterol levels, reduce the risk of cardiovascular disorders, and improve cognitive functioning. It's also commonly added to nutritional supplements for enhanced athletic performance. It improves bone health and detoxifies the body from the inside.

These sun-loving plants prefer slightly acidic to neutral soil. They are also surprisingly easy to grow, as long as you time them properly. Ensure that the spot selected for growing garlic receives 6-8 hours of sunlight daily. Mixing aged manure or compost into the soil, and letting it stay for 1 week before planting, is a brilliant idea. To further strengthen the nutrient profile of the soil, add a little bone meal, or a well-balanced fertilizer such as a 5-10-10 fertilizer. They require well-draining soil.

You can grow garlic from store-bought bulbs, but it is not a good idea. Most of the garlic available in normal grocery stores will yield extremely small bulbs. The ideal time to plant garlic is in the fall, and you can harvest them in the following summer. The garlic cloves must be planted 6-8 weeks before the first frost in areas that receive a hard frost. If you want to harvest them during the summer, the cloves must be planted before the ground freezes.

Garlic thrives when it can go through a period of dormancy during cold weather, when the temperature is no less than 40° F. If the bulbs are planted during the fall, they get sufficient time to develop a healthy root system before the ground freezes and the temperatures drop drastically. During this stage, they will focus only on the growth of the roots instead of any above-ground foliage. As spring approaches, these bulbs come out of their dormant phase and produce foliage, followed by bulbs that can be harvested during the summer.

Planting and Growing

To get started, you will need to opt for cloves that are healthy, big, and free of any diseases. The size and health of the bulb are directly proportional to the size of the cloves you are using. The larger the clove, the better the harvest. Break the bulb apart, and you will obtain the cloves. Do this a couple of days before planting. Ensure that you do not remove the papery husk, or the covering on the cloves. The cloves must be planted 2 inches deep in the soil, and they must be 4-8 inches apart. Plant the cloves such that the pointy end faces upward, while the wider part faces downward. The rows must be 6-12 inches apart for best results.

If you reside in an area where the temperature drops rather drastically, then mulching the beds with straw and leaves ensures the overwintering of the cloves. As soon as spring sets in, remove the mulch layer. These shoots cannot survive a temperature that is lower than 20° F. As the sun warms up, the temperature of the soil will increase. This, in turn, encourages the young seedlings to start appearing. If any flower shoots crops during spring, get rid of them because they reduce the size of the bulb. These plants are heavy feeders, and therefore, side-dressing them with nitrogen-rich fertilizer or blood meal is a good option halfway through the growing season. They will need to be fertilized right before the bulbs begin to swell. If the foliage turns yellow, it will need to be fertilized again. These plants require 1 inch of water per week.

Harvesting

Usually, garlic will be ready for harvest within 90 days of seeding. The simplest sign that the bulb can be harvested is when the foliage turns yellow. Harvest garlic once their tops fall over and start yellowing as well. Don't wait until the foliage dries out, because the flavor of the bulb will be altered. Sample one bulb before you dig up all the plants. Lift the bulb to see whether it is ready or not—if the bulb is pulled too early, then the covering on the cloves will be thin and their shelf life will reduce. On the other hand, if you leave them in the ground for too long, their skin will split—this exposes the bulb to insects, pests, and diseases. Gently dig around the plant using a garden fork or trowel. Be careful while doing this, because the chances of accidentally hurting the bulb are quite high.

Onions

The botanical name of the onion is Allium cepa. Onions contain potent plant compounds, along with different vitamins and minerals. Their medicinal properties have been recognized since ancient times, and have been used for treating different heart diseases, mouth sores, and even headaches. These nutrient-dense vegetables are rich in vitamin C, B complex vitamins, potassium, and helpful antioxidants. It is known to reduce cholesterol levels, reduce the risk of heart diseases, tackle oxidative damage, and reduce inflammation on the inside. It also helps regulate blood sugar levels, has cancer-fighting compounds, and promotes bone density. In addition, it has several antibacterial properties that promote immune functioning, and the fiber present in it helps with better digestion.

These cold-season crops are quite easy to grow. The ideal time to plant them is early in the spring, so that they are ready for harvest during the fall. You can grow onions from seeds, seedlings, or sets. Starting onions from seedlings is preferred (though you can plant them as seeds as well), because they establish quickly. An onion set essentially refers to onions that are ready for harvest within 14 weeks of planting. They are sturdy enough to withstand light frost, and their success rate is higher when compared to directly sown seeds in the garden. They resemble tiny bulbs of onions, and are usually found at grocery stores. As the stalk matures, it develops into a full-size onion underground. Usually, you should opt for a set that is ¾ inch wide. Any bigger than this, and the chances of them going to seed are higher. If you choose to plant them as seeds, the ideal soil temperature for germination is around 50° F. Start the seeds around 6 weeks before the last frost, and then you can transplant them outdoors as the temperature warms up.

An important thing about onions that you should not overlook is to avoid planting them in the same spot after every growing season. Unless you practice crop rotation, the chances of the subsequent onion plants being plagued by insects, pests, and diseases increases. Onion plants require plenty of sunlight, and you must select an area that receives at least 6-8 hours of direct sunlight daily. The size of the bulbs produced is directly proportional to the sunlight they receive. So, if you want larger bulbs, ensure the plants are exposed to plenty of sunlight. Mix some compost or manure into the soil before planting to improve its texture and nutrient profile. There shouldn't be any debris or rocks in the soil; instead, it must be well-drained. Bulb development is harmed if the soil is compact.

As soon as the ground can be worked during the spring and the temperature will not be less than 28° F, it is time to plant the onion sets. If you are starting with seeds, start them indoors at least 6 weeks before the last frost. Transplant them into the garden once the soil temperature is around 50° F. If you are planting them during the fall, then be prepared to give the onions at least 6 weeks of the dormant period. As soon as the ground warms up and the soil temperature increases, the seedlings will appear. These plants are heavy feeders, and require regular nourishment. If you want big bulbs, then start with a nitrogen fertilizer at the time of planting.

Planting and Growing

Bury the onion set so that they are 1 inch deep in the soil. The sets must be 2-6 inches apart, while the rows must be 12-18 inches apart. If you are starting the seeds indoors, seedlings must be placed in the outdoor garden so that they are 4-5 inches apart. While planting the sets, the pointy end of the bulb must face upward, and the flat end must be downward. Never plant 2 sets close together, because this hinders bulb development. To retain moisture and avoid weed growth, mulching around it is needed.

Even though onions are bulbs, treating them as a leaf crop is a better idea. By encouraging the growth of healthy foliage, the plants will have sufficient energy to produce larger bulbs. Use a layer of light mulch to protect the immature bulbs. This layer must be removed, however, as soon as you notice the first signs of seedlings starting to appear. Every couple of weeks, fertilize the plants using a nitrogen-rich fertilizer. As soon as the onions push the soil away or the bulb's top is visible, it is time to side-dress it with fertilizer. Usually, these plants require up to 1 inch of water per week.

Harvesting

If you notice that any of the onion plants have flowers or have started flowering, then uproot them immediately. The flowering stalk signifies that the bulb formation has come to an end. If you planted onions during the spring, they will be ready for harvest by midsummer. As soon as the foliage turns yellow or falls away from the onions, then you can harvest it. The ideal time to harvest is by late summer when the weather is still dry. While harvesting, loosen the soil around the onion using your hands or a garden trowel. After this, simply remove the bulbs.

Spring Onions

The botanical name of the spring onion is Allium fistulosum. Spring onions are also known as scallions or green onions. They are filled with vitamins A, B2, and C, and are a rich source of copper, magnesium, potassium, and phosphorus. Apart from all the different nutrients present in them, their unique taste instantly elevates the flavor of any dish they are added to. Spring onions are commonly used in Chinese cuisine. Their bulbs aren't always white—they can also have a tinge of pink or yellow. These vegetables can be either cooked or eaten raw depending on your preferences. The dietary fiber present in them is known to improve digestive health, support immune functioning, and regulate blood sugar levels. It also has certain anti-cancer properties, keeps the bones strong, and promotes better eye health. The potent plant compounds present in it also tackle inflammation and offer anti-aging benefits.

Spring onions are essentially immature onions harvested before the bulb is fully mature. They usually have a dark green stem and a white bulb that has roots attached to it. The ideal soil temperature for germination of spring onions is between 65° F and 85° F. As with onions, you can either use seeds or sets to grow spring onions, too. These plants prefer well-drained soil with a pH between 6 and 7.5. Mix the soil with aged compost or manure before planting. They must be fed a well-balanced fertilizer during the growing season.

Planting and Growing

Sow the seeds such that they are ½ inch deep in the soil. After this, cover them with another layer of soil. You can also start the seeds 6-8 weeks before planting. The ideal time to do this is as soon as the spring sets in. The onions must be placed 2 inches apart, and the rows must be up to 12 inches apart. Maintaining these plants once they are well-established is quite easy, since they hardly have any other requirements. Ensure they receive 1 inch of water per week for good growth. The soil must be evenly moist without being too wet or soggy. If at any point the soil feels dry to the touch, then it must be watered. If the temperatures soar during the summer, be extra vigilant about their watering needs. Mulching is a good idea at this stage.

Harvesting

The ideal time to harvest spring onions is when the stalks are young and tender. You can harvest them as soon as they are 6-8 inches tall, and the bulbs start to swell. If you want fully-grown bulbs, then wait until the stalks wither and turn brown. The usual maturity period of spring onions is between 70 and 90 days from planting. A subsequent batch can be grown from the existing ones. Harvest the bulbs such that 1 inch of the bulb (along with the roots) is left undisturbed in the soil. Simply cover them with a layer of soil and water. Within a couple of weeks, the green tops will resprout. As long as the weather conditions are ideal, you can obtain multiple harvests from the same starter batch.

Chapter 14:

Roots and Tubers

In this chapter, you will learn about different types of roots and tubers that can be grown at home. From the benefits they offer to their ideal growing conditions and step-by-step instructions, this chapter offers a wealth of information.

Beets

The botanical name of beets is Beta vulgaris. Beetroots are also commonly known as beets, which are an incredibly vibrant vegetable. Their flavor and aroma are their distinguishing characteristics, and the addition of beets brings a bright pop of color to any plate. They are extremely nutritious and filled with much-needed minerals, vitamins, and other helpful plant compounds. They are a rich source of copper, manganese, magnesium, potassium, iron, and vitamins B6 and C. A combination of all these factors is believed to regulate blood pressure, promote athletic performance, and tackle inflammation. They also improve digestive health, support cognitive functioning, and improve your overall energy levels. Furthermore, they are versatile and can be easily incorporated into your diet.

These sun-loving plants prefer slightly acidic to neutral soil. Their tasty roots and green tops can both be consumed. Growing this dual-purpose plant is quite easy—they are a cool-season crop, and you can grow them by directly sowing the seeds in well-prepared soil. They can survive near-freezing temperatures, as well as frost. This makes them an ideal fall crop. If you are just getting started and reside in warm climatic temperatures, it's better to look for varieties that are bolt-resistant. Beetroots come in different shapes, colors, and sizes. You can start harvesting them when they are the size of a golf ball or a tennis ball. The younger ones taste quite delicious, while the more mature ones are slightly woody and tough to eat.

When selecting a spot to grow beets, opt for one that receives at least 6 hours of sunlight daily. The ideal pH is between 6 and 7. They thrive in well-prepared and fertile soil, but do well in soil of average quality, too. If the soil's pH is less than 6, beets will not grow properly. Also, you should thoroughly inspect the soil in the growing area to make sure there are no rocks or other obstacles—these can prevent the roots from developing, and getting rid of them is needed. Another thing you must remember when it comes to growing beets is to avoid planting them where you have recently grown either spinach or Swiss chard. All of these plants belong to the same family—and therefore, if the previous crop was infested by any pests or diseases, it can pass on to the subsequent ones as well.

The time to start planting beets is once the soil is workable; this is usually during early spring. Keep making successive plantings every 3 weeks or so until midsummer, in order to receive a continuous harvest. As long as the daytime temperature is not more than 75° F, beets will germinate and grow. The ideal soil temperature for germination is 50° F. If the ideal temperature and soil conditions are maintained, they will germinate within 5-8 days of planting, whereas they can take up to 3 weeks if it is colder. If you want to quicken the germination process, soak the seeds in water for up to 24 hours before sowing. The ideal time to get started with beets is 4-6 weeks before the first fall frost date, if you want a fall harvest.

Planting and Growing

You can either start with seeds or start-up plants, but the choice is yours. The seeds can be started indoors or outdoors depending on your preference. That said, it's easier to start them outdoors. Beets can tolerate being transplanted, provided you are careful while moving their roots. They are cold-resistant plants, and starting them outdoors or indoors should not be a problem as long as they have the required temperature. To get started, sow the seeds ½ inch deep in the soil. They must be placed 1-2 inches apart, whereas the rows must be 12-18 inches apart. Use a thin layer of soil to cover the seeds after sowing.

If you look at the beet seeds, you'll realize each of these wrinkled seeds is a cluster of 2-4 seeds. This is one of the reasons why the plants must be thinned once the greens crop up. Once the beet greens are 4-5 inches tall, thin them such that they are around 3-4 inches apart for best growth. This also gives the plants the needed space for proper root growth. While thinning, avoid pulling the plants since this might result in disturbing the roots of the plants next to them as well. Instead, simply pinch or snip the greens off the plant. These greens can then be consumed just like any other leafy vegetable. Only the young and tender leaves taste good.

These plants need to be watered regularly—ensure they receive at least 1 inch of water per week. They require plenty of moisture for proper root growth and development. While watering, please be gentle, because they have shallow roots that will be easily disturbed. Extra fertilizer is usually not needed. If you want to fertilize, ensure that you opt for one that is not too heavy on nitrogen. Excess nitrogen results in lush green foliage, but tiny bulbs.

Harvesting

Depending on the variety of beetroot you are growing, they are ready for harvest within 55-70 days of sowing. Within 2 months after planting, the beets will be ready. The ideal time is to wait until they're the size of a golf ball, or even a little larger. However, if they become too large, they are tough and do not taste as good as the young ones. Loosen the soil around the plant you want to harvest, and then gently pull it up. This ensures the root is intact.

Turnips

The botanical name of turnips is Brassica rapa. This root vegetable belongs to the cruciferous family that includes Brussels sprouts and kale. It is one of the most important crops grown across the world, because it's used to feed not just humans, but cattle as well. Turnips can be green, red, or purple on the outside with a white-fleshed bulb. The roots and the leaves of this plant are edible. Turnips contain healthy dietary fiber, protein, folate, phosphorus, calcium, and vitamins A, C, and K. They help regulate blood sugar levels, tackle inflammation, promote internal healing, protect the body from harmful bacteria, aid in weight management, strengthen bones, and protect the liver.

These cool-weather vegetables are ideal for growth in both the spring and the fall. They germinate rather quickly and their greens, as well as their roots, are perfectly edible. Since these sun-loving vegetables thrive in the spring or the fall, they don't like hot summers. Usually, the crop that's grown in the spring is sweeter than others and more resistant to fighting pests as well. The ideal way to get started is to directly sow the seeds in the garden, because they do not transplant well. Also, they will germinate within a few days—and within a month or so, the greens can be harvested. Within 2 months, their swollen roots can be harvested.

The ideal time to plant turnips is 2-3 weeks before the last date of spring frost. They require plenty of sunlight, and the ideal temperature for their growth is between 40° F and 75° F. Work the garden soil with 2-4 inches of aged compost or manure to improve its drainage. If the soil is heavy or clayey, you'll need to add more to promote better drainage. Apart from compost or manure, using an organic and well-balanced fertilizer such as a 5-5-5 is a good idea, too. If they don't have the required nutrients, the roots will not grow properly. If you want to harvest them during the fall, then start them late in the summer or early in the fall.

While preparing the growing area, overfertilizing—especially with nitrogen—must be avoided, because it promotes leafy foliage instead of big roots. Therefore, opt for a balanced fertilizer. Consider using row covers to protect the crops from the time of planting.

Planting and Growing

Plant the seeds so they are 1 inch deep in the soil—they need to be 1 inch apart, while the rows need to be 12-18 inches apart. Alternatively, the turnip seeds can be scattered and then thinned later. Don't forget to cover the seeds using ½ inch of soil to protect them from the elements and other pests. Regularly and properly water the plants for the best growth. As soon as the seedlings are around 4 inches tall, it's time to start thinning them. This promotes healthy growth of the plants, and reduces the chances of malformed or small roots.

Thin the plants such that they are 4-6 inches apart—they will not grow properly if they are closer than 4 inches. The area must be free of weeds—but be extremely careful while weeding or mulching, because the roots are delicate and can be disturbed easily. These plants don't require much water, but the soil's moisture level must be consistent for the best growth. The ideal watering requirement of these plants is about 1 inch per week for best growth.

Even though these plants are usually treated as annuals, they are biennials. They flower and seed during the second year. Bolting is quite common during the first year, but it's usually due to lack of nutrients or water, or exposure to extreme temperatures. These elemental factors can result in little (or even no) growth of roots, or the growth of only leaves. To avoid bolting, ensure that you harvest them before the temperature is over 80° F.

Harvesting

If you want to harvest the greens, then do this when they are young and tender—this is when they taste the best. Ensure that you leave at least 2 inches of the stem above the base to promote the growth of foliage. Harvest only a couple of leaves at a time, especially if you are growing them for their roots. The young and small turnips are usually more tender and tastier, too. The ideal time to harvest them is around 5 weeks from planting. Some varieties are ready for full harvest within 6 weeks of sowing.

Parsnips

The botanical name of parsnips is Pastinaca sativa. This delicious root vegetable has been cultivated by humans for thousands of years across the world. It's quite similar to cabbage and parsley roots. The long and cream-colored tuberous root of this plant has a slightly nutty and sweet flavor. They not only taste incredible, but are also a powerhouse of nutrients as well. They're packed with important nutrients such as vitamins C, B6, K, and E, thiamine, magnesium, zinc, phosphorus, and plenty of dietary fiber. Parsnips are rich in antioxidants that reduce the risk of chronic health diseases, tackle inflammation, and support immune functioning. The dietary fiber in them promotes digestive health and assists in weight loss and management.

These cool-season plants are quite hardy, and thrive when they are exposed to full or partial sunlight. Whether it is a soup or stew, parsnips can be added to multiple dishes. The ideal time to get started with this delicious and versatile plant is during the spring, so that it can be harvested right before the ground starts freezing. These plants were introduced to the Americas by ancient Greeks and Romans, and they belong to the parsley and carrot family. Even though they are biennials, they're grown as annuals across North America. They require a prolonged growing season, and the ideal time to harvest is after a couple of fall frosts. The roots will be small if planted too late in the season.

The area where you want to grow these vegetables must get plenty of sunlight, and the soil must be loose. Move the soil around to ensure that it is free of rocks or any other obstacles that will prevent root growth. If the soil is compacted or clayey, the roots will be thin and misshapen. Before you start planting, ensure that you get rid of weeds in that area under the soil using well-rotted compost or manure. Alternatively, you can also use a neutral fertilizer to improve soil fertility. The ideal time to start sowing seeds in the soil is during the spring, when the ground is still workable. The required soil temperature for germination is around 50° F to 54° F, but they can still germinate if the soil is as low as 48° F.

Planting and Growing

An important consideration when it comes to planting and growing parsnips is to opt for fresh seeds. If the seeds are over a year old, the rate of germination will be extremely low. Instead of starting them indoors, it is better to directly sow them in the garden soil. They must be sown ½ inch deep, and no more. The rows must be 18-24 inches wide for best results. These seeds are rather slow to germinate, and usually take around 2-3 weeks—even longer if the soil temperature is not ideal. Make sure the soil is moist to quicken the germination process.

Thinning will be needed to promote better growth of the plants. The young plants must be 3-4 inches apart as soon as they are 2-3 inches tall. While doing this, ensure that you don't disturb the roots of the seedlings around them. To thin the plants, simply snap off the green tops. Do not pull the seedlings or try to uproot them by grabbing them, because this will certainly harm the other plants around them. To deter pests or any other insects, using row covers is a good idea—especially when they're quite young. The plant beds must be free of weeds, and mulching is a great way to achieve this goal. They require around 1 inch of water per week, and need a fair amount of moisture to form healthy root systems. Fertilizer is not needed if you start with decent or high-quality garden soil. If there is excess nitrogen in the soil or the fertilizer used, this will result in excess foliage growth instead of root formation. Hill the soil around the base of the plant once the roots are formed, in order to prevent the greening of its shoulders.

Harvesting

A word of caution—always wear gloves or long sleeves while harvesting or handling these plants. The leaves—and their sap—are skin irritants. Usually, you can start harvesting parsnips within 24 weeks of planting. The ideal time to harvest them is once their roots are around 1 inch wide. Let the roots stay in the ground for a couple of frosts before harvesting, as this intensifies the flavor. However, don't forget to harvest them before the ground freezes. If you want to, you can also leave them in the ground for the winter after covering the soil with a thick layer of mulch. Then, they can be readily harvested in the spring as soon as their growth starts and the ground thaws. If the flower stalk crops up, this means the roots have become woody.

Celeriac

The botanical name of celeriac is Apium graveolens var. rapaceum. Celeriac, or celery root, is steadily gaining popularity these days. It's filled with several important vitamins and minerals, offering impressive health benefits. It is quite versatile, and can be used as an alternative to potatoes and any other root vegetables. This root vegetable is closely related to parsnips, celery, and parsley. It almost looks like a misshaped turnip, and has a knobby and rough surface covered in tiny rootlets. Its white-colored flesh is quite similar to that of potatoes. Celeriac is quite popular in European regions, especially during the winter months. Its impressive nutrient profile includes plenty of dietary fiber, vitamins B6, K, and C, manganese, fiber, phosphorus, and potassium. These low-carb vegetables are packed with healthy antioxidants that tackle inflammation and reduce the risk of chronic illnesses, support and strengthen cardiovascular functioning, improve digestion, strengthen bones, and improve immune functioning.

This cool-season crop is usually grown as an annual, but is really a biennial. The ideal time to harvest them is when the weather turns cold. Ideally, the seeds can be started indoors and transplanted at a later stage into the garden. You can do this 10 weeks before the last frost date. The maturity period is between 90 and 120 days for most varieties. Though it belongs to the celery family, the root of this plant resembles the root of the turnip, and also grows similarly. The ideal plants for companion planting are peas, lettuce, and spinach.

Planting and Growing

They thrive in colder climatic conditions, especially when the nights are cold. If you reside in an area that receives cold winters, the right time to grow them is during the spring. Late summer is ideal if you have relatively warmer winters. They take plenty of time for germination, and the right way to get started is by using transplants. The seeds can be sown 10 weeks before the last frost date in spring. They require up to 120 days to fully mature and be ready for harvest. If you are growing them late in summer, the seeds can be directly sown in the soil.

Sow the seeds such that they are ½ inch deep in the soil. Cover the area with burlap or seed cloth to keep it moist until the seedlings appear. Thin the plants once they are 3-4 inches tall, such that they are 6-8 inches apart. This is also the right time to transplant them if you were growing the seeds indoors. Space the rows such that they are 24-30 inches apart. Since these are shallow-rooted plants, be extremely careful while watering them. The soil must be moist without becoming too damp. Ensure that you keep the growing area free of weeds to prevent the plants from competing for the available water and nutrients. Since these plants have shallow roots, be careful while removing weeds. The side roots must be snapped as the main route develops. To blanch the bulbs, hill the soil over them. Even if the outside of the root blanches white, the flesh will have a brownish tinge on the inside.

Harvesting

These plants usually don't have any serious pest or disease problems, and are quite easy to take care of. Most varieties of celeriac are ready for harvest within 120 days of seeding. The right time to harvest is when the root is 3-4 inches in diameter, or even a little bigger. Use a sharp knife to cut the root close to the stem, and then lift it using a garden fork. The young and tender leaves can also be used to flavor stews and soups.

Carrots

The botanical name of carrots is Daucus carota subsp. sativus. It is said that carrots were first grown somewhere in Afghanistan around 900 A.D. They are best known for their orange color, but come in different shades including red, purple, white, and even yellow. Orange carrots were introduced in central Europe sometime during the 16th century. Carrots are a rich source of essential vitamins and minerals including vitamins A and K, potassium, calcium, dietary fiber, and iron. They are filled with antioxidants that tackle inflammation as well. Carrot consumption reduces the risk of certain types of cancer, improves eye health, and regulates blood sugar levels. They also strengthen the functioning of the immune system, relieve constipation, strengthen bones, and regulate diabetes.

This cool-season crop usually thrives in the spring, and loves plenty of sunlight. Carrots are not only delicious, but come in a variety of colors and shapes as well. Whether it's purple or white, there's plenty to choose from. Usually, these plants have a reputation of being a little tricky to grow—especially if the soil is compacted and heavy. However, with the right information and a little conscious effort, growing carrots is not challenging.

Before you get started, you will need to select a location that receives around 6-10 hours of sunlight daily. The soil must be free-draining. This is one of the few plants that prefer sandy soil instead of other variants. However, if the soil is too loose, the roots will not be able to reach down. Similarly, if it is compacted or heavy, it will need to be loosened using manure or compost. The ideal time to get started is 2-3 weeks before the last date of spring frost. The soil must be a little dry and warm after the last frost. The ideal soil temperature for germination is 40° F, but it should not exceed 75° F. The quality and taste of the harvest are reduced if the temperature increases.

Planting and Growing

Ensure that you till the soil at least 10 inches deep in the garden—there shouldn't be any soil clumps, rocks, or stones. The soil can be amended using compost, or by adding another 6 inches of sandy topsoil. Double digging is an ideal practice to ensure that the soil is aerated and loose. Instead of transplanting them, it is better to directly sow the seeds in the garden. They have a delicate root system that doesn't do well when transplanted. The seeds must be sown ¼ inch deep in the soil and 2-3 inches apart—each row must be 1 foot apart. Distribute the seeds evenly so that they don't grow too close together. The seeds are quite tiny, and sowing them too thickly is easy. To ensure that the seeds are sown evenly, simply mix them with a little fine sand. Now, sprinkle the sand-seed mixture 2-3 inches apart. After this, cover them with another layer of topsoil.

The soil must be moist, so therefore, you'll need to water them frequently. Deep watering is not recommended, though. The soil must not have a hard crust on top—if it does, then the seeds will not germinate. Use a fine layer of sand, compost, or vermiculite to cover the seeds to ensure a crust doesn't form. The ideal way to check whether the soil conditions are perfect for germination or not is by doing the finger test. Simply stick your finger into the soil—it needs to feel moist until mid-knuckle. If it doesn't feel moist, then it's time to water the plants. If you want a continuous harvest throughout the growing season, successive planting must be done every 4 weeks or so.

To retain moisture and speed up the germination process, gentle mulching is needed. As soon as the seedlings are 3-4 inches tall, or have 3-4 true leaves, start thinning. The plants must be 3-4 inches apart. Use a pair of sharp scissors to simply snap their tops off instead of pulling them off. Since their roots are delicate, you must be extremely careful here. Carrot plants require around 1 inch of water every week. Avoid overwatering if you want a good harvest later, and be extremely diligent when it comes to removing weeds. The ideal time to fertilize the plant is 5-6 weeks after seeding. Always opt for a fertilizer that has relatively low nitrogen to promote the growth of roots instead of foliage.

Harvesting

Since these plants grow underground, how do you know when they are ready for harvest? The simplest and most effective means to do this is to poke around the roots a little, and check the approximate width of the root's neck. Usually, the first root is ready within 2 months of sowing. Their taste is directly proportional to their size—so, the smaller the carrots, the better the taste. The ideal time to harvest is as soon as the root is ½ inch wide, or the size of your thumb. Simply grip the base of the plant and tug. This is an ideal way to harvest, especially when the roots are young and shallow. If the roots are longer or larger, you'll need a gardening fork to loosen the soil and then harvest them without damaging the other plants. You will have a staggered harvest that spans over a couple of weeks if you harvest in stages fully. Ensure that they are harvested before the temperatures soar, because this affects the taste and flavor of the roots.

Potatoes

The botanical name of the potato is Solanum tuberosum. Did you know that potatoes belong to the nightshade family? This is the same family that tomatoes, peppers, and eggplants belong to. Potatoes are usually a cool-weather crop. Usually, the tuber develops within 5-7 weeks of planting. They are one of the oldest vegetables that humans have been cultivating. In fact, the earliest record of potatoes was traced back to the ancient Incan civilization in Peru. It arrived in the American colonies in 1621, and has since been a staple in most cuisines across the world. Potatoes are not only versatile, but healthy, too!

These vegetables are a source of essential carbohydrates the body needs. They are rich in vitamin C, potassium, folate, niacin, iron, zinc, magnesium, and riboflavin.

Potatoes prefer full exposure to the sun. They are related to eggplants and peppers since they belong to the nightshade family, instead of carrots or other roots, as most might think. If the climate is warm, these cool-weather plants can be grown as a winter crop as well. The underground part of the plant, which is edible, is known as the tuber. Usually, they can be harvested and developed within 5-7 weeks after planting.

The patch where you want to grow potatoes must receive at least 6 hours of direct sunlight daily. These plants require well-trained and loose soil—if the soil structure is compact, the tubers will be misshaped. The ideal pH of the soil is between 5.8 and 6.5, and it thrives in slightly acidic soil. The required soil temperature for optimal growth is between 45° F and 55° F. When you start planting, ensure that you amend the soil with some organic matter or compost to ensure the soil is loose and fertile.

The right time to sow the seeds directly in the garden is as soon as the soil is workable—this is usually around 2 weeks after the last date of spring frost. If the crops are sown too early, the roots can rot. Instead of focusing purely on the calendar, it is recommended to pay close attention to the soil conditions and structure as well. If the soil seems too warm, or if it's sticking together, it will be hard to work. Apart from all this, the plants will grow better if the soil dries out a little, and you can start planting after this condition is met.

Planting and Growing

When you decide to grow potatoes, you should always opt for certified seed potatoes—such potatoes have eyes, or birds, that protrude from the spud. Seed potatoes are not potato seeds, or the varieties you find at a local grocery. You can purchase them from a local nursery or garden store. Use a clean and sharp paring knife to cut the large potato into golf ball-sized pieces. Each piece must have at least 1 or 2 eyes, and this must be done at least 2 days before planting. This will give the potatoes sufficient time to form a protective layer over their surface that improves rot resistance, as well as moisture retention. If the seed potatoes are smaller than the size of an egg, plant them as it is instead of cutting them any further.

The rows must be spaced 3 feet apart for best results. Now, it is time for a little elbow grease. You need to dig a trench that is around 6 inches wide and deep. The bottom of the trench must taper to around 3 inches. Mix some aged manure or compost into it. In each trench, the seed potato must be placed such that its cut side faces the ground. Place the potatoes 12-14 inches apart. Within 16 days of planting, the growth must be visible. At this stage, cover the trench further with another 3-4 inches of soil to ensure the plants are not exposed to direct elements. Until the entire trench is filled to ground level, you will need to keep repeating this process. The rows must be mulched to maintain the soil temperature, prevent weed growth, and improve moisture retention.

Ensure even moisture is available for the plants, especially once the flowers bloom. These plants require up to 2 inches of water every week. If you don't water them or they are overwatered, their ultimate growth will be misshapen. If the foliage turns yellow or the plant starts dying, it's usually a sign of the plant being overwatered.

One thing you must remember is to keep the potatoes covered, so that they are not directly exposed to sunlight. The depth at which they are planted, along with the darkness provided, influences the flavor of potatoes. As the plants start growing, periodically mound the soil and compost around them to ensure that only the top leaves are sticking out. If the spots are exposed to sunlight, they can turn green, which further destroys their flavor profile.

Hilling must be done early in the morning, especially when the plants are at their tallest. This is because the plants start drooping as the sun rises. Once the plant blooms, or it is around 6 inches tall, you can stop hilling.

Harvesting

The ideal time to harvest potatoes is when the weather is dry. On such days, simply dig the soil gently to harvest. Be extremely careful while doing this, because you might unknowingly end up hurting the tubers. Digging and harvesting become easier when the soil is loose and not compact. These tubers can withstand a light frost but don't forget to harvest them right before the first hard frost. New potatoes (or small ones) are usually ready for harvest within 2-3 weeks after the plant starts flowering. The mature ones are ready for harvest after the foliage has died back.

Sweet Potatoes

The botanical name of sweet potatoes is Ipomoea batatas. Sweet potatoes not only taste incredible, but are also a powerhouse of different nutrients your body requires. They are rich in vitamins B and C, iron, magnesium, calcium, phosphorus, zinc, and potassium. The carotenoids responsible for the sweet potato's rich color are helpful antioxidants. A combination of all these different nutrients within it helps lower the risk of certain types of cancer, heart diseases, and macular degeneration. They also lower inflammation and strengthen cardiovascular functioning. Regular consumption of sweet potatoes is known to stabilize blood sugar and cholesterol levels.

These sun-loving plants thrive in warm weather. You can have a generous harvest of this delicious root vegetable by just growing a couple of sweet potato plants. It's essentially a tropical plant that belongs to the morning glory family. The foliage and flowers of the sweet potato plant closely resemble those of the morning glory flower itself. Despite their name, they are not related to potatoes that belong to the nightshade family. Unlike potatoes, the edible part of the sweet potato plant is not a tuber, but its roots. Technically, it is a modified stem instead of a true tuber.

They require warm soil for germination, and need warm weather for their growth for at least 4 months. They are heat and drought-tolerant, to a certain extent. These plants aren't grown from seeds; instead, you will need slips. Slips are sprouts obtained from an existing sweet potato plant. You can obtain slips from local nurseries, garden centers, and even local farmers. Before purchasing slips, ensure that you have at least 90-120 days of ideal growing conditions, because this is how long the plants take to mature.

These plants require well-drained soil and a sunny spot. They are not too picky, but if the soil is on the sandy side, their growth will be stifled. They require plenty of air in the soil so that their roots can grow. If the soil is compacted, rich in clay, or rocky, a raised bed is a better option. Alternatively, planting them in loamy soil can be created by mixing regular soil with compost and coconut coir, or perlite. Do not use any animal manure, because this can result in stained or spindly roots later. Also, avoid using a nitrogen-rich fertilizer, because it promotes the growth of foliage instead of the tuberous roots.

The right time to start the slips outdoors is 3-4 weeks after the last date of spring frost. You should wait until the soil is at least 65° F, while the nighttime temperature should be no lower than 55° F—anything lower than this, and the plant will not grow. The idea is to plant them early in the season, so they have sufficient time to mature. However, you must not plant them so early that they are harmed by the last spring frost. Sweet potatoes must be protected from late frosts or colder nights, especially when they're tender. Using row covers is a good idea. Remove them during the daytime to ensure the plants get sufficient sunlight.

If you do not want to purchase slips or want to start them on your own, it takes a little while longer. You must start with unblemished, organic, and smooth sweet potatoes. Purchase them at least 8 weeks before the last spring frost. The entire sweet potato must be placed in a bin or a pot that has around 3 inches of light, well-drained and organic soil. Place the potatoes in it such that there is 1 or 2 inches between them. Cover the potatoes with 2 inches of the same soil. Now, ensure that the soil is moist without becoming soggy or damp. The soil temperature, as well as that of the surrounding area, must be between 75° F and 80° F. If this temperature cannot be maintained, or you believe the plants will not receive sufficient sunlight, then artificial growing lights can be used. As soon as the slips emerge from the soil, you can move them outdoors. However, this process itself takes 6-8 weeks. The slips must be at least 6-12 inches long, with multiple leaves and roots, before they can be transplanted. If you believe it is still too early to start transplanting them outdoors, keep them indoors only for 2 weeks or until the last frost has passed. Harden the slips by exposing them to outdoor sunlight for 1-2 weeks before transplantation.

Planting and Growing

To plant the sweet potato slips, you will need to create mounds that are 6-8 inches tall. Each mound must be at least 12 inches wide. There must be 3 feet between each mound, so that the vines have sufficient space to grow. Ideally, they must be transplanted to the garden only when the soil temperature is around 60° F, and no less. Only the top leaves must be present on the slips, and the lower ones should be broken off—this promotes the growth of roots instead of foliage. The slips must be placed deep enough in so that the roots are covered while the leaves are visible. Use a liquid fertilizer high in phosphorus at this stage to ensure that the roots become strong. You'll need to water them regularly for the next 7-10 days.

After 3-4 weeks of transplantation, side-dress the plants with a 5-10-10 fertilizer. Beds must be regularly weeded once every 2 weeks after planting. Do not dig deep or use any tool that will disturb these rather delicate feeder roots. During midsummer, the plants must be watered regularly. After the temperature soars, deep watering is required to improve the yield. Avoid pruning the vines, because these must be vigorous for better growth. To ensure that the skin of the sweet potatoes does not crack or break open, you must reduce the amount of water given to the plants.

Harvesting

The right time to harvest them is once their leaves, as well as the ends of their vines, turn yellow. Usually, this takes around 100 days from planting. Gently loosen the soil around the plant—do this so that the root isn't harmed. The vines must be cut away at this stage. The primary crown of the plant must be pulled up, while the root must be dug by hand. Be extremely careful while doing this, because they bruise rather easily. Any excess dirt must be shaken off, and avoid washing the roots. The harvest must be complete before the first fall frost.

Yuca

The botanical name of yuca is Manihot esculenta. Yuca root is also referred to as cassava root—it resembles a combination of sweet potatoes and potatoes. It is a dark brown tuber that's been cultivated in Africa and South America for centuries, and is an excellent source of several antioxidants, vitamins, and minerals. It includes vitamins A and C, phosphorus, potassium, choline, and magnesium. A combination of all these helpful compounds is known to promote eye and brain functioning, tackle the damage caused by free radicals, stabilize the digestive system and improve its functioning, and regulate blood glucose levels.

The yuca plant (also known as tapioca) is a perennial woody shrub that belongs to the spurge genus. Do not get this confused with the yucca plant. Even though their spellings and pronunciations are almost the same, one is edible while the other is not. In this section, you'll learn about growing yuca (or cassava) roots.

These sun-loving plants thrive in tropical and subtropical climatic regions, and take at least 1 year to mature. They also prefer sandy and loamy well-drained soil that is slightly acidic to neutral, and amending the desired area with manure or compost before planting is a good idea. When it comes to the cassava plant, starting with seeds is not possible. Instead, propagate them from cuttings. This is a simple way to ensure that you are not growing bitter varieties of cassava. The stem cuttings obtained from this plant also root rather easily in the garden, and can be planted directly into the soil provided the ideal climatic conditions are prevalent. The cuttings will be fully established in a couple of months. You just need one healthy cutting to propagate future plants.

Planting and Growing

Once you have selected the ideal growing area, it's time to get started. Ensure that these plants are exposed to full sunlight for at least 8 hours daily—heat and humidity are vital for its growth and development. As long as the pH of the soil is between 5.5 and 6.5, you will obtain good results. The right time to start planting is once the temperature is at least 70° F. If the temperature is not at this level yet, you can always start the cuttings inside and then shift the transplants outdoors later when the conditions are ideal. To start the cuttings indoors, you will need a couple of containers or a growing tray. Layer it with the ideal soil, place the propagated stems in it, and water it lightly. Ensure the soil is slightly moist without becoming too damp. Expose them to sufficient sunlight and keep them away from the cold. Within 6 weeks, these transplants can be shifted outdoors. If the temperature is less than 50° F, the plants will stop growing altogether.

While planting the stems in the garden, ensure that ¼ of the stem is steadily planted within the soil. If the stem has a couple of nodes on it, within a week or two, you will see new leaves appearing. The plants must be spaced 3 feet apart, and there must be at least 3-16 feet between each row. As long as you have prepared the soil with well-rotted manure or any other compost before planting, all good. However, you need to side-dress it 2 months into this process using a good quality manure liquid fertilizer. These plants are drought-resistant, and therefore, their watering requirements are quite lower than other plants growing in your garden. As long as the roots get sufficient water without becoming too damp or soggy, they should be fine.

Harvesting

Once you follow all the steps mentioned until now, your first cassava is ready for harvest. Wait for 1 year if you want an even better harvest. If you have more patience, you can wait for up to 18 months. If it looks like the entire plant is dying, uproot it because the root must be ready for consumption. On the other hand, if the plants are still green, be careful while harvesting. As mentioned, these plants grow well from propagated stems. Therefore, while harvesting, hold on to a couple of cassava stems and you can use them for the subsequent crop.

Use a sharp knife or a machete to harvest or cut the entire plant down, such that you have at least 1 foot of the stem left behind. Dig the soil away carefully from the plant so that you're not hurting its roots. Be extremely careful while harvesting, because the roots can get damaged quite easily. If the roots are a dark brown color and seem a little flaky on the surface, then it is perfectly mature!

Daikon Radish

The botanical name of daikon radish is Raphanus sativus var. longipinnatus. It is also referred to as oilseed, and icicle radish. This variety is native to Japan and China. It's also considered to be a winter radish. Daikon radish is a low-calorie and high-fiber vegetable that contains plenty of vitamins C and B, calcium, potassium, and copper. The active plant compounds in it promote the functioning of the immune system, tackle inflammation, aid in weight loss, and reduce the risk of chronic conditions such as neurodegenerative diseases and diabetes.

If you are just getting started, this is the perfect plant for your garden. They are incredibly easy to plant, and require little maintenance. Also, they are ready for harvest within 3 weeks. On average, these vegetables weigh around 1-2 pounds each. The roots of this plant are usually white, but the color varies depending on the variety. For instance, the

Korean varieties have green-colored roots. It's not just the root that is edible—even the flowers can be used as a garnish, too. It's also commonly used as a cover crop. This plant belongs to the brassica family, and is an annual variety. It can grow 8-24 inches tall, and requires plenty of sunlight. It prefers mildly alkaline and well-drained soil.

The ideal time to start planting daikon radish is in the early fall or late summer. While planting, ensure that there is at least 8-12 inches of space between each plant and each row—they need a little space to grow properly. They need at least 6 hours of sunlight daily, while the pH of the soil must be between 5.8 and 6. If the soil is not well-drained, supplement it with some compost or aged manure, and then start planting. The nitrogen level in the soil must be relatively low for this plant to survive—if not, the roots will not flourish, and the foliage will keep growing instead.

These plants thrive when the temperature is between 50° F and 60° F. That said, they can survive even if the temperatures are as low as 30° F—but not any lower. Ensure that there is no imminent frost when you get started with daikon radish. They don't require any additional fertilizer, provided you have amended soil before getting started. Halfway through the growing season, you need to side-dress it to promote better tuber growth.

Planting and Growing

As with any other variety of radish, direct seeding is the best way to go about growing daikon radish as well. The seeds must be sown around 2 months before the first frost date. This, in turn, will help achieve a quicker harvest. The seeds must be sown 12-18 inches apart. Ensure the seeds are not sown more than ½ inch deep in the soil. Also, don't forget to prepare the soil before you start seeding. If the soil is compacted, it will not grow properly. Loosen the soil and mix it with sufficient aged compost or manure. However, do not mix too much nitrogen into the soil, because this will result in smaller roots and larger greens. Once the seeds are sown, the soil must be sufficiently moist for a couple of days, then the seedlings will appear. As soon as they are 2 inches tall, you'll need to start thinning them such that they are 4-6 inches apart.

You will need to water the plants regularly. The soil must be moist without becoming too damp. Also, don't worry if a little bit of the root is visible above the ground. You will also need to keep pruning the plants regularly, because these plants attract a variety of garden pests and insects. The tender edible greens can be harvested at any time.

Harvesting

The ideal time to harvest daikon radish is once they are in-ground for at least 3 weeks. As soon as the greens are about 8 inches tall, pluck them out of the ground. Be careful while harvesting these radishes, because they bruise rather easily. Carefully dig around the plant roots to loosen the soil, then simply pluck them out of the ground.

Salsify

The botanical name of salsify is Tragopogon porrifolius. Salsify contains a variety of minerals, vitamins, and other helpful nutrient components. It contains vitamin C, riboflavin, choline, omega-3 fatty acids, dietary fiber, potassium, sodium, iron, zinc, copper, magnesium, and calcium. Consuming salsify regularly strengthens bone health, supports immune functioning, improves digestive health, reduces the risk of diabetes, and improves cardiovascular functioning. Since it is rich in dietary fiber, it also helps reduce body weight and tackle obesity.

This rather old-fashioned vegetable is not easy to find in the local grocery store. That said, growing it is quite exciting and fun. Salsify is also known as a vegetable oyster or oyster plant, due to its flavor that is reminiscent of oysters. Planting salsify is incredibly easy, and the right time to start is the early spring. This is needed especially if the area receives snow, but is not needed during the fall. These plants require up to 100-120 days to fully mature, and then you can harvest them. These cool-weather plants can be started from seeds, and they are slow-growing plants. They cannot survive if the temperature is any higher than 85° F. If the temperature is any higher than this, the roots become quite tough and fibrous. So, don't hesitate to use row covers or offer them some shade if the temperatures soar.

Planting and Growing

The ideal pH of the soil for this plant is between 6 and 7. They prefer deep and fine-textured, well-drained soil. If the soil is too compact or cannot retain too much water, you need to work it with some compost or aged manure. Ensure that you do this before you start planting. Once the soil is ready, it is time to get started. The seeds must be sown such that they are ½ inch deep in the soil, and no more. The seeds must also be placed 1-2 inches apart in each row. Within a week, the seeds will germinate, provided the climate conditions are ideal. If not, it can take up to 3 weeks. Once the seeds have sprouted, it's time to start thinning them. Thinning can be done only once the seedlings are around 2 inches tall. Thin them such that they are 2-4 inches apart for best results

These plants barely require any pruning, because they are slow-growing plants. Since the roots of these plants will grow bigger, ensure the soil is moist at all times. They will need up to 1 inch of water per week, and more if the temperatures are higher. Taking care of these plants is rather easy once they are well-established in the garden. Even when you are mulching, be careful to not hurt their roots or disturb them.

Harvesting

Salsify will be ready for harvest during the fall if you planted it in the spring. If you planted it in the fall, then it will be ready for harvest in the subsequent spring. When it comes to harvesting salsify, remember that they have extremely deep roots. At times, their roots can be up to

1 foot deep in the soil. To carefully harvest, you will need to remove the entire root without hurting or breaking it. To do this, you will need a shovel or a spading fork. Carefully move the soil, along with the plant, while avoiding its roots. Once the soil is loose enough, simply pluck the plant, and the root is ready for harvest.

Chapter 15:

Stems

In this chapter, you will learn about different stem vegetables that can be added to your home garden. You will not only learn about their growing requirements, care, and harvesting techniques, but the different benefits they offer as well.

Asparagus

The botanical name of asparagus is Asparagus officinalis. Asparagus has an impressive nutrient profile, and is low in calories—half a cup of cooked asparagus has only 20 calories. It is filled with dietary fiber, vitamins A, C, K, and E, potassium, phosphorus, and folate. It also includes other helpful micronutrients such as zinc, iron, and riboflavin. It is an excellent source of potent antioxidants that combat chronic inflammation and other conditions associated with it. It promotes digestive health, reduces blood pressure levels, and can assist in weight loss.

These sun-loving plants require neutral to slightly acidic or alkaline soil. The ideal bloom time for them is in the spring, and this is the first plant that will greet you during springtime. It's a perennial plant, which means that once the roots are established, they will return yearly provided you take care of them. Apart from that, the benefit of growing asparagus is that they are aesthetically pleasing. These summer plants are usually grown in temperate regions, but can tolerate a long winter as well. The young stem (or the shoot) is the only edible part of the plant. Unless the soil temperature is above 50° F, the shoot will not emerge. An important thing you must remember is asparagus must not be harvested during the first couple of seasons. Instead, allow them to establish themselves, so that you will have a sustainable harvest later. With asparagus, patience is needed—a little effort and patience go a long way. Once the plants are fully rooted and established, they can last for a couple of decades, not just one growing season.

As mentioned, a newly planted asparagus plant will take around 2-3 years to fully produce delicious stems. They are relatively quick producers once you get through the first year or two. After this, during the spring, you'll notice fresh spears every couple of days. Since this is a perennial plant, care must be taken before you start planting or sowing the seeds. This is because once the plants are established, they will keep growing in the same site every year. So, the chosen area must receive around 6-8 hours of direct sunlight daily. The ideal way to plant asparagus is to use them to line the edge or the border of the garden. Select a place that will not be regularly disturbed by any other activity.

The soil must be well-draining, but not too moist. These plants require water, but not too much of it. If the soil is neutral to slightly acidic with a pH of 6.5, then these plants will thrive. Before you get started, it is better to loosen the soil using some manure or compost—especially if the soil is a little compact. If you want the spears to grow properly, the soil must be loosened up to 15 inches deep, and there shouldn't be any rocks or other obstacles.

Planting and Growing

The ideal time to get started with planting and growing asparagus is once the soil can be worked. So, the early spring works perfectly well for these plants. If you are growing potatoes, then you should start asparagus at the same time. The 1-year-old plants that are used for growing asparagus are known as crowns. You can also start them with seeds if you want. However, starting with crowns is easier, and it reduces the tedious process that starts from seeding to production.

If you are starting with seeds, then it is better to start them indoors and then transplant the seedlings once they are 12–14 weeks old. The seeds must be started indoors in the spring, and the transplantation can take place before the last spring frost. Before you start the seeds, soak them in water for up to 24 hours to quicken the germination process. Sow the seeds in a growing tray, and once they are 12 inches tall, harden them for 1 week to 10 days. After the last frost goes by, transplant them to the garden.

If you want to start asparagus by using crowns, then you need to first find an ideal spot in the garden. The crowns must be planted deep in the ground to ensure they are not easily harmed by aboveground activities. Start by digging a trench that is 12-18 inches wide—this must be at least 6-8 inches deep as well. Once the trench is dug, ensure the subsequent trenches are at least 3 feet apart. The asparagus crowns must be briefly soaked in lukewarm water before you plant them. A 2-inch-tall ridge of soil must be made along the center of the trench, and the asparagus crowns must be placed on the top of this mound. Ensure that you spread their roots evenly.

After this, you can either fill the trench with soil and compost mixture all at once, or do it one step at a time. If you are doing it gradually, then you will need to keep adding more soil to the trench as the spears grow. Once the spears are 2-3 inches tall, you need to add 2 inches of soil, and so on. Keep repeating this process until the trench is entirely filled. This is entirely up to you, and it depends on your convenience. That said, ensure that the soil is fairly loose, or else the asparagus spears will have trouble breaking through the soil surface.

Once you have filled the trench, adding a 4-to-6-inch layer of mulch is a particularly good idea. This not only derails the growth of any weeds, but also ensures the soil is moist enough for the roots to take hold. Weed management is one of the biggest challenges any gardener must face when it comes to growing asparagus, especially during the first 2 years. Their roots must not be disturbed—therefore, you will need to carefully pull the weeds using your hands and not any other tools. Usually, these plants require 1-2 inches of water per week during the first 2 years. If they don't receive sufficient water, the plants will not grow properly. You will also need to keep side-dressing the plants with an organic fertilizer during the growing season at intervals, to ensure better growth and harvest.

Harvesting

As mentioned, asparagus must not be harvested in the first and second growing years. If possible, wait until the third year—this way, the harvest will not only be better, but tastier too. Once the crowns are fully established, you'll have more asparagus plants growing in the same spot in the subsequent years as well. If the plants are young, the entire growing and harvesting season exceeds just 2-3 weeks. After the first 2 years when the plants are fully established, however, this season stretches to up to 8 weeks. Therefore, patience pays off when it comes to asparagus.

These plants must be tracked every other day to ensure that you did not miss any spears that are ready for harvest. If they become too woody, the stems will not taste good. The ideal time to harvest them is once they are 8-10 inches tall. For best results, the stalks should not be more than ½ inch wide. The tender and thinner the stalk is, the better the taste. Use a sharp knife or scissors to cut the spear at ground level—this is the best way to harvest them to avoid breaking the spear at any stage. If the diameter of the spear is less than that of normal size, it is better to harvest it instead of letting it grow.

Fertilize the part of the plant that is left behind after harvest in the early summer. Use a well-balanced organic fertilizer to top-dress this. Alternatively, you can also use decomposing mulch or weed-free compost. Through the growing season, ensure that you leave at least 2 or 3 spears for better growth next year. The remaining stems must not be cut down during the summer, or the asparagus bed will be ruined. Instead, let them grow and mature. This replenishes the soil and ensures the subsequent batch of asparagus will have plenty of nutrients. The fronds must be cut back only after the foliage has died, or it has turned yellow or brown. This usually happens once the ground freezes.

Bamboo Shoots

The botanical name of bamboo shoots is Bambusa vulgaris. Bamboo shoots are commonly used in Asian cuisine—they have a mild and earthy flavor, with a crisp texture. There are over 1,500 species of bamboo. Out of them, the most common ones used for cooking include Bambusa vulgaris and Phyllostachys edulis. They are a rich source of dietary fiber, copper, vitamins B6, E, and K, riboflavin, phosphorus, iron, and potassium. Bamboo shoots can reduce cholesterol levels, strengthen cardiovascular functioning, and promote gut health. Regular consumption of bamboo shoots is also ideal for those interested in weight loss and maintenance.

The tender shoots are the edible part of the bamboo plant, and they usually look like asparagus stems. They also grow from the ground during the spring. There are hundreds of species of bamboo across the world, and most of them are edible. Some are tastier, but aren't as productive as others. You must be careful about the type of bamboo you are growing, because not everything tastes good, and all the species are not edible. The tender and tastiest species that produce abundant shoots include Sweet shoot bamboo and Moso bamboo. When it comes to bamboo, one thing you must remember is that size is not directly proportional to the flavor they offer. If the cane is too large or the shoots are too big, you might have a bigger harvest, but it will not be as tasty.

Most varieties of bamboo are quite tall, and at least 2 inches wide. They prefer hardy to different climatic conditions as well. Some species can even withstand a temperature of 0° F. That said, a temperature between 15° F and 30° F works well for most species. Bamboo is nothing but a variety of giant grasses, and this makes it incredibly easy to grow. They require sufficient sunlight for better growth, and need rich and well-drained soil. As long as they have ample moisture in the soil, you'll have an abundant harvest. The lusher the growth, the sweeter and more tender the shoots will be. The soil should not just be irrigated at the top level, but even the roots must obtain it. Additional fertilizer is not needed if the soil is prepared before planting. The simplest way to do this is by mixing the garden soil with some aged manure or compost. If you want more shoots, using a nitrogen-rich fertilizer is a wonderful idea. Even though animal manure is rich in nitrogen, avoid using it because the pathogens in it can quickly harm the tender shoots that sprout from the ground.

Planting and Growing

Bamboo offers rapid growth, and this is one of the reasons why it's an excellent choice for most gardens. Starting with seeds is possible, but it is extremely time-consuming. Instead, opt for a clump. Depending on the variety, a bamboo clump is usually 3-10 feet in diameter. Bamboos are classified as clumpers and runners. A clump forms compact clumps, or stays rooted in the spot where planted. On the other hand, runners are the reason why bamboo gets a bad reputation as a spreader in the garden. As the name implies, they spread quickly and result in the growth of new plants all over the place. Such species can quickly end up colonizing significant garden space. Therefore, always opt for clumpers. Once you have taken care of the abovementioned soil conditions, it is time to get started with planting.

Start with a young bamboo shoot. Dig a shallow hole using a hand trowel or a shovel. The bamboo shoot can be used as a guide to dig a hole. Ensure that the hole is not any deeper than the depth at which the shoot was growing previously. You will see a muddy soil line on the shoot, and ensure this is the same depth as the hole you are digging. The hole must be twice as wide as the base of the shoot. Now, place the bamboo shoot in it and replace any soil to ensure that the shoot will hold. Once you are happy with the positioning, gently find the roots in the bottom of the hole and push some soil back onto them. The entire hole must be filled with soil until it is at the same level as the rest of your garden.

Once the bamboo shoot is in place, it's time to gently water it. Use a sprinkler or water can at this stage. Do not add too much water, or the roots will rot. Usually, they require up to 1 inch of water per week, and no more. Every spring, side-dress these plants using a 10-10-10 fertilizer.

Harvesting

The ideal season to harvest them is in the spring. Keep a close watch on your plants at this stage. The right time to harvest is when the young shoots emerge from the ground. The smaller the shoot is in diameter, the better its taste. Do not wait until the shoots are tall, or they will not taste good. Cut them before they are 6 inches in length. During this season, bamboo can grow anywhere between 6 to 12 inches every day. Therefore, you'll need to harvest them within 24 hours, or it will be too late. To harvest the shoots, slice the stem close to the ground using a sharp blade. This will quickly detach them from the root system without harming the roots below. Around 30%-50% of the shoots must be harvested every year, so that new shoots can grow in the same spot.

Kohlrabi

The botanical name of kohlrabi is Brassica oleracea var. gongylodes. This vegetable belongs to the cabbage family, and is extremely popular in Asia and Europe. These days, it is steadily gaining popularity across the world for all of its different health benefits and culinary applications. Kohlrabi is also known as a German turnip. In spite of its name, it doesn't belong to the turnip family, and instead belongs to the brassica family which includes cauliflower, cabbage, Brussels sprouts, and broccoli. Its texture and taste are quite similar to that of broccoli stems, as well as cabbage. It contains plenty of dietary fiber, vitamin B6, potassium, manganese, iron, and folate. It is rich in antioxidants that reduce the risk of inflammation, improve cardiovascular health, and support immune functioning. The soluble and insoluble fibers present in it support and promote digestive health as well.

Kohlrabi loves plenty of sunlight, and thrives in neutral to slightly acidic soil. It is a cool-season vegetable, and is usually overlooked because of its strange appearance. However, it's one of the quick-growing vegetables and is incredibly tasty and healthy. Even though it is a cool-season vegetable, you can grow it during the spring or the fall as well. That said, if the temperature is too hot during the summer, this stresses the plant and results in misshapen growth. Kohlrabi can be purple or green. This biennial plant usually produces bulb-shaped stems, and seeds and flowers are produced during the second year. Don't forget to remove the outer layer, because it is quite tough and inedible. On the other hand, once you remove it, the inner flesh is white, sweet, and tender with a mild pepper flavor. They are easy to grow, mature quickly, and are usually pest-free and resistant to a great extent.

Before you can start growing kohlrabi in the garden, ensure that the area you select receives around 6 hours of direct sunlight daily. It's even better, though, if the kohlrabi plants get more sunlight than this. They prefer slightly acidic and rich soil that is well-draining. It is not a heavy feeder, and once you dress the soil before planting, it should be sufficient throughout the growing season. Ideally, dress the soil with at least 1 inch of compost and leave it for 1 week before you are ready to plant. Another thing you must remember is to not plant kohlrabi where any other brassica family plants were grown in the last 2-3 years.

As mentioned, you can either grow it in the spring or the fall. Wait until the temperature is around 45° F if you want to grow it in the garden outdoors. Alternatively, you can also start the seeds indoors 6-8 weeks before the last spring frost. Once the seedlings emerge, you'll need to harden them before transplanting them to the garden outside. The seeds can be directly sown outdoors sometime during mid-to-late summer if you want a fall harvest. If the region you reside in is slightly warmer, you can also grow it as a winter crop.

Planting and Growing

Once you have taken care of the abovementioned requirements, it's time to get started. The seeds must be sown ¼ inch deep in the soil, and not any deeper. Cover the seeds with another layer of topsoil. The seeds must be placed 2-3 inches apart, whereas the rows must be 10-12 inches apart. Usually, the seedlings will emerge within 4-7 days. As mentioned, it is a quick-growing plant. Once the seedlings emerge, you'll need to start thinning them. Thin the seedlings such that they are 5-8 inches apart. Consider stagger sowing the seeds once every 2-3 weeks throughout the growing season for a continuous harvest later.

Ensure that the soil is relatively moist—they need around 1 inch of water per week. If the soil seems to be drying out quicker, you'll need to water them more regularly. You can also add 1 inch of mulch over the top layer of the soil to ensure sufficient moisture is available for their growth. Be extremely diligent when it comes to weeding around these plants. Do not disturb their roots, especially when they're young. If you do, then all the efforts you have made until now will go to waste.

Harvesting

Harvesting kohlrabi is incredibly simple, and it can be done in no time. You will need a sharp knife to do this. Simply cut through the root at the ground level. The ideal stage to harvest is once the stem is 2-4 inches wide. If you allow it to become any bigger, it not only is more bitter, but becomes tougher as well.

Celery

The botanical name of celery is Apium greveolens. Crunchy and crispy stalks of celery offer a variety of health benefits. They are a rich source of antioxidants—namely beta-carotene, flavonoids, and vitamins A and C. These antioxidants reduce inflammation, and promote digestive health and the overall functioning of the body. They also contain important minerals such as potassium and folate. Celery offers all these benefits without causing any spikes in blood sugar levels. It has an alkalizing effect, which is essential for different body functions.

Growing celery at home is not only simple, but quite rewarding as well. Also, it is much better than any store-bought celery. These vegetables are usually grown in colder regions, and do well when planted early in the spring. If you are residing in a warmer area, then plant them in mid-to-late summer for a good harvest. This sun-loving plant prefers neutral soil. Usually, it takes up to 140 days until they are ready for harvest. They require a long growing season, but you have other varieties which mature quicker than this. It is a hardy biennial (though it's usually grown as an annual plant), and can produce stalks that are 12-18 inches tall. The ideal way to go about growing celery is by starting the seeds indoors, because finding a hardy transplant is not easy. Also, it might not be the best way to go about it.

There are two types of celery available, and they are known as trenching celery and self-blanching celery. With trenching celery, as the stem starts growing you will need to mount soil against it to ensure the stem is pale and crisp. Usually, planting this in a trench is the best method, hence its name. As the plant grows, you can keep filling up the trench until it is at garden level. On the other hand, all these steps are not needed if you opt for self-blanching celery.

Ensure that you opt for a site that receives around 6-8 hours of direct sunlight every day. Without this, celery plants will not grow properly. They require nutrient-rich and loose soil. Loosen the soil to around 12-15 inches deep by using a garden fork, then mix in 2 inches of compost or aged manure. Alternatively, you can also use a 5-10-10 fertilizer before you start planting. This will give the celery plants sufficient nutrients to take root and thrive. The ideal pH of the soil is between 5.8 and 6.8. Therefore, ensure that you maintain these conditions. They also prefer soil that can retain moisture and does not drain away too quickly. That said, if the soil is too moist or damp, the roots will rot. It is a thirsty vegetable, and therefore, maintaining a consistent watering schedule throughout the growing season is needed.

Because it requires a long growing season, it's best to start the seeds indoors. If you want a spring crop, start the seeds 1o-12 weeks before the last spring frost. On the other hand, if you want a fall crop, then it must be started 10-12 weeks before the first frost date.

Planting and Growing

Now, let's look at how the seeds can be started indoors as well as how to transplant the seedlings outdoors. Before you can start the seeds, it's important to soak them overnight to quicken the germination process. These seeds are incredibly tiny, so you will need to be careful while handling them. You will need seed pots that are filled with some high-quality seed starting mix in them. Gently press it down until the entire pot is full. The soaked seeds must now be gently pressed into the starting soil. Don't cover the seeds. The simplest way to sow the seeds is to gently tap the packet of seeds above the potting mix. The seeds must be usually placed 1 inch apart, but you can always thin them later. For now, the idea is to get as many seedlings out of it as possible.

Instead of using soil to cover the seeds, you'll need to cover the pots or trays using a plastic wrap. This helps retain moisture that's needed for the seedlings to germinate. Usually, the germination takes place within a week of sowing. If the climatic conditions are not ideal, this process can take up to 3 weeks, so you will need to be patient. They need solid sunlight every day. If you are starting them indoors, expose them to fluorescent growing lights for up to 16 hours daily. You will need to do this until the seedlings appear. The ideal temperature to be maintained during this duration is 70° F to 75° F. Instead of watering, use a spray can and gently mist the seeds.

Once the seedlings are around 2 inches tall, you can transplant them into individual pots. Ensure that the new pots they are transplanted into are deep enough to accommodate the roots. Before they can be transplanted outdoors, you need to harden the seedlings. To do this, place them directly under sunlight for a couple of hours daily. Gradually increase the duration, and then you can move them outdoors. Ensure that you do not transplant the seedlings outdoors until the ideal climate conditions prevail. The nighttime temperature must be no lower than 40° F, whereas the soil temperature must be at least 50° F. If the temperature gets any colder, this will result in bolting. While you place the seedlings outdoors, ensure that they are at least 8-10 inches apart in all directions. Don't forget to water the plants thoroughly.

The three important things you must remember when it comes to celery are to take care of the climatic conditions, water requirements, and organic matter in the soil. Since they have shallow roots, you need to water them regularly—if they do not get sufficient water, the stalks will become tough, stringy, and small. Similarly, fertilizer must be applied to the top layer of the soil so that the entire plant gets its required nutrients. During the growing season, especially if the weather is hot and dry, don't forget to water the plants regularly. You will need to side-dress them using good compost during the growing season. As soon as the plants are around 6 inches tall, prune them to not just maintain the ground temperature, but to also ensure weeds don't grow. Because they have shallow roots, you must be extremely careful while weeding. If you disturb the roots, the entire efforts made so far will go to waste.

Depending on whether you are growing trenching or self-blanching celery, the care needed will vary. For instance, the trenches need to be gradually filled with soil for every 2 inches of stem growth. You will need to keep doing this until there is no more room left. The stalks must be covered or wrapped to ensure that they are green and pale. This is known as blanching. Anything that will keep the lights out, such as cardboard or even a brown paper bag, can be used for security. However, only the stem must be covered, not the leaves.

Harvesting

You can harvest celery from summer until the fall ends—right before the first hard frost. Since it has grown as a biennial, it can overwinter if the climatic conditions are milder. In such instances, it will produce a couple of occasional stems, even when the weather is quite cold. The entire plant can be harvested, but it's better to pick or cut the individual stems as and when needed. This, in turn, ensures that the plant keeps producing for a prolonged period. The stalks are the main part of the celery plant that is harvested. Whenever you want, simply pick a stalk. Usually, the tender and the younger the stalk is, the better it tastes. You can start harvesting the stalks as soon as they are around 8 inches tall.

Rhubarb

The botanical name of rhubarb is Rheum rhabarbarum. Rhubarb is rich in vitamins A, C, and K, helpful antioxidants, dietary fiber, potassium, magnesium, folate, calcium, and manganese. The vitamin K it provides is needed for improving and strengthening bone health, the dietary fiber regulates cholesterol levels and promotes digestion, and the antioxidants tackle inflammation and reduce the risk of certain types of cancer. The red color of rhubarb is associated with powerful plant compounds known as anthocyanins and proanthocyanidins. These anti-inflammatory compounds also have antibacterial and anti-cancer properties that reduce the risk of cardiovascular disorders, cancer, and diabetes.

These sun-loving plants require plenty of daily sunlight. Also, these plants can grow for up to 10 years and are resistant to most pests and insects. It is incredibly simple to grow rhubarb. It is a perennial vegetable with ruby- or green-colored stems that are quite sturdy. Whether it is a pie, crumble, sauce, or jam, you can use it for different purposes. The ideal time to plant rhubarb is early in the spring or late in the fall. It's only at this time that you can start with rhubarb, because the soil is workable. Even though it originally came from Asia, it was introduced to Europe sometime during the 1600s, and to America later. It requires a colder climate to thrive, and is incredibly popular in North America. If the average temperature is around 75° F in the summer and the winter temperatures are around 40°F, these plants thrive.

The stalks are the only part of the plant that is edible. They have a tart flavor when cooked. The leaves are toxic, however, even though they look quite similar to the stalk. The leaves contain an irritant known as oxalic acid that causes distress when ingested. Despite this fact, a wonderful thing about this perennial is that it can be harvested for 5 or more years when it takes root in your garden. This is one of the reasons why you need to find a specific spot in the garden where the plant will not be disturbed while growing. Any soil that has been amended with compost or even well-rotted manure is the best to use when starting rhubarb.

They require soil that is fertile and well-drained. Good drainage is crucial, and if it's absent, the roots will rot. Compost, rotted manure, or any other fertilizer rich in organic matter will help amend the soil and make it ideal for rhubarb. They are heavy feeders, and therefore, they require plenty of organic matter throughout the growing season. These plants require plenty of growing space as well. When fully mature, a single plant can grow up to 2-3 feet tall, as well as wide.

Planting rhubarb in the early spring or in late fall is recommended. If you are planting in the early spring, the crowns can be placed in the soil as soon as it is workable. At this stage, the roots are still dormant, and the growth begins as the temperature rises. The ideal soil temperature for the growth must not be less than 50° F. If you are starting in the fall, the rhubarb crowns must be planted after the dormancy sets in. This way, the plants will appear during spring.

Planting and Growing

These plants cannot be started with seeds. Instead, opt for rhubarb crowns. You will need a rhubarb crown that is at least a year old. These can be easily obtained from a local nursery or garden center, or even ordered online. The plants are usually sold as bare-rooted specimens. You might also notice that some rhubarb plants are sold as young ones growing in pots.

Before you start planting it in the soil, ensure that all perennial weeds are eliminated from the growing site. Holes need to be dug in the ground that are the size of a bushel or a basket. Rhubarb plants must be planted such that they are 2-4 feet apart from each other, and there must be at least 3-4 feet between each row. While planting, ensure that the crown with the eyes is facing upward. They must not be sown more than 2 inches deep in the soil. The buds must always face upward. At this time, you'll need to water them properly. A common problem with this specific plant is overcrowding. If the plants are overcrowded, their growth will be poor. After every 3-4 years, the rhubarb roots must be dug and split evenly.

A simple way to overcome any problem with weeds or overcrowding is by mulching generously. Use a heavy layer of straw for improving the moisture level within the soil while discouraging any growth of weeds. The plants must be watered regularly and consistently, especially when the days are hot and dry. They need at least 1 inch of water per week, and even more during hot summer days. As soon as the seed stalks appear, they must be removed. By doing this, the plant will focus on growing more of its edible stalk instead of the foliage. During the fall, old plant debris must be removed, too. If the ground freezes, cover the rhubarb plant with 2-4 inches of organic mulch. Preferably, opt for well-rotted compost. During early spring, applying a well-balanced 10-10-10 fertilizer can be used for side-dressing. During the fall, add some nitrogen-rich fertilizer to the garden soil to ensure the plants are well prepared for spring.

Harvesting

It can be quite tempting to harvest the stalks as soon as they appear. However, please be patient with these plants. Instead of harvesting them immediately, let them grow for the first year. During the second year, you can harvest it provided you are a considerate harvester. During the third year, you can harvest as much as you want. At this time, the harvest period will be between 8-10 weeks and will go up to midsummer. The stalks must be harvested when they are around 12-18 inches tall, and up to ¾ inch wide. Do not harvest when the stalks become too thin, this is a sign that the plant is struggling to find the nutrients needed for its growth. In such instances, you need to fertilize the plant.

To harvest, grab the base of the stalk and tug it away from the plant. Be gentle while doing this, because the roots need to stay underground, and the idea isn't to uproot the plant entirely. While harvesting, ensure that you leave at least 2 stalks behind so that the rest of the plant can keep growing from it—this will also give you a bountiful harvest. If you take care of them, these plants can grow for up to 2 decades, and you will have a good harvest.

Florence Fennel

The botanical name of Florence fennel is Foeniculum vulgare. Fennel is an extremely flavorful culinary herb, and it is also known as finocchio. It has several medicinal values, and the bulb and seeds have a mild licorice-like flavor. The bulb, seeds, and stem are all edible. It is an incredible source of dietary fiber, vitamins, iron, calcium, potassium, and magnesium. In addition to the abovementioned nutrients, fennel is also low in calories. It contains several potent plant compounds that have an anti-inflammatory effect on the body. These antioxidants are known to reduce the risk of cardiovascular disorders and neurological diseases, and even regulate type 2 diabetes. It acts as a natural appetite suppressant, improves cardiovascular health, and has certain cancer-fighting properties. Is also known to increase milk secretion in breastfeeding women. Other potential benefits of fennel include its ability to improve mental health and relieve menopausal symptoms.

This is a cold-weather plant that is usually grown as an annual plant across the United States. It has a bulbous base and leafy stalks that can be used almost like any other vegetable. It is a stocky plant that can grow up to 25 inches tall, and looks pretty much like celery because of its fleshy stalk and feathery leaves. Sweet fennel (or Florence fennel) refers to a cultivar that is specifically grown for its leaves, as well as seeds, for their herbal properties. These leaves and seeds are also used as a seasoning. It produces a cluster of small golden flowers that are flat-topped. All types of fennels are actually members of the parsley family.

The ideal time to start growing fennel, especially if it is in the garden, is 2-3 weeks before the last frost in spring. Florence fennel is grown specifically for its stalk, and requires anywhere between 90 to 115 frost-free days for growing before it is ready for harvest. The ideal time to sow it, especially if you want a fall crop, is mid-to-late summer. They require plenty of sunlight, and ensure that the spot you opt for receives anywhere between 6 to 8 hours of sunlight daily. The soil must be well-drained and rich in organic matter. It is better to prepare the bed or the soil in advance by mixing some aged compost or manure into it. The ideal pH of the soil for growing this plant is between 5.5 and 6.8. The ideal temperature for the seeds to germinate is around 60° F. That said, they can tolerate cold when they are closer to maturity.

Planting and Growing

Once you have taken care of the soil requirements, it is time to get started. The seeds must be sown ¼ inch deep, and they must be 4-6 inches apart to begin with. The rows must be 24-36 inches apart for best growth. Once the seedlings appear and they are 2 inches tall, it's time to start thinning them. The seedlings must be 12 inches apart—if not, they will become overcrowded, and the growth will not be good. They require evenly moist soil without becoming too damp or wet. Therefore, mulching during the hot season is better to ensure that it also retains moisture. During midseason or halfway through the growing season, side-dress the fennel plants using compost or manure. They don't require excess care or attention. Once they take root, the plants are easy to maintain. The lowest stem of the plant must be blanched for them to develop a bulb. If you want to do this, you will need to blanch the stems. To do this, the lowest stem must be wrapped in cloth, or you can mulch such that the lower part of the stem stays covered. This ensures the harvest is sweet and tender. Any seed stalk must be removed—and if you leave it unattended, this plant will self-seed. If you do not want your garden taken over by fennel plants, then you need to pay attention to this.

Harvesting

As soon as the stalk is around 3 inches or more in diameter, it is ready for harvest. The plant can be harvested just like celery. You need to cut it right below the point where the individual stalks join the primary stem. The leaves can also be harvested once they are the size you need. That said, waiting until the entire plant is up to 18 inches tall is a good idea. As mentioned, Florence fennel is usually harvestable within 115 days of sowing.

Chapter 16:

Pods and Seeds

In this chapter, you will learn about different pod and seed vegetables that can be easily added to any garden. Growing them is not only simple, but fun as well. Apart from learning about their planting, growing, and harvesting requirements, you will also learn about the different health benefits they offer.

Black Beans

The botanical name of black beans is Phaseolus vulgaris. They are usually classified as legumes. Because of their hard black shell-like appearance, they are also known as turtle beans. These beans are grown for their edible seeds. The beans are rich in dietary fiber, potassium, phosphorus, magnesium, zinc, sodium, folate, iron, and vitamin C. They also contain different phytonutrients that offer a variety of antioxidant properties. These beans belong to a type of carbohydrate known as complex carbohydrates. They require plenty of time to be digested, and prevent any spikes in blood sugar levels. Regular consumption of these beans is believed to improve bone health, reduce blood pressure, and reduce the risk of heart diseases. It is also a great way to manage diabetes, promote digestion, and assist in weight loss.

There are different varieties of black beans available, but the ones that home gardeners opt for are black turtle beans. They are believed to have originated in Central and South America, and belong to the same species as snap beans. However, they're grown specifically for their dried seeds instead of the mature pods. This is one of the reasons why black beans require longer time for harvest than snap beans. Usually, black beans can be harvested about 95-105 days after planting. These are warm-season vegetables, and the ideal time to grow them is between the first and last frosts.

Unlike other varieties of beans, you don't need any trellises, but a couple of bamboo sticks or posts will give these short runners the needed support for a better harvest. They require plenty of sunlight and fertile soil. The seeds are usually sown during the spring after the frost has passed. The ideal temperature of the soil for germination is between 68° F and 80° F. If you rush into this, the cold or wet climate will hamper their germination.

You will need to find the right site before you can start growing these vegetables. They need around 6-8 hours of direct sunlight daily along with well-draining soil. Therefore, the soil must be amended with well-aged manure or compost, at least 1 week before planting.

Planting and Growing

These plants are ideal for direct seeding, and germinate quickly. While sowing, ensure that the seeds are ½ inch deep in the soil and at least 3 inches apart. The rows must be 15-18 inches apart. This offers the plants sufficient space to grow, while the canopy they create discourages the growth of weeds. Once the seedlings appear and they are 2 inches tall and growing well, thin them such that they are 6 inches apart. The seeds can also be started 3-4 weeks before the last spring frost. To do this, you will need to start them indoors and use grow lights. Ensure that you harden off the seedlings for 1 week before transferring them to the garden. They require deep watering once planted.

These are relatively low-maintenance crops, and offer a significant yield. With a little extra attention toward watering, weeding, and side-dressing, you can boost their overall yield. Since they are shallow-rooted plants, you will need to water them carefully for good growth. If the soil feels too dry, it will need additional watering. As a rule of thumb, they need up to 1 inch of water per week.

Harvesting

Timing is crucial when it comes to these plants. It is also the difference between a poor-quality versus a high-quality yield in the end. As the summer ends, keep checking the plants every week to determine whether the pods are mature or not. As soon as the pods turn brown and feel dry to the touch, or take on a straw yellow color, they are ready for harvest. You need not wait until they are completely dry on the plant for harvesting. These beans should also be harvested before the hard frost sets in. Freezing temperatures damage the seeds, and the quality of the harvest as well. You can either pick the pods individually, or harvest the entire plant by cutting it at the soil level. Leaving the roots in the soil ensures the bacteria in its nodules infuse the soil with nitrogen. Avoid pulling the plant using your hands, because doing this may damage the pods themselves. Instead, use garden shears to snip them.

Black-Eyed Peas

The botanical name of black-eyed peas is Vigna unguiculata, and they are also known as black-eyed beans or goat peas. This is one of the most common varieties of beans that are grown across the world. It's believed to have been introduced to the West Indies by the West Africans sometime during the 1600s. They have a creamy white body with black marks or eye-like structures, which show where the bean was once attached to the pod. Black-eyed beans contain plenty of protein, dietary fiber, calcium, iron, vitamins A and K, magnesium, copper, manganese, and folate. They also have a variety of antioxidants that help your body fight different diseases, while supporting the immune system as well. A wonderful thing about these beans is that they can be consumed at any stage of development. Growing them is not only easy, but quite rewarding as well. Ensure that you amend the soil with some compost or manure and leave it for 1 week before planting.

Planting and Growing

The ideal time to start planting black-eyed peas is when the soil temperature is around 65° F. They require an area that receives around 6-8 hours of direct sunlight daily. You can purchase the seeds online, or from a local gardening store. Ideally, opt for seeds that are wilt-resistant to reduce the risk of these plants succumbing to wilt disease. You should also practice crop rotation, too. Do this by rotating them to a different area once every 3-5 years. To get started, plant them in rows that are 2-3 feet apart. The beans must be sown 1-1.5 inches deep in the soil, and must be 2-4 inches apart. Keep the soil moist at this stage to promote quicker germination. Ideally, these plants need around 1 inch of water per week. You don't need too much fertilizer, because excess nitrogen results in the growth of foliage instead of peas.

Harvesting

Most varieties are ready for harvest within 60-90 days of planting. They keep producing peas for a couple of weeks during the growing season, depending on the variety. The young and tender leaves of this plant are edible, too, and can be utilized just like any other greens.

Fava Beans

The botanical name of fava beans is Vicia faba, and they are referred to as broad beans as well. They are essentially legumes that come in pods with edible seeds on the inside. They have a slightly sweet and earthy flavor, and are quite popular across the world. They are filled with a variety of vitamins, minerals, and protein, as well as dietary fiber—this makes them a powerhouse of nutrients. In addition, they contain plenty of copper, manganese, magnesium, iron, zinc, and thiamine. They also contain calcium as well as selenium, in trace amounts. Regular consumption of fava beans is known to improve cognitive functioning while reducing the risk of Parkinson's disease, the folate in them promotes the growth of a healthy fetus, they have immune-boosting properties, and they are good for bone health as well. They also reduce any symptoms of anemia, while regulating blood pressure levels. If you want to regulate your cholesterol levels or wish to shed those extra pounds, adding fava beans to your diet is a wonderful idea.

This is a cool-season, fast-growing vegetable that's usually grown as an annual. You may need to plant them during the spring or the fall. They require plenty of sunlight for their growth and do well in loamy, moist, and well-drained soil. The ideal soil pH is between 6.2 and 6.8 for these beans, and an ideal temperature for their growth is between 65° F and 75° F. As long as there is sufficient moisture in the soil, humidity is not a problem—and some plants can even tolerate temperatures as low as 40° F, but not any lower.

Planting and Growing

Once you take care of the soil and temperature requirements, it is time to get started. The seeds must be planted 1-2 inches deep in the soil, and 6 inches apart. The rows must be 2-3 feet apart. While the plants are still young, stake them for structural support. Avoid disturbing the roots once the plants start maturing. The water requirements of this plant are average, and some of them are even drought-tolerant. They usually require up to 1 inch of water per week. As with any other beans, even these are capable of fixing nitrogen requirements in the soil by themselves—so if the soil is low in nutrients, working some compost into it is a good idea. Once the seedlings are 2 inches tall, start thinning them so that they are 4-6 inches apart.

Harvesting

Usually, they are ready for harvest within 80-100 days after seeding. This can vary depending on the climatic conditions, as well as the variety you are growing. The right time to harvest them is once the pods are plump and glossy. Gently twist it off the plants or cut it off by using scissors. If you wait too long, the beans will become dry fruits.

Groundnuts

The botanical name of groundnuts is Arachis hypogaea. They are also known as peanuts. This legume is believed to be native to South America, and has been introduced to other parts of the world as well. Despite the name, they are not like any other tree nuts. Instead, they belong to the legume family and are closely related to soybeans and other lentils. Whether it is roasted peanuts or peanut butter, this ingredient is incredibly popular in a variety of cuisines. It's not just used in snacks and sauces, but it also comes in handy when making desserts and other confectionery items as well. Peanuts are rich in protein, dietary fiber, healthy fats, copper, iron, manganese, biotin, vitamin E, magnesium, thiamine, and phosphorus. They also contain other helpful plant compounds and antioxidants that improve the functioning of the immune system, reduce the risk of heart diseases, and reduce the risk of developing gallstones as well. Apart from this, they also assist in weight loss and maintenance.

Groundnuts require a long and warm growing season, and the right time to get started is usually mid-to-late spring and through summer. The soil must be sandy and well-drained, while also rich in organic matter. They require plenty of direct sunlight daily—at least 6-8 hours.

Planting and Growing

To get started, you need to sow 3-5 seeds such that they are 2-3 inches deep in the soil. Ensure they are 7-8 inches apart, while the rows must be at least 24 inches apart. Once the seedlings are around 6 inches tall, you'll need to add a layer of mulch to ensure the weeds are under control. They also require calcium for the growth and development of pods. As soon as the plants start flowering, adding gypsum to the soil is a good idea. They need up to 1 inch of water per week.

Harvesting

Most varieties of groundnuts are ready for harvest within 120-150 days of seeding. The right time to harvest them is in early fall or in late summer—this is when the peanuts taste their best. The hull color of the pod changes from white or yellow to dark brown. Gently dig the plant, shake the excess soil, and then harvest the individual pods.

Lima Beans

The scientific name of Lima beans is Phaseolus lunatus. These legumes have a buttery and mild flavor. They are known for their unique color, which can be anywhere between cream and green. They are also commonly known as wax beans, butter beans, and double beans. They can be consumed in mature, as well as immature, stages. These days, you can obtain them in different colors and varieties. These beams are a powerhouse of nutrients. They include dietary fiber and a variety of vitamins and minerals including manganese, magnesium, copper, iron, potassium, vitamin C and B6, thiamine, and phosphorus. They are especially rich in manganese, which plays a crucial role in overall body metabolism. The health benefits offered by lima beans include stabilizing blood sugar levels, promoting heart health, supporting weight loss and maintenance, and better metabolism.

Planting and Growing

Growing these beans is not difficult, but planting them is, because they're quite averse to frost. For direct seeding, ensure that the outdoor temperature is at least at a consistent 65° F. For a successful harvest, planting every 2-3 weeks throughout the growing season is a good idea. This will give you a continuous harvest, too. Ensure that the growing site that you opt for receives 6-8 hours of direct sunlight daily. You will need to loosen the soil by adding some well-rotted manure compost to it. The ideal soil pH must be between 6.0 and 6.8.

Sow the seeds such that they are 1 inch deep and 2 inches apart. As soon as the seedlings appear, thin them such that there are 4 inches between each plant, and around 24 inches between each row. They need 1 inch of water per week for the best growth and development.

Harvesting

These beans are usually ready for harvest within 60-90 days of seeding. A sign that the pods are ready for harvest is when they are firm and bright green-colored. Simply pluck the individual pods to harvest.

Soybeans

The botanical name of soybeans (or soya beans) is Glycine max, and they are native to eastern Asia. In fact, they are a crucial part of the Asian diet and have been consumed for thousands of years. They are primarily grown in North America, Asia, and South America. These beans are not just consumed in their whole form, but a variety of products are also made from them such as soy milk, oil, and even tofu. These beans are a rich source of antioxidants as well as phytonutrients that offer a variety of health benefits. These extremely nutritious beans are an incredible source of fiber, and contain healthy fats that are good for the heart. They also contain a variety of vitamins and minerals such as vitamin K, folate, manganese, thiamine, and phosphorus. A variety of other bioactive plant compounds present in them are also good for your overall health. These beans are known to reduce the risk of certain types of cancer, alleviate symptoms of menopause, promote bone health, and assist in weight loss and maintenance.

Planting and Growing

These plants are fairly easy to grow, and require an ideal soil temperature of around 50° F for optimal growth. Ensure that you are not rushing during the cold season to start planting, because the cold will prevent the seeds from germinating. Instead, it's better to opt for staggered planting every couple of weeks for a continuous harvest throughout the growing season. Sow them 1 inch deep in the soil, and ensure that they are 2-3 inches apart. The rows must be 2 or 2 ½ feet apart for best growth. The maturation and germination are quite long for these plants when compared to others. They require moist soil without being overly wet. Usually, they need around 1 inch of water per week.

Harvesting

These pods can be harvested when mature, or even immature. The young pods are known as edamame, and the best time to harvest them is when they're still young and crisp to the touch. The entire plant can be removed from the soil, or the individual pods can be picked to harvest.

Runner Beans

Runner beans belong to the same genus as snap beans, but are a different species altogether. The botanical name of runner beans is Phaseolus coccineus. These beans are low in calories, naturally fat-free, and filled with healthy dietary fiber. Around 90% of the calories present in them are in the form of healthy protein the body requires. They are also a rich source of folate that is needed for immune functioning and overall energy levels. Apart from this, they are also a great source of vitamin C.

Planting and Growing

This is a type of pole bean, and the best way to grow them is by planting them in soil that is amended with well-rotted manure or compost. The ideal time to sow them is in the spring. Staggered planting every couple of weeks ensures that you have continuous harvest throughout the growing season. They do not like the cold, so wait until the soil is at least 50° F before you start planting. To warm the soil, use a row cover or place a sheet of black plastic on the growing area for 1 week. Once the soil is of the right temperature, start planting. Before planting you need a couple of support structures to support the lanky beans. These plants can grow up to 5 feet tall, or even more—therefore, they will require frames or trellises to climb on. During the initial stages, the young plants might have to be tied to the stakes to support their growth.

Plant the seeds such that they are 1 inch deep in the soil and 8 inches apart. Sow a couple of seeds to ensure that you have a few steady seedlings. You don't have to thin them later, and can instead tie the seedlings to the frames previously installed. The rows must also be at least 24 inches apart.

Harvesting

Ensure that you regularly water these plants—they need around 1 inch of water per week. Occasionally, using a liquid fertilizer will also be needed for better growth—especially during midsummer. The ideal time to harvest is when the pods are still young, to avoid any stringiness. These beans grow at a rapid rate, so it is important to keep an eye on them.

Chapter 17:

Miscellaneous

Until now, you were introduced to different categories of vegetable plants that can be grown at home. Now, let's look at some basic herbs that can be easily added to your garden. Growing herbs is not only simple, but most can be harvested within a few weeks as well. Also, their maintenance requirements are quite low. Herbs don't need much space to grow, and are aesthetically pleasing, too. In this chapter, we'll look at some basic herbs you can grow at home, how to grow them, how to take care of them, how to harvest them, and also their health benefits.

Mint

Mint is the common name that is used to refer to over a dozen plants belonging to the species. It includes peppermint and spearmint, and belongs to a specific genus known as Mentha. It comes in a variety of colors and flavors, too. Mint is incredibly versatile. It is not only easy to include in your diet, but also offers a variety of benefits as well. It is low in calories and contains plenty of vitamins and manganese. Apart from all this, it has a dynamic flavor that is instantly refreshing. It is known to reduce the symptoms of irritable bowel syndrome, release indigestion, improve cognitive functioning and concentration, and reduce any pain associated with breastfeeding. It also helps mask bad breath and improves the symptoms associated with a cold, too.

Planting and Growing

These vigorous perennials require light and well-drained soil. They grow well in the sun or partial shade, and some varieties require protection from direct sunlight. You can either use cuttings or purchase transplants to get started. It's not ideal to start them from seeds. The cuttings or the purchased plant must be placed 2 feet apart in the garden soil. You don't need multiple plants; just one or two will easily cover the entire ground. Since it is an invasive crop, you will need to be careful, or the runners will quickly overrun your entire garden. Ideally, growing it in its separate area, a raised bed, or a container is the best option. To make sure that this plant doesn't become invasive, it's better to plant it close to tomatoes or cabbage to ensure that it doesn't spread.

This plant hardly requires any care once it takes root, and a light layer of mulch will do the trick. This keeps the soil moist and keeps their roots clean. They are shallow-rooted plants, and are quite easy to pull out. Therefore, you don't have to worry too much even if they are spreading because they can be easily uprooted.

Harvesting

One thing you must remember is to regularly harvest to ensure the mint plant is at its best. The young leaves usually are more flavorful and tender than the mature ones. Cut the stem 1 inch from the ground right before it starts flowering. You can harvest the plant 2-3 times during a single growing season, or can alternatively pick the leaves as and when needed.

Cilantro

The botanical name of cilantro is Coriandrum sativum. It is a wonderful addition to any garden, and is quite easy to grow. It's also known as coriander. Cilantro is quite commonly used in Asian, Middle Eastern, and Indian cuisines. This herb can be easily incorporated into a variety of dishes. Cilantro and its seeds help regulate blood sugar levels, antioxidants present in it have immune-boosting properties and tackle inflammation, it promotes heart health, and improves cognitive functioning. Apart from this, the active compounds present in it support digestion for better gut health, help fight infections, and improve skin health as well.

The ideal time to plant it is in the early spring, but you can start a little early as well. Usually, the leaves can be harvested within 30 days of seeding. It is an annual herb that requires plenty of sunlight and does well in loamy, well-drained, and moist soil with a pH between 6.2 and 6.8. The ideal temperature for their growth is between 60° F to 70° F.

Planting and Growing

Once you take care of the soil conditions and temperature requirements, it is time to get started. It is a cool-season plant, but thrives in sunlight. Ensure that you don't plant it too close to taller plants, because their shade will prevent cilantro's foliage growth. The seeds must be sown ½ inch deep in the soil, and must be 1-2 inches apart. As soon as the seedlings appear, thin them such that they are 6-8 inches apart for best growth. The rows of plants must be at least 1 foot apart. You'll need to give them 1 inch of water per week, and no more than this, because these plants don't require much water and simply prefer moist soil. As long as the soil is of the right type, you don't need to apply any additional fertilizer. If needed, mix some organic matter or manure into the soil right before planting the seeds.

Harvesting

This plant will be ready for harvest within a couple of weeks. You can start harvesting as soon as the plant is around 6 inches tall. Simply pinch back the portion of the stem to harvest the leaves. This, in turn, promotes newer and fuller growth of the plant as well. Ensure that you do not harvest more than ⅓ of the leaves at any point. If you want to harvest its seeds, let the plant flower, and then leave the seed heads to dry out on the plant itself. Simply shake them into a paper bag, or snip the entire seed head and dry it, to harvest the seeds.

Parsley

The botanical name of parsley is Petroselinum crispum. This is a flowering plant that is quite hardy. The most common types of parsley are Italian flat-leaf parsley and French curly leaf parsley. It is an herb that can be used in its fresh and dried forms. It contains vitamins A, C, and K, potassium, and a variety of antioxidants. The antioxidants in it reduce the risk of type 2 diabetes, improve heart health, support bone health, and have cancer-fighting properties. Apart from all this, it is also rich in different nutrients that are needed for improving eye and heart health. The extract of this plant has antibacterial properties.

This plant is native to the Mediterranean and Europe, and is grown as a biennial. That said, you could grow it as an annual in the home garden. These plants thrive when exposed to direct sunlight, but do well in shade as well. They prefer slightly acidic to neutral soil with a pH of 6.0. If the soil is well-draining and rich in organic matter, then these plants will thrive. You can either start the seeds indoors, or directly sow the seeds in the garden. Ensure that you are extra careful while transplanting them, because their roots are delicate. To get a head start, start the seeds in pots indoors 6-8 weeks before the last frost. The ideal temperature for their germination is around 70° F, but they can tolerate temperatures as low as 50° F, and no less.

Planting and Growing

To get started, soak the seeds in water for an hour or two before planting. Sow them ¼ inch deep in the soil, and 6-8 inches apart. The rows must be spaced 10 inches apart for best growth, and the soil must be moist for germination and growth. The seedlings will appear within 2-4 weeks. Ensure the plants have sufficient water to get through the hot summer months. Lightly mulching around the plants is a good idea, too.

Harvesting

Harvest parsley as soon as the leaf stems have around 3 segments. Snip the leaves from the outer stem to ensure the inner stem grows further. Give the plant up to 2-3 weeks after a significant harvest. Replant it in a pot and place it in a sunny spot if you want a continuous harvest through winter.

Rosemary

The botanical name of rosemary is Salvia rosmarinus. It is a perennial evergreen shrub that sports pretty blue or purple flowers. Its sweet and distinctive aroma gives it a special place in the culinary world. Rosemary is native to the Mediterranean coasts, and thrives in humid and warm weather. This shrub can be 2 feet tall when fully mature. It is commonly used as a seasoning for poultry and meat-based dishes, along with soups and stews. In addition to being a seasoning, it also has different medicinal uses. It is rich in manganese that's important for metabolic health. It also contains different phytochemicals that improve eye and liver health, and powerful antioxidants capable of reducing the risk of certain types of cancer. From strengthening the functioning of the immune system to reducing stress and improving concentration, it offers a lot.

This is a sun-loving herb that prefers slightly acidic to neutral soil. These plants can be started from seeds, or from cuttings taken from established plants—even though you can grow them from seeds, the germination rate is quite low, and they are extremely slow-growing plants. Using a cutting helps speed things up. If you want a head start on the growing season, then start the cuttings or seeds 8-10 weeks before the spring frost. The seeds can take up to 3 weeks to germinate, so be patient.

The area you decide to grow rosemary in must receive plenty of sunlight, and the soil must be well-drained without being too damp or moist. Also, ensure the plants have sufficient space to grow, because they can grow up to 4 feet tall and wide when fully mature. The ideal soil temperature must be around 70° F for best growth.

Planting and Growing

Now, it is time to start planting. Start by placing the fresh cuttings that are about 2 inches tall in a pot or tray lined with perlite and peat moss. Ensure there aren't any leaves on the lower two-thirds of the plant, and regularly water the cuttings and expose them to sufficient sunlight. Within 1 week to 10 days, the cuttings will be hardy enough, and then you can transplant them to the garden outdoors.

The transplants must be placed around 2-3 feet apart in all directions. These shrubs are drought-tolerant once fully established. Ideally, they need up to 1 inch of water per week. Avoid overwatering or underwatering them for good growth. Rosemary isn't a heavy feeder, and if you mix some compost into the soil before getting started, this should be sufficient. Pruning the plant helps promote its growth, but never prune more than one-third of the plant at any time. Also, pruning is needed after flowering.

Harvesting

Harvesting rosemary is incredibly simple. You can harvest it at any time, but its growth is the most active during the spring and summer. The leaves are extremely flavorful and aromatic right before the plant blooms. Use pruners to cut off the stem tips as needed.

Dill

The botanical name of dill is Anethum graveolens. This is an herb and spice that can be used to elevate the flavor of different dishes. The most common pairings it is well-suited for include yogurt-based sauces, salmon, and potatoes. This culinary herb is low in calories and contains vitamin C, folate, and manganese. It is an age-old remedy to treat colic in babies and relieve digestive troubles. The antioxidants present in it reduce damage caused by free radicals, and prevent the risk of chronic conditions such as arthritis, heart disease, and even Alzheimer's disease. Regular consumption of dill is known to improve heart health, regulate blood sugar levels, and reduce menstrual cramps. It's also good for bone health and has antibacterial properties.

This herb is not only easy to grow, but incredibly rewarding, too. These plants thrive when exposed to plenty of sunlight, and usually bloom during the summer. Their feathery green leaves are not only fragrant, but also look quite pretty. It's native to the Mediterranean and Eurasian regions, and usually grows in warmer climatic conditions. It is an annual herb and also helps attract beneficial insects to the garden.

Before you get started, ensure that the area you opt for receives 6-8 hours of direct sunlight daily. It should also be protected from strong winds, because the foliage of these plants is quite delicate. The soil must be well-draining and rich in organic matter. If it isn't, then amend the soil accordingly. The ideal pH is between 6.5 and 7.0. Plant it close to any members of the brassica family to improve their growth and reduce any pests. However, keep it away from carrots, because this can reduce their yield.

Planting and Growing

The right time to sow the seeds directly in the garden is after the first frost has passed. These plants do not transplant well, and therefore, do not start inside. The ideal temperature of the soil must be between 60°

F and 70° F. Plant the seeds ¼ inch deep in the soil. Within 10-14 days, the seedlings will appear. Wait for another 2 weeks to thin the seedlings such that they are 10-12 inches apart. Freely water the plants throughout the growing season without letting the soil dry out excessively. For a season-long harvest and a generous supply of fresh dill, staggered sowing every few weeks is a good idea.

Harvesting

The right time to harvest it is as soon as the plant has at least 4-5 leaves. Always start by harvesting the older leaves before moving on to the younger ones. The leaves can be either pinched off or cut from the stem using a pair of sharp scissors. The entire stalk can be taken if there are plenty of dill plants.

Basil

The botanical name of basil is Ocimum basilicum. This flavorful and leafy green herb is believed to be native to Africa and Asia. It contains vitamins A and K, calcium, manganese, iron, and a variety of antioxidants. It's a popular folk remedy to treat bug bites and nausea, and is also quite popular in traditional Chinese medicine, Ayurveda, and other holistic systems of medicine. It's known to reduce the risk of memory loss, elevate symptoms of depression or chronic stress, improve heart health, regulate blood sugar levels and blood pressure, and improve mental alertness.

This fragrant herb is a warm-weather plant, and tastes incredible in a variety of dishes. The seeds or transplants can be planted after the threat of frost has passed. They require more warmth and moist soil for abundant growth. Different types of basil are available, and their taste and color vary. For instance, sweet basil is different from Thai basil or purple basil. It is quite easy to grow, but should only be grown outdoors during the summer. The growing area that you opt for must receive 6-8 hours of direct sunlight every day. It requires well-drained and moist soil, with an ideal pH of 6.0 to 7.5.

Planting and Growing

If you want to start planting outdoors, then wait until the soil temperature is at least 50° F. If the temperature is a little higher, it is even better. Please be patient and do not be in a hurry while growing basil. Without the needed sunlight or warmth, the plants will not grow well. The seeds must be sown ¼ inch deep in the soil. As soon as the seedlings appear and have 2-3 pairs of true leaves, start thinning. The plants must be 10-12 inches apart at this stage, because they can grow up to 24 inches tall. If the variety of basil you are growing is even larger, then ensure that they are at least 16-24 inches apart in all directions.

Don't hesitate to mulch around the branches, especially if you reside in a warmer region. Prune the plant close to the second set after it has produced the first 6 leaves. This improves branching and results in better foliage. You need to prune the branch back to its first set of leaves as soon as it has 6-8 leaves. Using a 5-10-5 fertilizer during the growing season sparingly is a good idea for better foliage. To prevent early flowering, pinch the center shoot after 6 weeks of planting. If the flowers grow, simply cut them off to encourage foliage.

Harvesting

As soon as the plant is around 6-8 inches tall, you can start harvesting the leaves. Simply pick the leaves that you want. Try to harvest them early in the morning, because they taste the best at that time. Even if you don't need the leaves immediately, keep harvesting regularly to ensure that the plant produces more.

Lemongrass

The botanical name of lemongrass is Cymbopogon citratus. It is quite a popular ingredient in Southeast Asian cuisine. The different active compounds present are known to reduce anxiety, treat common colds and coughs, and regulate blood sugar and blood pressure levels. It is also used as a sleeping aid.

This citrusy herb is quite refreshing and rewarding to grow. Its slender and long gray-green foliage is an aesthetically pleasing addition to the garden as well. This is a perennial herb, and prefers plenty of sunlight. It requires loamy soil with a neutral pH. It usually grows in a tropical climate that is warm and humid. These plants will grow and multiply rather quickly once they obtain sufficient heat, light, and moisture. It is fragrant and acts as a natural pest repellent, too.

Planting and Growing

Ensure that the area where you want to grow lemongrass receives around 6 hours of direct sunlight every day. Before you get started, amend the soil using leaf manure, compost, or any other aged manure. They prefer moist soil and need 1 inch of water per week. Once the plant is established, it becomes more tolerant to drought. However, adding a layer of mulch helps retain soil moisture and creates the required condition for the plants to grow. Do not start planting it before the nighttime temperature reaches at least 50° F. Since it is a grassy plant, nitrogen-rich fertilizer is needed for the growth of foliage. Using a slow-release 6-4-0 fertilizer during the growing season is a good idea.

Even though these plants can be started from seeds, finding the right seeds is not easy. Therefore, it's better to start with a small potted plant. Simply plant it in the garden soil and take care of its other growing requirements. Alternatively, the seeds can be sown directly in the soil. Keep the soil moist to promote germination. The seedlings should appear within 10-14 days of planting. Once the seedlings are 3 inches tall, thin them such that they are 1 foot apart.

Harvesting

The leaves and shoots of this plant can be used for culinary purposes, as well as aromatherapy. The right time to harvest it is as soon as its leaves have grown, and the plant is 1 foot tall. Use a sharp knife or scissors to cut what you require. While cutting the stalks, ensure that you leave at least 1 inch of it close to the base to let the plant grow. Wait until the stalks are ½ inch wide if you want to utilize its tender core. However, harvest the stalks when small because they become fibrous as they grow. You can harvest multiple stalks by uprooting the entire plant at the end of the growing season.

Oregano

The botanical name of oregano is Origanum. This is a sun-loving herb that blooms in the summer. The flowers it produces are quite pretty and can be pink, white, or purple. This is a must-have in any culinary garden. It's not only easy to grow, but is easy on the eyes as well. It belongs to the mint family and is a woody perennial plant. It has a peppery bite with a minty aroma. The word oregano in Greek means, "joy of the mountain." Unsurprisingly, it's quite popular in Mediterranean cuisine. This herb is rich in antioxidants, helps fight disease-causing bacteria, has anti-cancer properties, reduces viral infections, and tackles inflammation.

Ensure that the area you opt to grow this plant in receives 6-8 hours of direct sunlight every day. The ideal time for growth is to wait until spring after the risk of frost has passed. The soil temperature must be around 70° F for best growth. If you want to get a head start, the seeds or cuttings can be planted 6-10 weeks before the last frost. Ensure that you mix organic matter as well as compost into the soil for the best growth.

Planting and Growing

Start the seeds indoors in a seed tray before the last frost. Place the tray or container in a sunny spot to let them germinate, which usually occurs within 1 week or so. Once the seedlings are 6 inches tall, thin them such that they are 1 foot apart. You can transplant them outdoors once the risk of frost has passed. Once the plant is established, it doesn't require much attention. These plants are usually drought-tolerant, and can take care of themselves. That said, give them 1 inch of water every week.

Harvesting

You will need a sharp pair of shears or garden scissors to harvest the leaves. Harvest them as soon as the plant is several inches tall, but do not harvest more than one-third of the plant at any time to promote better growth. Midsummer is when these plants produce their most flavorful leaves.

Part 3:

Tending to Your Garden

As a gardener, your job doesn't merely end after planting. You need to take care of the garden, too. This is an ongoing process. In this part, you will learn about different tips and tricks to tackle common pests and diseases and increase the yield.

Chapter 18:

Common Gardening Problems and

How to Fix Them

Gardening problems do not discriminate. It's not just the newbies who struggle, but even veteran gardeners might find themselves dealing with slow-growing plants or even seeds that refuse to sprout, regardless of what they do. These issues are common, and they can crop up in any garden at any time. So, do not panic, because you are not alone. Instead, take a look at your plants and you can usually identify the problem. Checking their leaves, blossoms, stems, and fruit will give you a better idea about what the problem is as well as its causes. Once you are aware of these things, finding a solution becomes easier.

It can be incredibly frustrating, but preparing yourself for different garden issues is the best option. Remember, there are a variety of factors outside of your control. The most common causes of garden problems are the environment, pests, and diseases. Some of these problems are trickier to deal with than others, but all of them can be tackled. Don't give up on your beautiful and bountiful garden. Instead, learn about some common problems and simple solutions given here.

Seeds That Do Not Sprout

If the seeds are not sprouting, this probably means the plants require a little while longer. Perhaps you are getting impatient. However, the first thing you need to consider is the weather conditions. Ensure that you are planting at the right time, and are not afraid to replant if necessary. In the previous part of the book, you were introduced to different vegetables you can start growing. You were also introduced to the climatic conditions they require. So, ensure that you have selected the right time to plant. After all, different seeds require different temperatures to start germinating.

The next probable cause is the soil. If the soil is too dry or wet, the seeds will not germinate. If the soil feels dry to the touch, water it immediately. If the soil is too wet, the seeds are probably rotted. In this instance, you will need to replant. It is okay to replant, and you have nothing to be ashamed of. If you are worried about soil quality, refer to the previous chapters where you were introduced to the right soil conditions and different suggestions for improving its profile.

The seeds used can also be a problem. Yes, seeds expire just like any other packaged commodity. So, check the expiration date on the seed packets. If you are using seeds from a previous season, ensure that they are not older than one or two years at the most. Usually, the germination rate of the seeds reduces as they get older. If the seeds are too old to germinate, or you have an inkling of doubt that this is the reason, then replant.

Another obvious, yet overlooked, problem is birds. Birds love to eat seeds. Perhaps there are no seeds left in the garden, and that's why they have not sprouted. In this instance, you will have to replant. If this becomes a recurring issue, consider covering the garden using bird netting or something along these lines to deter the repetition of this problem.

Young Plants Are Wilting

If young plants in your garden are wilting and dying, the primary cause can be dry soil. Ensure that the soil is evenly moist at all times. Another simple technique that can be used to ensure the seedlings do not wilt and die is to grow the seeds indoors. Once the seedlings appear, you can transfer them to the outdoor garden. Even if the seedlings are overwatered, they will die. Usually, a fungal disease known as damping off is quite common in areas with high humidity and warm temperatures. In such instances, ensure that the seed starting mix used is sterile and treat the soil with fungicide before getting started. If the stems or roots are rotting, the seedlings will wilt and die. Once again, you mustn't be overwatering. Instead, adding a layer of compost to the topsoil ensures this doesn't happen.

Fertilizer burn is also a common cause that is overlooked. Using synthetic fertilizer can cause the seedlings to wilt, or even die. Even organic fertilizer can result in this condition. The common cause of fertilizer burn is using a potent fertilizer in massive doses. Ensure that young plants are not exposed to such harsh chemicals. Usually, they require around ¼ dose of full-strength fertilizer when compared to fully grown ones. Even if you are using old seeds, this can be an issue. As mentioned, the seeds must not be older than one or two years.

Some types of insects, especially cutworms, can result in this as well. These are creatures you do not want in your garden. Your garden must be free of debris, plant residue, and weeds. If a plant is dead, get rid of it immediately. Usually, cutworm larvae are present at the base of the plants. If you notice them, uprooting the plant is a better idea than letting it fester in your garden. Aside from cutworms, even root maggots can be another cause of dying or wilting plants. They usually occur when moths or flies lay eggs in the soil close to the roots. If this is the cause, uproot the plant and use floating row covers to ensure it doesn't occur again.

Plants Turn Brown and Die

If you notice that the leaves and stems have dark spots or the plant is turning brown and then dying, a plant virus is the most likely cause. Remove all the plants that are infected along with their stems, as well as the leaves left behind. While doing this, remove all weeds around them as well. If you notice this becomes a pattern, chances are it could be a chemical or a fertilizer burn. Once again, follow the instructions on the bag of fertilizer you are using when it comes to young plants. Also, refer to the information given about plant nutrition in the previous chapters.

Weak, Frail, or Skinny Plants

If your plants start looking weak, skinny, or frail, this means they're probably not getting the required amount of sunlight. As a rule of thumb, ensure that the garden location you opt for receives at least 6-8 hours of sunlight daily. If the plants you are growing need more sunlight, cater to them. If the plants are overcrowded or the small plants are growing in the shade of larger ones, they will not get the required sunlight. Apart from sunlight, overwatering can also result in this. Water only when the soil feels a little dry to the touch. Usually, a good watering practice is to water when the top 2-3 inches of the soil feels dry to the touch. Adding peat moss, perlite, compost, or even vermiculite to the soil improves its drainage.

Nitrogen is an essential plant nutrient. That said, plants need it in an ideal proportion. If there is too much nitrogen in the soil, or the fertilizer used has too much nitrogen, your plants will look frail and skinny.

Wilting of Partially Grown Plants

If your partially or fully grown plants are wilting, then there are three things you need to do: check the soil, look for worms, and keep an eye out for diseases. If the soil is too dry, water the plant thoroughly. On the other hand, if it is too wet, do not water until the top 2-3 inches of the soil dries out. After this, focus on improving the soil drainage to ensure your plants stay healthy.

Chances are that plant disease has invaded your garden. The simplest practice is to ensure the garden is always clean and weeds are removed. Two causes resulting in the wilting of fully grown plants are vascular wilt and root rot—these are fungal diseases. Avoid overwatering, and regularly take care of the plants. Root rot nematodes can also kill your grown or partially grown plants. Crop rotation is a simple, yet effective, means to ensure that crawlies don't make their way to healthy plants. Also, these days, a variety of disease-resistant seeds are available. Opting for them will also help.

The Slow Growth of Plants

If the plants are growing slowly and their leaves are pale yellow or light green, it's probably because they are not getting sufficient sunlight. Perhaps the plants are overcrowded, and the larger ones are covering the smaller ones. Fix these issues immediately to ensure your garden stays healthy. Cold weather can also be a reason for this. During the cold months, opting for floating row covers keeps the plants warm and prevents direct exposure to cold. The ideal pH of the soil to be maintained for a healthy garden is 7.0. If the soil is too alkaline, use compost or sulfur to improve it. It can also be a nutrient deficiency in the soil. Again, compost will fix the situation immediately. Don't forget to check for insects or plant diseases, such as wilt disease or yellow disease. The simplest way to check for this is to notice whether one side of the plant turns fully yellow before the other. If this is the case, remove the entire plant to ensure the rest of your garden does not get infected.

Leaves and Stems Have Yellow or Brown Patches

A plant virus is the leading cause of any yellow or brown patches on the leaves. They can also be the reason for puckered leaves and stunted growth. If so, remove the infected plant along with all its foliage immediately. The next step is to carefully weed the garden and ensure there are no uninvited guests in it.

Shriveled and Brown Leaf Edges

If the margins or the edges of the leaves look brown and shriveled, this is due to dry soil. Watering the plants helps fix this situation. Alternatively, even fertilizer burn can be a cause. Regardless of whether it is a synthetic or natural fertilizer, ensure that you do not go overboard—use it cautiously. A potassium deficiency in the soil could also be a cause of this. If so, test the soil immediately and amend it with compost. A final cause of shriveling and browning of leaves is associated with the temperature, especially during cold weather. Floating row covers will be helpful if it is temperature-related.

Curled or Puckered Leaves

If the leaves look distorted, puckered, or curled, this is a sign of wilt disease. This attacks the vascular system of the plant. If only specific plants are exhibiting these signs, uproot them immediately—this ensures the disease is limited to the specific plant, and does not jump to the healthy ones. Following the practice of crop rotation every year is a great way to reduce the risk of wilt disease. Another issue could be aphids. Spraying the plants with neem oil, or any other insecticide, helps destroy them. If aphids affect any plant, remove it immediately because this can quickly spread to healthy plants in the garden.

Tiny White Dots on Leaves

If the plant leaves are speckled with tiny white dots, this is a sign of spider mites. An insecticidal solution of neem oil can be used to treat this problem. If spider mites aren't the cause, it can be a sign of air pollution. If so, gently hose the plants with water during the day.

A Powdery White Substance on Plants

If you notice a white powdery substance on the plant foliage, this is most likely a fungal disease known as mildew. If the weather is humid and the leaves are dry, this problem occurs. The simplest way to ensure this doesn't happen is by exposing the plants to direct sunlight. You should also make sure that there is sufficient air circulation. Any parts that have a significant concentration of the white powdery substance must be trimmed to ensure the disease doesn't fester.

Holes in the Leaves

If it looks like the plant or fruits are gnawed or chewed on, then this is a pest problem, and is the same reason for any holes in the leaves. The most likely culprits are rabbits, insects, slugs, rodents, and birds. Using floating row covers or fencing helps block these unwanted pests. You can also spray neem oil to kill unwanted guests in your garden. If the plants are exposed to hail or high winds, similar damage is caused. Floating row covers or barriers will once again help fix this problem.

Leaves That Are Shredded or Stripped From the Plant

If you notice that the leaves are shredded or stripped from the plant altogether, this is a sign of pest infestation. The most common culprits include slugs, deer, and even rodents. To block unwanted pests, opt for fencing or floating row covers. Another organic and helpful remedy to kill or discourage pest infestation is to spray neem oil on the plants.

Rotting Blossoms

If the weather has become extremely dry or wet all of a sudden, the blossoms on your plants can rot. This is especially true in the case of tomato and pepper plants. If you notice any drastic changes in the weather conditions, change how you water the plants. This can also be due to a calcium deficiency. If that's the case, add some lime to the soil, and it should suffice. If the plants are planted too deep in the soil, it can result in root injury. Even if you cannot fix this problem right away, you can learn from it and ensure you do not repeat this with the subsequent crop. Another reason is soil compaction. If so, the plants will not get the nutrients or water they need for growth and maturation. Adding compost is a quick fix for this.

Not Producing Fruit

If it looks like your plants are not producing fruit, the first thing you need to consider is whether you planted them at the right time or not. If the weather is not ideal for the vegetable plants you want to grow, they will not produce any fruit. If the plants are not pollinated, they cannot produce. Another obvious factor is that your plants are not yet mature. If so, you just need to wait for a while longer. This is why you need to be patient if you want to garden. If the plants are producing fewer fruits than you expected, or the fruits are small and not as tasty as you thought they would be, check the soil. If the moisture in the soil is uneven, mulching is recommended. Also, if the soil doesn't have the required nutrients for the blossoms to turn into fruit, you will need to add some compost at this stage.

Chapter 19:

Dealing With Pests, Insects, and Diseases

In the previous chapter, you were introduced to general suggestions and tips that can be used for tackling common garden problems. Pests, insects, and diseases are three things that can quickly spoil the most beautiful of gardens. Since your time, energy, effort, and money go into taking care of a garden, learning to deal with them is important. In this chapter, you will be introduced to the most common pests, insects, and diseases a vegetable garden is susceptible to and tips to tackle them.

Common Pests

It can be rather discouraging to see your entire garden wiped out by pests and insects. Once these hungry invaders make their presence in your garden, chances are they'll become a recurring problem. Dear gardener, you do not have to worry, because all hope is not lost. You can regain control of your garden from these pesky invaders. In this section, you will be introduced to the most common garden pests and insects. You will also learn how to recognize them based on signs and symptoms of their infestation and how to control them.

Colorado Potato Beetle

Beetles are an incredibly common form of pests. They migrated from west to east by feasting on potato crops during the 1800s. These dome-shaped insects are hardly an inch in length. Adult beetles are yellow with narrow black lines on their exterior. The larvae of the Colorado potato beetle look like any other beetle larvae. The soft-bodied larvae have two rows of black dots along the sides of the bodies. Check the underside of the leaves, because this is where they lay their yellow-orange eggs. They usually take cover in the soil during winters and emerge in spring. Their eggs are laid on the foliage, and as the name suggests, they prefer potatoes. The larvae are produced from the eggs within 10-30 days, and adults emerge within 2 weeks. These adults will then feed on your plants and reproduce. This, in turn, results in a full-fledged infestation.

These beetles not only favor potatoes, but are also a threat to tomatoes, eggplants, and other types of peppers as well. The adults and the larvae feast on the stems, foliage, buds, flowers, and fruits of the plant. They do not discriminate, and the entire plant will be lost within no time. If left unchecked, they will eliminate all the foliage on the affected plant along with the plants close to it. If you notice any signs of defoliation, immediately check for these beetle larvae.

Use These Control Measures to Tackle This Problem

Protect the young seedlings from beetle infestation by shielding them with a barrier made of cheesecloth. To destroy the adult beetles and their larvae, handpick them and toss them into a can of soapy water. Opting for plant varieties that mature quickly is also a good idea to prevent any damage by the second generation of beetles. Helpful insects such as stink bugs and ladybugs feast on these harmful larvae. So, focus on attracting them. Ensure that your garden is thoroughly weeded before spring to eliminate food sources for these pesky pests.

Cabbage Looper

Cabbage looper is a common pest that attacks crops belonging to the brassica family. They usually move like inchworms—in a looping motion, hence their name. The larvae don't have legs, and use the middle portion of their body for movement. Mature caterpillars are light green and have white stripes down their sides. The younger larvae are paler. The caterpillars turn into moths that are grayish brown in color. The simplest way to recognize them is to look for a distinct silver mark in the shape of the number eight on their body. The eggs of the cabbage looper are white or pale green. Check the upper portion of the leaves for these eggs. Eggs are deposited on the host plants by the moth, and they hatch between 2-10 days, depending on the climatic conditions. The damage caused by large caterpillars is conspicuous, unlike the larvae that feed on the lower surface of the leaves. Multiple generations of cabbage loopers can be produced during a single growing season.

If you are growing cabbage, broccoli, cauliflower, turnips, kale, mustard, or any other plants belonging to the brassica family, watch out for these insects. Other crops they can damage include squash, potatoes, beans, peas, tomatoes, peppers, cucumbers, melons, and cantaloupe. If you notice ragged holes in the leaves, this can be due to these insects. The damage caused by them is sufficient to stunt the growth of the plant, and prevent the formation of the flower head.

Use These Control Measures to Tackle This Problem

Common weeds that must be removed from your garden are wild cabbage, wild mustard, and peppergrass because cabbage loopers prefer them. Carefully check the plants susceptible to damage by these insects, and crush any eggs you notice before they hatch. As mentioned, the larvae are present on the underside of the leaves—and therefore, you have to check the entire plant thoroughly. Floating row covers can be used as a barrier to ensure moths do not deposit eggs on plants. You can also make an organic pesticide to kill them. To do this, you'll have to look for deceased caterpillars. They are highly susceptible to a virus that leaves them looking swollen, white, or yellow. Collect these infected caterpillars and blend them with water. Use this spray on other plants that are infected to kill further growth of cabbage loopers.

Cutworms

Cutworms cut down seedlings, hence their name. They destroy the seedlings close to the soil surface. The moths belonging to the family noctuid produce these caterpillars. Depending on the species, their color and markings vary; however, a common behavior displayed by them is to curl into the shape of the letter C when disturbed. A fully grown moth is medium-sized, and though it doesn't directly harm the garden, it does cause indirect damage. They usually overwinter in the form of larvae, and as soon as the temperature starts warming up, they feed on the plants in your garden. Caterpillars will tunnel into the soil to pupate during the spring, and moths emerge during the summer. A single female moth can lay hundreds of eggs! They usually lay eggs on weeds in the garden, and new generations of larvae are produced as long as the temperature is warm.

Cutworm species feast on a variety of plants, but the most common ones susceptible to their damage include potatoes, tomatoes, carrots, celery, peas, beans, peppers, eggplant, and lettuce. If you notice that young seedlings or plants are severed close to the soil surface, this is cutworm damage. This damage can occur overnight. Usually, cutworm infestation occurs during the spring. Some species feed on foliage, fruits, or buds—whereas others prefer the roots.

Use These Control Measures to Tackle This Problem

The simplest way to get rid of any overwintering cutworms is to turn and till the garden soil as soon as spring sets in, and right before planting. Usually, these caterpillars are active late in the day or early evening. If they damage any plants, ensure that you uproot them and check for their presence in the soil around the damaged plant. To create a barrier around seedlings, insect collars come in handy. You can also use empty cardboard toilet paper rolls for the same reason. To reduce any space available for the cutworms to seek shelter, get rid of weeds and plant debris. Don't forget to turn and till the garden soil at the end of the growing season to ensure there are no worms in the soil.

European Corn Borer

European corn borers are caterpillars, and are named so because they primarily feast on corn. However, the damage caused by them isn't restricted to this single variety. These brown-headed caterpillars can be gray or light pink-colored. They have dark spots along their sides. The pupae are usually yellow-colored, but are rarely seen. The metamorphosis usually occurs in the larvae tunnel underground. The moths have gray-brown wings, and are nondescript per se. The cream-colored eggs take on a tan or darker beige tinge as they age. The larvae usually overwinter in the corn stalks, and pupate during early spring. The moths emerge during the spring and summer. The females can deposit eggs in clusters of 15-20, and develop within a month. The larvae feed on the host plant. Multiple generations of these creepy crawlies can occur within a single growing season.

Even though they prefer corn, they affect other plants such as peppers, lima beans, snap beans, and potatoes. Cabbage, celery, beets, okra, tomatoes, and eggplants are also susceptible to damage caused by them. The corn borers usually feast on the leaves of the corn plant, and then move to the pollen and tassels. However, the mature larvae tunnel into the ears and stalks of the corn plant, too. In all other plants infested by them, the damage is usually restricted to the fruit.

Use These Control Measures to Tackle This Problem

At the end of the growing season, you'll need to get rid of all plant stalks and weed debris that are big enough to shelter the overnight borers. After harvest, corn stalks must be destroyed, and do not add them to the compost pile. This can encourage the borers to overwinter and infest the garden during warmer months. Beneficial insects such as parasitic wasps, ladybugs, and lacewings help destroy these larvae. Using a pesticide sprayer is needed if you notice the population of the European corn borer is significant in your corn or pepper plants.

Bean Leaf Beetle

If you are growing snap beans or any other legumes, you need to watch out for bean leaf beetles. They come in a variety of colors ranging from red to yellow and green. Their markings usually vary, but all bean leaf beetles have a distinct black triangle on their forewings. Usually, the adult beetles are easy to spot, and their young stay in the soil. If you notice oval-shaped, orange-red eggs, this is a sign of these beetles. The white larvae have black ends, and the pupae are a ghostly white rendition of the mature version.

These beetles attack all plants belonging to the legume family, including soybeans and snap beans. The larvae munch on the roots, whereas the adults feast on the pods and foliage. The most common signs to look out for are holes in the foliage, especially along the margins of the leaf. If the larvae are feeding on the roots, plant growth will be stunted. Another sign is to look for any damage caused to the pods late in the growing season.

Use These Control Measures to Tackle This Problem

You can handpick the adult beetles and kill them by dropping them in a mixture of soap and water. Usually, these beetles are quite active during the afternoon—therefore, pay extra attention to your plants during this time. Young seedlings are at a higher risk of being targeted by them, and you must be extra vigilant at this stage. As mentioned, the adults usually emerge in the spring, and so planting a little later in the season is an effective means to reduce the damage caused by them.

Aphids

In regulated numbers, aphids are not as harmful to garden plants as most seem to think. It is time to act the minute you notice curled leaves or any sooty mold on the foliage of your plants, though. Aphids are extremely tiny bugs, and they have piercing and sucking mouthparts designed to extract the juices from any plants. These pear-shaped bugs have two structures jutting out of their hind ends that look like tiny tailpipes. This is a differentiating factor between other soft-bodied insects and aphids. Depending on the species and the plants they are feasting on, their color will differ.

The life cycle of these bugs is rather unusual, as the females can give birth to live young ones even without mating. Usually, the eggs overwinter, and wingless females emerge in the spring. These females, in turn, quickly give birth to the next generation and the cycle perpetuates throughout the growing season. During the fall, the female produces males to mate with. This results in a cycle of conventional reproduction wherein they lay eggs in the soil. These eggs overwinter underground until the climatic conditions are ideal.

All garden plants are susceptible to aphid infestation. The most common targets include cucumbers, pumpkins, melons, beans, peas, cabbage, squash, tomatoes, and potatoes. They are also known carriers of a variety of plant diseases, too. The common signs to look out for include sooty mold or fine black dust-like deposits on the foliage, curling or yellowing of leaves, and stunted growth.

Use These Control Measures to Tackle This Problem

If the plants are sturdy enough, aphids can be knocked off using a strong spray of water. Beneficial insects also prey on aphids. Therefore, avoid using broad-spectrum pesticides to ensure you do not kill the beneficial insects. Make sure you do not overfertilize the plants, because aphids thrive when they have easy access to nitrogen. So, too much nitrogen essentially encourages aphid infestation. Any weeds need to be removed along with other infested plants to curtail the spread of aphids. Horticultural oil or soap, and neem oil are effective means to stop their spread. Always check the underside of the leaves, because these bugs usually take refuge there to avoid detection.

Cucumber Beetles

The two types of cucumber beetles you must watch out for are striped and spotted variants. These beetles not only feast on the seedlings, but also spread a disease known as bacterial wilt. The striped beetles have 3 stripes along the length of their wings; and the spotted beetles, on the other hand, have 12 spots on their exterior. Both beetles are oblong-shaped and have yellowish bodies with black-colored heads. The larvae resemble thin white grubs with brown capsule-like heads. The clusters of eggs are often yellow-orange and are oval-shaped.

The mature beetles overwinter and seek shelter in woodlands or dense grass. During the spring, they emerge and feed on plants and pollen. Once they discover their preferred crops, they move on to them and feast on the foliage until nothing is left. The females lay eggs in the soil, and each female beetle can lay hundreds of eggs. The larvae feed upon the roots and plant stems upon hatching until they pupate. The next batch of mature adults will emerge midsummer, and the cycle perpetuates.

As the name suggests, these beetles usually prefer cucumber plants. They are known to target melons, squash, cantaloupe, pumpkins, and gourds. Other plants susceptible to their damage include eggplants, potatoes, corn, peas, beans, and tomatoes. If you notice any scarring on the fruit, visibly damaged flowers and leaves, girdled seedlings, and flagging of leaves, this is a sign of these bugs. If the plants start wilting, their growth is stunted, and the foliage turns yellow while the entire plant eventually collapses, it's a sign of wilt disease spread by these bugs.

Use These Control Measures to Tackle This Problem

The crops must be fertilized early in the growing season to promote healthy growth of roots. Their ability to withstand infestation by these bugs also improves when they are healthy. The young seedlings can be protected from mature beetles by using barriers such as row covers or cheesecloth. Wait until later in the season to plant cucurbit crops. If you notice any plants that are infested by wilt, get rid of them immediately to ensure the disease doesn't spread further.

Squash Vine Borer

An entire year's labor and harvest of pumpkins, zucchini, and other squash plants can be wiped out by squash vine borers. This is essentially a type of a moth. The brown-headed larvae of these moths are cream-colored and can be up to an inch in length. The adult moths are quite similar to a red wasp, with black dots on their abdomens and a greenish tinge on their wings. Their brown eggs are flat and tiny. As with other pests and insects, these bugs pupate and overwinter, and mature adults usually emerge during June and July. The eggs are laid on the stems of the host plants right above the soil line. This process usually occurs during midsummer. The larvae eventually hatch and penetrate the plant stem and start feeding on the tissue. Within a growing season, you can encounter up to two generations of these harmful borers.

The preferred hosts for the squash vine borer include pumpkin, zucchini, squash melons, and even cucumbers. The surest sign of vine borers is the sudden wilting of young and fully-grown plants. This is because the larvae make their way into the plant stem and feed on it from the inside, which disrupts the flow of nutrients and water within the vine. Carefully check the stem, especially right above the soil line, for any entrance holes or visible larvae.

Use These Control Measures to Tackle This Problem

Using yellow plant traps is an effective way to curb the damage caused by adult moths. Fill yellow pans with water and place them close to the vine crops during the summer months. If there are any adult vine borers in the garden, chances are you will find them in the pan. So, don't forget to check the pans daily. Using barriers such as row covers helps protect the susceptible plants from the vine borers. Remove these barriers when the plants start to flower to promote pollination. To prevent the adults from laying eggs, carefully wrap the lower part of the stem with foil. Once again, check for any holes or frass, which are common signs that a vine borer has entered the stem of the plant. Make a slit along the length of the stem with a clean and sharp knife if you find any signs of vine borers, and remove them. This reduces the chance of them further harming other plants.

After removing any borers, make a mound of moist soil around the plant stem to promote its root growth. Any dead vines must be removed and destroyed immediately. At the end of the growing season, carefully turn and plow the garden soil to disrupt any borers overwintering in it. The same procedure must be repeated right before spring or the growing season.

Squash Bug

These bugs suck the sap from plants belonging to the cucurbit family such as melons, pumpkins, and squash. As with most bugs, squash bugs have wings folding over their bodies, and they are flat. They have light orange stripes along the edges of their abdomens, and the adult bugs can be black or brown. The newly emerged young bugs have black-colored heads and greenish bodies with black legs. The colors of the young bugs darken as they move to the adult stage. Their eggs can be usually found in clusters and are bronze or yellow-colored. So, carefully check the underside of the foliage for these eggs.

Usually, the squash bugs overwinter and seek refuge in garden debris, leaf litter, piles of wood, or any other protected place in your garden or yard. As the vines start running during the early summer, the adults will then mate and lay their eggs on the host plants. These eggs hatch within 10 days, and the cycle perpetuates. It is common to notice young bugs and adults at the same time during late summer. Both the adults and the young ones damage the plant by sucking on their sap. The most common signs of damage caused by them include yellow spots on the foliage, withering vines, wilting wines, or the entire vine turning black. Pay extra attention to the plants susceptible to damage by these bugs to ensure your garden doesn't become their victim.

Use These Control Measures to Tackle This Problem

Keep a can of water mixed with soap that can be used for destroying the adults and young bugs once they are handpicked. These bugs usually flee or hide when disturbed. So, handpicking them is not always easy. You can collect these bugs using trap boards, especially when the nights are cool. Don't forget to carefully check under the trap boards early in the morning. Do this before they become active, and destroy the ones present under it. Check the underside of the foliage to find clusters of their eggs, and crush them before hatching. Ensure that the vines are uprooted and destroyed at the end of the growing season, or after harvest, to ensure squash bugs aren't attached to them. Keep the garden clean at all times to reduce any places where the squash bugs can take refuge.

Flea Beetles

Flea beetles are incredibly small pests, and they take tiny bites out of their preferred plants. However, when they're all put together, the damage caused by them is significant. These pests are quite small, and they are usually a few millimeters in length. Most species of these beetles are dark-colored, and have a metallic tinge or shine to their exterior. They are named so because they are capable of jumping from one plant to another when disturbed, just like fleas. Leaf litter and garden debris are their favorite places for overwintering, especially the adults. The adults emerge and locate their hosts as soon as the temperatures rise in the spring. They feed on the weeds found in the garden until they locate their desired plants. The eggs are laid in the soil close to the base of the host plant by females during the spring. The larvae that emerge from the eggs munch on the roots and root hairs until they pupate in the soil. Multiple generations of these harmful pests can occur within a single growing season.

The most preferred plants of these pests include squash, melon, cucumber, eggplant, corn, pumpkin, lettuce, cabbage, tomatoes, gourds, sweet potatoes, spinach, radish, peppers, celery, carrots, and even watermelons. A sure sign of their infestation is the presence of extremely small holes in the foliage. Numerous tiny holes make the leaves look like they were buckshot. The seedlings start wilting and their growth is stunted when attacked by these pesky pests. Another sign is when the root crops look blemished or have pimple-like formations on them.

Use These Control Measures to Tackle This Problem

Ensure that your garden is free of all weeds, especially during the spring and early spring, to discourage the growth of adult beetles. If you want to grow any plants that are susceptible to damage by these beetles, changing your growing technique will do. Instead of directly sowing the seeds in the garden, transplant seedlings after you grow them indoors. To prevent flea beetles from feeding on your plants, opt for barriers such as row covers and start plants a little later in the season. Yellow sticky traps can also be used to attract adult beetles. You can easily purchase these from any gardening or home center. The flea beetles can be effectively lured away from their usual targets by growing a trap crop early in the season, such as radishes. Pull any weeds and get rid of plant debris from your garden at the end of the season to reduce any overwintering flea beetles.

Asparagus Beetles

As the name suggests, these beetles feast on asparagus plants. These oval-shaped beetles are hardly an inch long. There are two varieties of asparagus beetles you must be aware of, and they are the common and spotted variants. A fully-grown common asparagus beetle is quite colorful and has bluish-black wings with yellow markings on them, along with red margins lining the wing covers. The spotted asparagus beetle, on the other hand, has black spots on an orange body. The larvae of both species are light-colored and have black capsule-like heads. The eggs are oval for each variety. The spotted asparagus beetle usually lays eggs on ferns, whereas the common asparagus beetle lays them on stalks.

These beetles overwinter as adults, and seek refuge under tree bark, old stalks of asparagus, and even garden debris. They emerge during the spring, and feed on the tender shoots of young plants. After this, they mate and lay eggs on the host plants. The larvae usually hatch within a week and feed on the host plant. The mature larvae then borough underground to pupate, and adults emerge from the soil as the temperature rises. If your asparagus plants are bent, scarred, or brown, this is a sign of these bugs.

Use These Control Measures to Tackle This Problem

Regularly check your asparagus plants, and you might notice beetle adults or larvae. If you do, handpick them, and toss them into a can of soapy water to destroy them. Knock out the larvae to the ground by gently brushing the asparagus plants with a soft brush. The larvae usually die before trying to make their way up the plant. Ensure that you clean the garden and get rid of all weeds and debris at the end of the growing season to prevent the future growth of these beetles. If you notice any clusters of their eggs, crush them immediately.

Hornworms

Hornworms are essentially caterpillars, and come in a variety of colors. Usually, they range from white to yellow—and as they grow, they take on a greenish tint. The tomato hornworms have V-shaped markings on either side of their bodies. They have a horn-like projection on the last segment of their body, hence their name. These fat-bodied moths have small wings, and their eggs are usually green in color and oval-shaped. They are usually laid in a single line on leaf surfaces.

These worms overwinter in the soil as they pupate, and emerge from the soil as the spring sets in. They also mate and reproduce through eggs during the spring. So, within a single growing cycle, you can come across a few generations of these pesky pests. Some common plants they feed on include common garden weeds such as horse nettle and jimsonweed. The caterpillars mature within 4 weeks, and in the meanwhile feed on foliage. Eggplants, potatoes, peppers, and tomatoes are the preferred targets of hornworms. The common signs of their presence include defoliation of plants, especially close to their top. The rate of defoliation quickens as the caterpillars grow in size. If you aren't careful, they will quickly devour the entire plant! If you notice green or black frass on the lower leaves or close to the affected plants, it means the caterpillars are present nearby.

Use These Control Measures to Tackle This Problem

If you notice any adult caterpillars, handpick them and toss them into a can of soapy water to destroy them. These caterpillars are adept at camouflaging, so you will need to carefully check your garden, especially plants susceptible to their damage. At the end of every growing season, carefully turn and till the soil to disrupt any worms pupating or hiding underground. Solanaceae weeds are their preferred hosts, so keep your garden weed-free. Predatory wasps, ladybugs, and other helpful insects usually prey on these bugs. So, growing plants that attract them is a good idea.

Common Diseases

As with pests and insects, even certain diseases can quickly wipe out your garden. The only way to stay ahead of a possible infestation or plant disease is to be aware of what to look for. Once you are aware of the possible causes, the chances of saving your harvest are greater. You can also work on reducing the damage caused by them to save otherwise healthy plants. So, let's look at some common diseases that vegetable plants are susceptible to.

Leaf Spot

A leaf spot, or bacterial leaf spot, is caused by a specific type of bacteria that infiltrates the flowers of the plants. It results in the creation of visible spots on the leaves, and discoloration in mild situations. When left unchecked, it results in quick defoliation of the affected plant. It usually spreads during cold or wet seasons. The bacterium moves to the leaves when you water overhead, and the infected soil splashes onto the foliage. The bacteria tend to overwinter and harm any plants or weeds left in the garden if it is not cleaned during the winter. This problem becomes evident when you plant something in your garden the following growing season.

How Do You Deal With It?

A couple of simple solutions are available to prevent this disease from taking root in the garden. The first solution is to ensure that you water the plants from beneath, in order to make sure the bacteria present in the soil don't splash onto the foliage. Try watering earlier in the day so that even if any soil with the bacteria splashes onto the foliage, the sunlight is sufficient to kill them. Another benefit of watering plants early in the day is that they dry out before the cold air of the night hits them. When you water the plants later in the day, it offers moisture and a cold temperature, which is ideal for the spread of this bacterium.

Ensure that you clean the garden completely between the growing seasons. Any leftover weeds or dead plants should not be in the growing space. If there are any, they become a breeding ground for different types of diseases as well as pests. The final option is to treat the foliage with a fungicide. This gives you a good chance to save the plants from further damage caused by this disease.

Rust

The name of this disease by itself offers an accurate description of what it looks like. It results in discoloration of the foliage such that it looks like rust is growing on the plants. It is a fungal disease, and usually spreads in wet conditions—the spores are transferred from one plant to another by the wind. Once the spores land on the foliage of any plant, they start breeding. The most common vegetable plants affected by this disease include onions, asparagus, eggplant, peas, okra, corn, artichokes, beans, and sweet potatoes.

How Do You Deal With It?

With a little planning and preparation, you can stay ahead of rust. Whenever you are planting crops, you need to practice proper thinning techniques to ensure the plants are not overcrowded. When there is sufficient space present between the plants, the airflow increases. When the airflow increases, moisture that is held within reduces. This ensures the soil doesn't become a breeding ground for this disease. Another option available is to ensure that you practice proper gardening maintenance. The garden area must be cleaned at the end of every growing season to ensure the disease does not hide in the soil during the winter. Remove the damaged foliage as soon as you notice they have become infected by rust. After this, treat the rest of the plant using a fungicide especially made for this purpose. Follow the preventative measures mentioned above to reduce the chances of a subsequent outbreak.

Downy Mildew

Downy mildew is also another fungal disease that usually thrives in cold and damp climatic conditions, and spreads through the air as well. Another common cause of downy mildew is when the affected soil is splashed onto healthy plants. The fungal spores also transfer from one plant to another through your hands, as well as gardening tools. The earliest sign of this mildew is leaf discoloration. As the disease spreads, gray hair-like structures start appearing on the foliage of the plant. When left unchecked, it will quickly invade the entire plant and result in a complete loss of foliage.

How Do You Deal With It?

Use a soaker hose to water the plants from beneath to prevent the risk of downy mildew. You should also start watering the plants early in the day to give them sufficient time to dry out. If the temperature reduces at night, it creates the ideal breeding ground for this fungal disease. Don't forget to wash your hands and your gardening tools, or anything else that comes in contact with the plants affected by it. All the infected plants must be uprooted and thoroughly destroyed to prevent further spread of it. Treating it with a fungicide is possible, provided you catch it early on. Opting for specific varieties of disease-resistant plants you want to grow also gives them a better chance to avoid this disease altogether.

Early or Late Blight

A variety of vegetable plants are affected by blight. That said, the most common varieties susceptible to it include potatoes, tomatoes, and eggplants. Usually, early blight occurs in the form of dark spots on the plant close to the soil level. On the other hand, late blight appears as a dark spot on the stem that moves upward toward the foliage. This disease can survive because it overwinters in the soil, and it's usually transmitted to the plants once affected soil is splashed onto the foliage during watering.

How Do You Deal With It?

Once again, you must clean the garden at the end of every season to prevent blight from entering a healthy garden. Weeds and dead plants attract a variety of pests and diseases that no garden should have. Ensure that you are careful while watering the plants at soil level using soaker hoses. Similarly, water early in the day to ensure the plants are fully dry before sunset. Use a fungicide immediately to treat the infected plant. Further treatments of a fungicide might be needed to ensure the disease is treated and doesn't infest any other plants. If the plant seems too far gone, then remove and destroy it. This ensures that healthy plants are not affected.

Corn Smut

This is an interesting disease that occurs in vegetable gardens, and can ruin your corn harvest when left unregulated. It has a unique appearance, and is hard to miss. It reduces corn harvest and causes large growth on the parts of a corn plant that are above ground. So, if you are growing corn in your garden, be extra careful. Usually, this disease overwinters in the soil and spreads through the water, as well as wind. It thrives in dry and hot climatic conditions. Getting rid of it is difficult, because it can stay active in the soil for up to 7 years. If the plant is physically damaged or there are any openings in it, corn smut will take advantage of it.

How Do You Deal With It?

The simplest way to avoid it is by opting for disease-resistant varieties of corn. If there are any pest problems in your garden, treat them using insecticide to ensure this fungal disease doesn't enter the corn plants. Always opt for a balanced fertilizer. If there is too much nitrogen in the fertilizer or the soil, this disease thrives. Remove and destroy the corn crops that are infected by corn smut to prevent further spread.

Clubroot

Clubroot is a common disease that prefers acidic soil, especially soil with a pH less than 6.5. This disease affects plants belonging to the brassica family. If you are growing broccoli, Brussels sprouts, cabbage, cauliflower, radishes, and turnips, watch out for this disease. If your plants aren't growing as intended and you have ruled out any possible cause of a deficiency, then chances are it is clubroot. This disease also causes plants to wilt and turn yellow. If you uproot the plant, you will notice clubs or spindle-like structures that come in a variety of shapes. This is the surest sign of clubroot.

How Do You Deal With It?

Raising the pH of the soil is the best way to reduce the risk of clubroot disease. The pH of the soil should not be less than 7.0, and should not be any higher than 8.0. So, you will need to opt for plant varieties that prefer alkaline soil. Adding lime to the garden soil is also a great way of quickly improving the pH. Ensure that you always use a soil testing kit to check whether the soil's pH is at an appropriate level or not. If clubroot is present in the soil, it can stay dormant for as long as two decades. So, you will need to be quite careful. If any of the plants are affected by this disease, remove them completely. Every part of the root system should be removed—if not, the disease will spread. Sanitize the gardening equipment and any other tools used for dealing with the infected plants before using them again.

Blossom End Rot

This is a disease that affects plants when they are close to harvest. The plants will look healthy and strong throughout the growing season. However, the fruit they produce will be rotten. Most gardeners usually panic thinking that their entire crop is ruined. This is a perfectly treatable condition, though, and it occurs due to a calcium deficiency. So, there is a quick fix available. Do not feel defeated if you spot this problem in your garden, because with proper care and a little vigilance, you can reap a bountiful harvest. The most common plants susceptible to this disease include tomatoes and peppers.

How Do You Deal With It?

Usually, this condition is a sign of low levels of calcium in the soil. To prevent this problem from occurring, feed a calcium supplement to the plants. Even sprinkling powdered milk close to the base of the plants during the planting season helps. It's not too late to tackle this problem. Sprinkling powdered milk close to the base of the plants at the first sign of blossom end rot is the best option. This is a cost-efficient means, and gives plants the needed calcium to fight off the disease.

Mosaic Virus

This is another disease that no gardener will want to find in their garden. The trouble with this disease is its symptoms usually vary and once it takes root, there is no going back. There isn't much that can be done, so focus on preventing it. As the name suggests, it is a viral disease and spread through human contact. Unknowingly touching the infected plant and touching other plants later results in its transfer. The most common plants susceptible to its damage include corn, celery, cucumbers, tomatoes, peppers, spinach, beans, and potatoes.

This virus can stay dormant within the soil for up to two years. The most common signs of this disease include stunted growth of plants, reduction in the harvest, and curled foliage. As mentioned, the symptoms usually vary from one plant to another.

How Do You Deal With It?

If you realize or have an inkling that mosaic virus is present within the soil and is destroying your plants, the first step is to completely unroot the plant. After this, destroy it by burning it. Do not even think about turning this into organic compost or anything else along these lines. It is a viral disease, and will spread. Therefore, sanitize everything that came in contact with the infected plant. Sanitize all tools used to remove the plant before moving on to other plants. This also means you should sanitize your clothing, hands, and even the stakes used for supporting the plants. There are no treatment options available to deal with this disease. So, opting for disease-resistant varieties in the future is a good idea.

Verticillium Wilt

This is a rather troublesome disease once it hits your garden. The common symptoms associated with it include discoloration and wilting of foliage. The foliage also starts curling during the initial stages. If left unchecked, it will quickly kill the plant altogether. This is a fungal disease that attacks the plant from the soil. It infiltrates the plant's internal system and destroys it from the inside. The most common plants susceptible to its damage include pumpkins, cucumbers, tomatoes, peppers, potatoes, and eggplants.

How Do You Deal With It?

If it looks like your plants are suffering from verticillium wilt, there is nothing to do other than uproot the plants and destroy them. You are still not in the clear, even after the plants are destroyed. There are two options available at your disposal. The first option is to opt for vegetable plants resistant to this disease in the future. The second option is to eliminate all traces of this fungus from the soil using solarization. To do this, the top 6 inches of the garden soil need to be tilled. After this, wet the area using a garden hose and then cover it with plastic. Ensure you leave this plastic sitting for at least 1 month, and don't forget to secure it thoroughly. As the temperatures increase and the area is exposed to sunlight, the warmth is sufficient to kill any traces of fungus living in it. So, you will need to perform this procedure only when the temperatures are high. At the end of the month, your garden soil will be healthy, and you can start planting again.

Damping-off

This is one of the most common fungal diseases, and it usually affects young seedlings. The roots and stems of the seedlings start rotting. The fungus responsible for it prefers cold and damp climatic conditions, and the best chance to avoid this disease is by paying extra attention to the young seedlings.

How Do You Deal With It?

Once the seedlings have contracted this disease, you cannot reverse it. So, reducing the chances of it occurring is your best bet. The first step is to ensure that your soil is thoroughly sanitized before you plant. This helps to get rid of any hidden diseases present within. If you are starting seeds in pots or trays, sanitize them, too. Whenever you are starting seeds, sow them at an appropriate depth, and do not plant them too deeply. If the seeds are sowed too deep in the soil, then the seedlings will be overworked during the germination process itself. This increases the stress on the plant and reduces its ability to withstand diseases. Along with this, you must pay extra attention to the spacing between the plants while planting. The airflow available to the plants increases when there is sufficient space between them. If not, it increases the risk of this disease.

Always water the seedlings from beneath. So, any trays or pots used for growing should be placed in a dish of water, which ensures the roots absorb it. Another advantage is this ensures the seedlings do not get wet, but get the required water and nutrition. Since this disease prefers a humid and moist environment, offering the seedlings plenty of sunlight does the trick. Apart from all this, using a natural fungicide is always helpful. As soon as the seedlings start appearing, sprinkling a layer of the natural fungicide keeps the unwanted diseases away. An organic option available is to sprinkle a layer of cinnamon on the soil to fight these diseases.

It is more than likely that you will face some of these diseases, pests, and insects as you start gardening. With a little planning, preparation, and mindfulness, you can ensure your hard work doesn't go to waste. So, spend some time and learn more about the different problems associated with a vegetable garden. When you know what to look for and how to prevent or treat it, you can rest easy knowing that your garden is healthy and thriving.

Using Nutrients to Prevent Plant Problems

In certain cases, fungal, viral, bacterial, and other plant problems can be due to an insufficiency of certain nutrients. Plants are living beings, too—and just like us, they also have nutritional requirements. For instance, if your levels of vitamin C are quite low, this affects the immune system and increases your susceptibility to common infections, such as the flu. Similarly, the same happens to plants as well when they do not have the required level of nutrients.

Fungal plant diseases including fusarium and downy mildew attack plant tissues. This happens because their tissues are weak due to the absence of certain nutrients, or the lack of them. If you notice there is a significant increase in fungal diseases, then you need to increase the presence of phosphorus, calcium, or potassium in the soil. There must be balance in every facet of life. Similarly, giving your plants too much of a specific nutrient can also increase their susceptibility to viral infections and diseases. Excess of certain nutrients, especially phosphorus and nitrogen, increases the susceptibility of plants to viral diseases. To rebalance the nutrient profile of the soil, you will need to add more potassium. Their susceptibility to bacterial illnesses increases when the plants do not have sufficient nitrogen, calcium, and potassium. On the other hand, if the nitrogen level is too high, certain species of bacteria thrive and can wreak havoc on your plants.

If you notice that, even after adding amendments, the health of the plants doesn't improve or it is obvious they are not getting better, then you must look for other underlying diseases or problems to be safe. If the plants cannot recover even after all this, take it as a sign that they are too unhealthy, and remove them from your garden to save the other plants.

Aside from viral, bacterial, and fungal diseases—the lack of nutrients also influences the ability of the plants to fight certain types of pests, too. If the plants are depleted of their required nutrients, they are unhealthy. Such plants are automatically more vulnerable to pests when compared to healthier ones. The level of certain nutrients within the soil increases the susceptibility of the plants to pest outbreaks. Excess nitrogen can increase the population of arthropods, including mites and aphids. When the plants are undernourished, the chemical signals sent by them attract different pests. On the other hand, when the plants are healthy and have the required nutrients, they start attracting helpful and desirable bugs that help the other plants in your garden as well. So, ensure that your plants have all the nutrients they require to prevent plant problems.

Chapter 20:

Tips All Gardeners Should Know

Until now, you were introduced to all the information you require to grow and maintain a healthy vegetable garden at home. By now, you would have also realized that gardening is not an activity restricted to only certain people. It is neither complicated nor difficult, by any means. All it requires is the right information, a positive mindset, and plenty of patience. In this chapter, you'll be introduced to some basic tips that all gardeners must know.

Plant Position and Location

The most important consideration of a good and healthy garden is the position and locations of the plants you want to grow. Spend some time doing this, and use the suggestions discussed in the first part of this book about garden planning and the basic soil and sunlight requirements. While choosing the right spot for your garden, consider where you want to place the plants, too. For instance, some require shade while others thrive in the sun. Similarly, consider whether you want to sow the seeds directly in the garden or want to start them indoors. A little planning certainly goes a long way in ensuring the health of your garden.

Height Arrangement

A common mistake newbies make is failing to consider the height of the plants they are growing. Saplings are small, but fully grown plants aren't. If you grow large plants next to small ones that require sunlight, the plants will not thrive. Remember, plenty of your time and effort go into gardening. Once again, this can be easily fixed by spending some time planning the garden. A simple and effective technique to create a balanced garden is to plant the tall ones at the back, and then move on to the shorter plants. This also makes it easier to tend to their needs.

Right Timing

Certain plants are ideal for certain seasons. Selecting the right time for the plant varieties you want to grow is needed, because it has a significant effect on their overall growth and development. The right time to plant in most cases is the dormant season. Usually, sowing the seeds during the late fall or early spring ensures the plants have the required climatic conditions to grow. Before you get started, go through all the information discussed in the second part of this book to ensure that the varieties you choose will thrive in the existing season. Some grow throughout the year, but their requirements will be different. So, cater to all your plant requirements with a little planning and preparation.

Soil Type

You should not start a garden without testing the soil. You must be aware of not just the soil's pH, but its nutrient profile as well. If the soil itself is poor or not the ideal type, then the plants will not grow. It is as simple as this. Knowing the type of soil in your garden ensures that you can easily amend it to fit the requirements of the plants. The simplest way to know the soil type is by conducting a rapid soil test. Information about this was discussed in the previous chapters. You should pay attention to the soil type and its nutrient profile, because amending the soil means you are feeding the plants. Understanding the plants you want to grow, along with the nutrient profile of the soil, ensures you are selecting the right amendments.

Organic Compost

A natural fertilizer that is ideal for any type of garden is compost. It is made of decomposed organic matter that enhances the nutrient profile of the soil. Garden compost can either be made at home, or even purchased from a local gardening store.

Gardening Journal

A simple, yet effective, means to ensure your garden is always healthy is to maintain a gardening journal. Regardless of whether you are just getting started or are a veteran gardener, maintaining a journal is a brilliant idea. In this journal, you should make a note of the existing soil conditions, any amendments made to it, and the plants you want to grow. Along with this, also make a note of the locations of the different plants you are growing. Make this journal as detailed and comprehensive as you possibly can. Don't forget to include information about the watering and feeding requirements of all the plants you decide to grow. This is the best way to ensure that you are aware of the assortment of plants in the garden. Along with all of this information, make a note of any plant diseases, pests, or other insects you have noticed in the garden. Your observations about this will go a long way in ensuring the health of the garden.

Garden Arrangement

A common mistake most gardeners make is when they plant vegetables and flowers next to each other. Ensure that you do not do this. Vegetable plants require different soil conditions for their growth. Pay extra attention to where the vegetable plants are placed, especially if you want to grow and harvest them later. Also, the shade from tall flower plants can stunt the growth of the vegetable ones.

Mindful Watering

The importance of watering your plants cannot be stressed enough. This is one point that's been repeated in all the chapters, because not watering the plants or overwatering them will kill the entire garden within no time. Therefore, ensure that you are aware of the water requirements of all the plants you grow. They have varying watering needs, and you must be mindful of them. This is another reason why maintaining a gardening journal makes things easier. The ideal time to water the plants is usually early in the morning or evening. Avoid watering them at around noon when the sun is at full mast.

Native Varieties

You can pretty much grow anything you want these days. That said, opting for native varieties is always a good idea. This is because certain plants are already accustomed to growing in the present soil conditions of the area you live in. They are also acclimatized to the weather and temperature, which means the chances of a healthy garden increase. Also, tending to native varieties is easier. If you are growing any plants that are not native to the region you reside in, ensure that you pay extra attention to them. They will have varying growing conditions, and you must cater to their needs.

Crop Rotation

A common mistake most gardeners make is they end up growing the same variety of plants every year. This is even more harmful if you have small space available for the garden. Without crop rotation, the plants will drain all the nutrients present in the soil. In the end, you will be left with lifeless soil that will prevent any growth of plants. Just because you've had a bountiful harvest by growing certain varieties, avoid giving in to the temptation of regrowing them. Instead, opt for other plants that will replenish the soil.

Plant Herbs

Growing herbs is not only easy, but incredibly fruitful as well. They are low-maintenance, and most varieties are hardy. This means they are resistant to a variety of climatic conditions and thrive in most regions. Some varieties produce beautiful flowers, too. Ensure that your garden is diverse and that you are not restricting yourself to one or two varieties of herbs.

The Gardening Tools Matter

If you want to paint, you will need painting supplies. You cannot paint without them. Similarly, you will need the right set of tools if you are serious about gardening. Investing in the gardening tools you were introduced to in the previous chapters in this book will help. Regardless of the type of garden you opt for, you will need some basic tools to get things done. A recap of essential gardening tools includes a shovel, fork, rake, spade, shears, gloves, and scissors.

Companion Planting

Humans are social beings, and we thrive in groups. Similarly, certain types of plants go well together. This is what companion planting is about. Some plants are mutually beneficial. For instance, cabbage, onions, tomatoes, and carrots go well together. The nutrients that one plant requires from the soil are fulfilled by the nutrients released by the other into the soil. Also, they have similar growing conditions. It makes your job easier as a gardener.

Container Gardening

This is one of the most popular forms of gardening. If you have an in-soil garden outdoors, consider container gardening for an indoor space. Whether it is herbs or any vegetable plant of your choice, you can grow anything in a container garden. Since you are already tending to a full-fledged garden outdoors, this added space will give you a bountiful harvest.

Use Kitchen Waste

One of the best starters for seeds is an eggshell—eggshells are rich in calcium, which is a natural nutrient required by most plants. You can start the seeds in eggshells, and then plant them. Alternatively, even adding eggshells to the plants is a great way to ensure the soil is nutrient-rich. Crush the eggshells and add them to the soil just like a fertilizer. Plants such as eggplants, tomatoes, peppers, broccoli, and cauliflower usually benefit from the addition of eggshells. You can also use citrus peels just like eggshells. If the soil isn't acidic enough and the plants require acidic soil, add citrus peels. Rinse the peels of citrus fruits, grind them, and then add them to the soil. This is a great way to repurpose any kitchen waste.

Mulching and Weeding

One thing you shouldn't forget is to regularly mulch the garden. Adding a layer of mulch close to the roots of the plants ensures they are protected from extreme weather conditions. Mulch also offers the nutrients young plants require. Regular mulching reduces the chances of any pest infestation, and also protects the roots from direct sunlight or harsh cold. If you mulch regularly, the soil will stay moist, weed growth will reduce, and the soil temperature will be regulated. A combination of these factors automatically results in better plant health and growth.

Ensure that you regularly remove any weeds or grass you notice in the garden. They need to be rooted out without any hesitation. If you don't, weeds will quickly overrun your beautiful garden. These additional invaders will leech the nutrients present in the soil that your vegetable plants need. As with weeds, ensure that you regularly rake fallen leaves as well. If you are not careful, fallen leaves can become a source of nourishment for harmful pests and other critters.

Start Small

If you are just getting started with gardening, chances are you are tempted to plant everything at once—this can be overwhelming for a newbie, though. It can also result in disorder and chaos. There are multiple factors you must pay attention to if you want a fully-functional garden. If you try to do too many things at once, chances are you will end up making the mistakes discussed previously. Whether it is not selecting the right spacing or ignoring other aspects important for their growth, this will make things complicated. It is always better to start small—and once you get the hang of it, you can start growing more plants.

Be Patient

Another obvious, yet commonly overlooked, mistake most make is they become impatient. Understand that you cannot grow a garden overnight. Even if you are using fully-developed plants, you still need to tend and maintain them. If you do not do this, your garden will not be healthy. You cannot obtain the harvest you want. The maturation cycle for different plant varieties is different. However, they take a couple of weeks at the least. You will also need to be patient depending on the weather conditions. Certain plants are ideal for specific growing seasons or climatic conditions. Gardening is an activity that takes plenty of time, consistency, and love. Once you commit to this and are patient, the results will leave you pleasantly surprised.

Chapter 21:

Increase the Yield From Your

Garden

Until now, you were used to different suggestions about a variety of factors associated with gardening. You might be interested in growing as much of your produce at home as possible. If you love the idea of eating fresh produce and want to have sufficient produce left over, then the obvious answer might be to grow more plants. However, if the space available is limited or there are any other problems associated with your garden, the yield will reduce. Use the suggestions given in this chapter to increase the yield from your garden, while optimizing the space available.

Hybrid Seed Varieties

Hybrid seeds are different from genetically modified ones. Hybrid seed varieties are plants that are specially bred and crossbred to improve certain characteristics. The difference between heirlooms and hybrid seeds is that the latter will not produce seeds that can produce plants with the same characteristics as that of the hybrid parent.

However, hybrid seeds are hardier and have increased vigor—this means they are resistant to the common diseases plaguing vegetable plants, and are unappealing to most pests. You can also use such variants to extend the growing season, or grow plants that have a quicker maturity. If there isn't sufficient time between frosts, then you can start growing during the colder seasons by using hybrid varieties.

Hybrid seeds are usually preferred because of the size of harvest they offer. One thing you must remember is to carefully check whether the seeds you are opting for are hybrid or genetically modified ones. Stay away from genetically modified ones, and ensure you are purchasing the seeds from an authentic and dependable supplier.

Old Seeds

Avoid wasting the garden space available, along with your time and effort, by using seeds that will not grow. Usually, this is the case with old seeds. Therefore, ensure that you check the viability of the seeds before sowing. A simple rule you can remember is to always oversow. If there are too many seedlings that crop up, you can thin them later. This is so much better than spending your time sowing seeds and taking care of them, only for nothing to grow.

Fast-Maturing Varieties

In addition to hybrid seeds, there are some fast-maturing varieties of seeds available, too. Select them if you are in a hurry to harvest vegetables at home. Most vegetable plants take only a couple of weeks to reach that full maturity. On the other hand, some plants take months together. For instance, the maturity period for tomatoes can be anywhere between 55-85 days. If you want to improve the yield from your garden and optimize the space available for growing, then opt for faster-maturing varieties.

All Compost Is Not Equal

Compost is the best way to improve the nutrient profile of the soil, along with the organic matter in it. The nutrients present in compost not only support plant growth and health, but also improve the soil structure as well. It also transports nutrients present in the soil across a larger area. So, adding compost regularly to the soil ensures its health and nutrient profile. However, it's important to remember that all compost is not the same.

If you are purchasing compost, carefully read through its nutrient composition. The ratio of carbon and nitrogen (C:N) in the compost determines whether it is ideal for your plants or not. If the C:N ratio is too high, this means the compost needs more time to age before it is ideal for use. In such cases, buy the compost in advance and let it age before you add it to the garden. This increases the availability of nutrients in it for the plants. The ideal ratio of carbon and nitrogen in compost for plants is 15:1. Anything more than this ratio means the nutrients in it will be utilized by the compost itself for its decomposition.

A Little Investment

Growing your own vegetables at home will significantly reduce your grocery bill. However, there is a little up-front investment in this world as well. Investing in the right tools might be a little expensive initially, but it is needed in the long run. Selecting the right soil amendments and fertilizers, supplies for starting seeds, insect nets, or even gardening tools, can quickly add up the costs involved. Opting for higher-quality tools will further increase the cost. When you look at all the costs involved, it probably looks like gardening is an expensive hobby. However, with the right tools, equipment, and appropriate information, you can significantly reduce your grocery bills later. Think of it as an investment instead of an expenditure.

Starting Seeds

The variety of plants you can grow in the garden will increase when you start your seeds at home. You can opt for seeds that will perform best in the existing garden soil, or select ones for the quantity of yield they offer. Even if you want an organic garden, opting for seeds that have an increased vigor will improve their chances of survival. Starting seeds at home is not only simple, but quite cheap as well. This is a cheaper alternative to purchasing grown plants or seedlings ready for transplant. That said, the choice is entirely yours. All the information you need to start seeds at home and grow a variety of vegetables was discussed in the second part of this book.

Undersowing and Interplanting

Undersowing is the simple practice of planting some specific plants that benefit from a cooler microclimate under larger plants that are sun-loving—thus, their ideal climate is created. The vegetables you plant in this way must be light feeders, so that they don't leach all the nutrients from the soil that the neighboring plants need. Light feeders refer to plants that don't require any nutrients in the soil for their growth. For instance, planting lettuce under tomato plants is the best example of undersowing. When the climate needed for lettuce is cool and wet, the harvest is better, and it does not become bitter as it matures. By planting it right under tomato plants, an ideal microclimate is created for lettuce to thrive.

Interplanting essentially refers to the practice of planting different vegetable types in the same plot. You should do this with the knowledge that one will be harvested before the other. This means you are making room for the subsequent crop even before harvesting the first one. For instance, interplanting kale with garlic during the spring is an incredible idea. This is because garlic is usually harvested earlier in the summer, and kale a little later. Even after harvesting one plant, you don't have to worry that the soil is empty, because there is another batch of plants growing there.

Encouraging Pollinators

All insects are not bad—some might destroy your crops, while others increase the yield. Hummingbirds, butterflies, and honeybees are excellent pollinators. If the rate of pollination increases, more flowers will bloom in the garden. This, in turn, means more vegetables will grow and increase the yield.

If you want to attract more pollinators to your garden, here are some suggestions you can follow. The first suggestion is to avoid using any toxic weed killers and pesticides. The problem with such pesticides and chemicals is they not only destroy any harmful disease-causing pathogens, but they also harm the beneficial insects and creatures you want to attract as well. Instead, opting for organic pesticides and weed killers is a better option. Even if you are interested in growing only vegetables, planting the right flowers is needed for attracting pollinators. Sunflowers, blanket flowers, and butterfly bushes are some common flowers you should start planting in your garden to attract beneficial insects.

If you offer adequate shelter, you will end up attracting more bees, pollinators, and butterflies. This is not a complicated process. Even letting a log decompose on the property, or placing artificial nesting boxes strategically around the garden, will do the trick. Apart from shelter, ensure that these pollinators you are trying to attract have sufficient water and food as well. Setting up hummingbird feeders will help attract more hummingbirds, as well as butterflies, to your property. A bird bath, a shallow catch basin for rainwater, or even a water fountain will help achieve this purpose.

Fertilize

Fertilizing the vegetable plants at the right time not only promotes healthy growth, but increases the yield, too. This is because they are obtaining the required nutrients regularly. The plants automatically become hardier and productive, and their ability to withstand diseases and pests also increases. Depending on the type of plants you are growing, the amount of fertilization they need will vary. Frequent fertilization is needed for heavy feeders such as cucumbers and tomatoes, whereas lettuce and kale are light feeders that don't need much fertilization. Usually, light feeders require a little boost maybe once, or at the most twice, during a growing season.

Record the Yield

Ensure that you record the yield obtained from the plants you are growing. Keeping a good gardening record of the yield, along with the expenses involved, will prove to be a game changer. You need not rely on memory from previous seasons to determine the varieties that produce the highest yield; you simply need to compare the observations through different growing seasons and determine which varieties offer better results and are the least expensive. These days, a variety of online tools and management applications are also available that can be used for keeping track of all this information. Or if you are old-school, you can maintain a gardening journal.

Succession Planting

Crops such as leafy greens, lettuce, beet, radishes, and carrots require only a couple of days to start germinating. You can plan for a continuous harvest by using the technique of succession planting. Sow a couple of new rows of these plants every week to ensure you will have a continuous harvest of the desired vegetable. Also, this is a great way to ensure that you are growing only as much produce as will be consumed immediately. As you harvest a batch of veggies, the next will be ready if you opt for succession planting. Once again, you will need to sit and carefully plan all this out if you want to improve your harvest.

Rainwater Catchment

Previously, it was mentioned that you should avoid using treated or softened water for your garden. If the water is softened using chemicals, its pH and mineral profile are significantly altered. So, using rainwater whenever possible is an excellent idea. The chemicals present in rainwater are relatively low, and it has more nutrients. This is also a great way to ensure that your garden is environmentally friendly. If you want to harvest rainwater, then using rain barrels or any other harvesting technique is a good idea.

Extend the Growing Season

You can harvest more and for longer by extending the growing season. Whether you are using greenhouses or cold frames, offering plants some much-needed insulation from cold weather will promote their growth. This is another aspect of gardening where maintaining records will be extremely helpful. However, it requires a little bit of trial and error. You can determine the cost-effective systems by trying out different varieties. Your records will also give you a better insight into the right time to start certain varieties.

Harvesting Young Crops

If you want mature plants to keep growing and produce more vegetables, then you must harvest when the fruit is young. For instance, picking zucchinis when they are just 6-7 inches long instead of waiting for them to grow in size is a better idea. When you harvest the vegetables young, they not only taste better, but this also encourages the plant to keep producing more fruit. If you regularly do it, the yield obtained will automatically increase.

You do not have to start implementing all of these suggestions at once. Instead, simply remember them as guidelines while planning your garden. Also, know that even implementing a couple of these practices in your garden will result in a better yield.

Conclusion

I want to thank you once again for choosing this book! I hope it proved to be an enjoyable and informative read!

Perhaps you were always interested in gardening, but never got around to it. Or maybe you are looking for a new hobby. Regardless of the reason, it is never too late to learn. Gardening simply refers to the act of growing and taking care of plants in a garden. It is one of the best hobbies anyone can develop. If you love the idea of growing your vegetables at home, then this book will act as your guide through every step along the way. In this book, you were introduced to all the information you will need to get started with gardening. Since gardening is not an overnight process and requires serious commitment, understanding the benefits it offers is a good starting point.

When you grow vegetables at home, you have complete control over what you feed the plant and soil. This helps improve your relationship with the environment. Gardening promotes mindfulness, reduces stress, improves mood, creates better bonds with others, and is extremely rewarding. What more? You can attain all these benefits while getting your daily dose of exercise. By now, you would have realized that there are multiple options available when it comes to the garden type you can choose. Whether it is a traditional in-soil garden or the modern vertical garden, space isn't a worrisome factor anymore. You can start a garden in a container, on your balcony or terrace, and even in grow bags. These options offer convenience and comfort, along with excellent space utilization.

Careful consideration is needed before you can start a garden, since it involves plenty of planning and preparation. A garden is a living, breathing thing. It is a complex ecosystem by itself. The factors that play a role in any garden are the quality of soil, sun and shade requirements, watering and maintenance, and the plants you want to grow. In this book, you were introduced to all these aspects of gardening in comprehensive detail. From helping you select the right type of soil to the tools you will need, this book is your step-by-step guide to gardening.

You can grow a variety of vegetables in your home garden. Whether it is leafy vegetables, herbs, bulbous vegetables, or tubers, the options are once again—endless. You were also given information about all the steps involved in growing a variety of vegetables. Once you select a garden layout and all the other factors are taken care of, the next step is to simply choose what you want to grow. After this, you need to gather the required tools and supplies and get started. Well, your job doesn't end here. It is not just about planting or sowing seeds; you must tend to the garden, too.

Regular maintenance and upkeep are needed if you want a healthy and thriving garden. Follow the information given in this book to take care of these needs. From understanding how to water the plants to tackling common challenges, a wealth of information was covered. There is no such thing as knowing it all when it comes to gardening. By following the information in this book, you can avoid mistakes most gardeners make. You can also increase the yield received.

Now that you are armed with the information needed about gardening, the next step is to get started. Take some time to plan your garden carefully. From considering what and how you want to grow and amending the soil, to choosing a garden type and selecting a watering system, planning is needed. Remember, failing to plan is synonymous with planning to fail. So, increase your chances of success as a gardener by utilizing the information given in this book. Ensure that you are consistent, patient, and conscious in your efforts. A variety of factors play a role in the health of your garden and the harvest you receive. This book will be your step-by-step guide. Spend some time and carefully go through all the information given in this book. Knowing what to do and not to do will improve your ability to become an excellent gardener. So, what are you waiting for? Simply follow the information given in this book, select the vegetable plants you want to grow, get started, and maintain them. It is as simple as this!

Thank you and all the best!

Glossary

Regardless of whether you are a newbie or a veteran gardener, learning horticulture lingo is needed. Here is a list of some basic words all gardeners must familiarize themselves with:

Aerate: Loosening the soil to improve the air and drainage is known as aerating. The simplest way to do this is through tilling.

Annual: Any plant with a life span of a single growing season is known as an annual. The usual growing time for these plants is in the spring and summer. They die during the first frost. However, certain annuals can survive through the cold season as well, and set seed and die when the weather starts warming up during the spring.

Average Frost Date: The average date of the first or the last frost, in the fall and the spring respectively, in the area where you reside is the average frost date. The first frost in the fall is known as the first frost, whereas the last one in spring is known as the last frost.

Bare Root: Any plant that's sold without any soil or pot around the roots is known as a bare root. Usually, these plants are available in the winter or early spring, when the plants are usually dormant.

Biennial: Any plant with a lifecycle spanning over two growing seasons is known as a biennial. They usually produce only leaves during their first growing season, and start to flower or set during the second one.

Bolt: When an annual plant shoots up a flower stalk and starts to seed, it is known as bolting. This word usually refers to cool-season vegetable plants that seed prematurely due to the hot weather.

Brassica: The plants that belong to the Brassicaceae family are commonly known as brassica. Some common examples include cauliflower, kale, broccoli, collard greens, and arugula.

Clay: The smallest particles present in soil are known as clay. They are usually smaller than 0.002 mm. Clay soil is better at holding nutrients, as well as moisture. If the soil has too much clay, then it becomes extremely hard when dry and doesn't drain well.

Cold Frame: This is a small greenhouse-like structure that goes over a planting bed. It encloses the bed with a transparent lid or cover to ensure the heat of the sun during the spring or fall is contained within, ensuring better growth of plants. This is how it acts like a greenhouse. It usually has a lid that is made of plastic, sheet glass, or any other transparent material to allow sunlight in.

Cool-Season Crop: Plants that thrive during cool seasons such as potatoes, peas, lettuce, radishes, beets, and even broccoli, are known as cool-season vegetables. Usually, the ideal daytime temperature required for their growth and development is between 60° F and 80° F.

Cover Crop: This refers to certain species of plants that are specifically grown for improving the quality of soil, instead of just obtaining a harvest.

Crop Rotation: This is a conscious practice of planting a variety of crops in different places every year, to ensure that there is no buildup of pathogens within the soil left behind by the previous crops.

Cross-Pollination: Cross-pollination occurs if two or more plants belonging to the same species are pollinated using each other's flowers. This is usually required to produce a crop, especially for fruit-bearing trees.

Cucurbit: All the plants that belong to the Cucurbitaceae family are known as cucurbits. The most common examples include different types of melons, cucumbers, and squash.

Cultivar: Any plant that is specially developed via selective breeding is known as a cultivar. It's usually developed for different purposes such as flowering, fruiting, or even their disease-resistant characteristics. These days, most vegetables are usually bred in a combination of different cultivars that offer a variety of traits.

Cutting: A small piece of a plant that is clipped off to be used for propagation is known as a cutting. These are usually planted or stuck in a rooting or growing medium, and exposed to a humid environment to grow. This encourages the stalk to start developing its own root system.

Damping-off: This is a disease that usually targets seedlings and kills them off right before they start sprouting. The best ways to prevent this are to avoid excess moisture in the soil, promote better airflow, and use potting soil or a mixture that is sterilized.

Days to Maturity: This refers to the average number of days, or the period a plant requires from seeding, until it is ready to harvest. If you are using seeds, the information about the same is usually printed on the packets.

Digging Fork: This is a gardening tool that helps loosen the soil, especially while preparing for planting.

Direct Seeding: If the seeds are placed where they will be growing, then this is known as direct seeding. This is quite different from sowing seeds that are placed in pots that are later transplanted to the final growing area.

Double Digging: This is a special technique used for preparing the growing area for creating soil that is loose and rich.

Drainage: This refers to water's ability to freely pass through soil. The soil must have good drainage to prevent water logging. If water keeps getting logged, or there is excessive moisture within the soil, this harms the roots and the growth of seedlings. It also increases the risk of root rot.

Drip Irrigation: This is a type of irrigation system when water drips out slowly close to the base of the plant.

Dwarf: Any plant that is bred to be smaller than what is considered to be typical for its specific species is known as a dwarf.

Evergreen: Any plant capable of retaining its foliage throughout the year is known as an evergreen.

Family: The rank above genus, but below order in taxonomic classification, is known as a family. The family name is usually written in Latin. Some varieties of plants are also referred to by their family name such as brassicas, which belong to the Brassicaceae family.

Genus: The rank above species, but below the family name in taxonomic classification, is known as the genus. This is also known as the scientific or the Latin name of the plant, and is capitalized.

Grafting: When two parts of a plant are spliced together so that they fuse and grow as a solid unit, this is known as grafting.

Green Manure: The plants that are grown for the specific purpose of accumulating organic matter nutrients into the soil, that is then tilled to improve the soil quality, are known as green manure. Green manure and cover crop are two terms that are often used synonymously.

Ground Cover: Any plant that can spread across the ground, while rooting itself in the process, is known as a ground cover. Usually, these species are opted for the landscaping of a rather large area within a budget.

Harden Off: This is the practice of gradually exposing young plants to outdoor conditions before transplantation. Usually, seedlings are placed outdoors for a couple of hours every day for a week, in order to ensure they do not suffer a shock while being transferred to the garden. Their exposure to the outdoor elements is increased daily.

Heavy Feeder: Any plant capable of producing a good result in highly fertile soil is known as a heavy feeder. Some common examples include broccoli, cabbage, and celery.

Herbaceous: Any plant that doesn't have any woody stems, but instead has soft green stalks and leaves, is known as herbaceous.

Humus: Humus refers to a complex soil substance created due to the decomposition of organic matter. If the soil is rich in humus, it is highly fertile.

Hybrid: If a plant cultivar is obtained via intentional cross-pollination of two varieties or species that are closely related, it is known as a hybrid.

Invasive: Any plant capable of spreading aggressively across the garden is known as an invasive variety. Such plants are usually quite tough to remove as well.

Light Feeder: Any plant capable of producing good results, even in soil that is marginally fertile, is known as a light feeder. Some common examples include root crops, herbs, and leafy greens.

Loam: Well-draining and fertile soil is known as loam. It's usually a perfect combination of silt, sand, and clay, along with plenty of organic matter and humus.

Microclimate: When the environmental conditions—including temperature and moisture—are determined by different elements of the landscape such as slope, structures, pavement, or even a tree canopy, it is known as a microclimate. Understanding these conditions makes it easier to determine the right place to start planting.

Micronutrients: The different trace elements required by a plant for its optimal growth in small amounts are known as micronutrients. Some common examples include zinc, copper, iron, and manganese.

Mulch: An organic material that is made up of straw, leaves, or even woodchips, and used for protecting soil, is known as mulch. It reduces the risk of soil erosion, infuses organic matter into the soil, helps retain moisture, and regulates the soil temperature.

N-P-K: This is shorthand used for expressing the ratio of nitrogen, phosphorus, and potassium in a fertilizer. These are the basic nutrients all plants need, and the three numbers that are listed on a bag of fertilizer correspond to the actual percentage of the nutrients in the product.

Nightshade: All plants that belong to the Solanaceae family are known as nightshade. Some common examples include eggplants, different types of peppers, tomatoes, and even potatoes.

Nitrogen: An essential nutrient plants require for the growth of foliage is known as nitrogen, and it's usually represented using its chemical symbol—N. Common sources of organic nitrogen include blood and fishmeal, and animal manure.

Nitrogen-Fixing: All plants that can form and sustain a symbiotic relationship with microbes present in the soil to convert atmospheric nitrogen into a soluble form are known as nitrogen-fixing plants. This is an essential nutrient, because it's responsible for the green growth of plants. Legumes usually belong in this category.

Organic Matter: Any dead or decaying plant or animal matter including manure, roots, leaves, or even bodies of microbes and earthworms when mixed, is known as organic matter. Compost is a primary source of organic matter, and when mixed into soil, it improves its fertility.

Peat Moss: Peat moss is the most common ingredient used as potting soil. It is a highly spongy material with an incredible capacity to retain water, and is ideal for acid-loving plants that require a low soil pH.

Perennial: All plants that can live for years together, such as woody trees and shrubs, are known as perennials. Usually, a variety of herbaceous species are considered perennials.

pH: This refers to the measure of soil's acidity or alkalinity. The usual pH for most plants is between 5.5 and 7.

Phosphorus: The essential nutrient plants require for performing metabolic functions and photosynthesis is phosphorus. Rock dust and bone meal are the primary sources of organic phosphorus for plants.

Pinch Back: A common technique of removing the tip of a plant-growing stem using your fingers or hand pruners is known as pinching back. This practice stimulates the main branch of the plant to grow, and encourages the overall growth to be short and bushy.

Potassium: This is an essential nutrient that plants require for performing different metabolic functions, and is usually represented using its chemical symbol—K. Sources of organic potassium include wood ash and kelp meal.

Rhizome: The fleshy roots that grow laterally close to the surface of the soil, or on the surface from which new stems sprout, are known as rhizomes.

Sand: This is the largest particle found in soil, and is usually between 0.05 to 2 mm in size. If the soil contains plenty of sand, it drains rather easily—but due to this, even the nutrients present in it are washed away.

Self-Pollinating: Plants that can pollinate themselves are known as self-pollinating plants—this means they can produce fruit using their pollen. This is especially helpful when space is limited, and you want a good yield.

Side-Dress: This refers to the practice of applying fertilizer to established plants in order to ensure that their nutrient requirements are met, especially during the growing season.

Silt: This refers to intermediate-sized soil particles that are between 0.002 and 0.05 mm in size. Silt has a perfect combination of the traits exhibited by sand and clay particles—it can effectively retain moisture, while promoting free drainage and better nutrient retention.

Slow-Release Fertilizer: This is a type of fertilizer wherein the granules are coated with a substance that ensures all the nutrients aren't leached into the soil at once.

Soil Amendment: If any substance is added to a specific growing area for improving the soil quality or conditions, this is known as a soil amendment. Some of the most common examples include fertilizers and compost.

Subsoil: This refers to the infertile layer of soil right under the nutrient-rich topsoil. This layer usually has little, or even no, biological activity or organic matter. It is also referred to as mineral soil.

Top-Dress: When fertilizer or compost is spread over the soil surface right before planting, it is known as a top-dressing. In this, the amendments are not filled or mixed into the soil—instead, it is simply spread over it. This technique is also used to meet the nutrient requirements of well-established plants.

Topsoil: The most fertile layer of the soil close to the biologically active surface is known as the topsoil. It includes different microbes, insects, earthworms, and organic matter such as humus.

References

Andrychowicz, A. (2014). *How to design a vegetable garden layout*. Get Busy Gardening. https://getbusygardening.com/vegetable-garden-design

Decker, K. P., Peglow, S. L., & Samples, C. R. (2014). Participation in a novel treatment component during residential substance use treatment is associated with improved outcome: A pilot study. *Addiction Science & Clinical Practice*, 9(1). https://doi.org/10.1186/1940-0640-9-7

Ekblom-Bak, E., Ekblom, B., Vikström, M., de Faire, U., & Hellénius, M.-L. (2013). The importance of non-exercise physical activity for cardiovascular health and longevity. *British Journal of Sports Medicine*, 48(3), 233–238. https://doi.org/10.1136/bjsports-2012-092038

Ersek, K. (2012, September 11). *The 6 essential nutrients for healthy plants*. Holganix. https://www.holganix.com/blog/the-6-essential-nutrients-for-healthy-plants

Gardening Know How. (n.d.). *Tips & information about vegetables*. Gardeningknowhow.com. https://www.gardeningknowhow.com/edible/vegetables

Gonzalez, M. T., Hartig, T., Patil, G. G., Martinsen, E. W., & Kirkevold, M. (2011). A prospective study of group cohesiveness in therapeutic horticulture for clinical depression. *International Journal of Mental Health Nursing*, 20(2), 119–129. https://doi.org/10.1111/j.1447-0349.2010.00689.x

Grant, A. (n.d.). *Growing soybeans: Information on soybeans in the garden*. Gardening Know How.

https://www.gardeningknowhow.com/edible/vegetables/soyb ean/soybean-growing-information.htm

Grow a Good Life. (2020). *7 Simple techniques to improve garden soil.* Growagoodlife.com. https://growagoodlife.com/improve-garden-soil

Hall, C., & Knuth, M. (2019). An Update of the literature supporting the well-being benefits of plants: A review of the emotional and mental health benefits of plants. *Journal of Environmental Horticulture,* 37(1), 30–38. https://doi.org/10.24266/0738-2898-37.1.30

Iannotti, M. (2021, October 20). *Vegetable seeds or seedlings? Find out which is best for your garden.* The Spruce. https://www.thespruce.com/vegetable-garden-seeds-or-seedlings-1403412

Lam, V., Romses, K., & Renwick, K. (2019). Exploring the relationship between school gardens, food literacy and mental well-being in youth using photovoice. *Nutrients,* 11(6), 1354. https://doi.org/10.3390/nu11061354

Leichty, C. (n.d.). *17 Common garden problems (& How to fix them!).* Do Not Disturb Gardening. https://donotdisturbgardening.com/17-common-garden-problems-how-to-fix-them

Litt, J. S., Lambert, J. R., & Glueck, D. H. (2017). Gardening and age-related weight gain: Results from a cross-sectional survey of Denver residents. *Preventive Medicine Reports,* 8, 221–225. https://doi.org/10.1016/j.pmedr.2017.10.018

Lowry, C. A., Hollis, J. H., de Vries, A., Pan, B., Brunet, L. R., Hunt, J. R. F., Paton, J. F. R., van Kampen, E., Knight, D. M., Evans, A. K., Rook, G. A. W., & Lightman, S. L. (2007). Identification of an immune-responsive mesolimbocortical serotonergic system: Potential role in regulation of emotional behavior.

Neuroscience, 146(2), 756–772. https://doi.org/10.1016/j.neuroscience.2007.01.067

Hanelt, P. (Ed.), & Institute of Plant Genetics and Crop Plant Research (Ed.). (2001). *Mansfeld's encyclopedia of agricultural and horticultural crops: Except ornamentals*. (2001st Edition). Springer Publishing.

Mead, M. N. (2008). Benefits of sunlight: A bright spot for human health. *Environmental Health Perspectives*, 116(4). https://doi.org/10.1289/ehp.116-a160

Now from Nationwide ®. (2020, August 9). *How to plant a vegetable garden*. Nationwide.com. https://blog.nationwide.com/tips-for-planting-garden

Old Farmer's Almanac. (2012). *Growing guides*. Almanac.com. https://www.almanac.com/gardening/growing-guides

Park, S.-A., Lee, A.-Y., Park, H.-G., & Lee, W.-L. (2019). Benefits of gardening activities for cognitive function according to measurement of brain nerve growth factor levels. *International Journal of Environmental Research and Public Health*, 16(5), 760. https://doi.org/10.3390/ijerph16050760

Sharples, A. (2020, April 21). *Your guide to different soil types*. Garden Benches Blog. https://www.gardenbenches.com/blog/different-soil-types

Thompson, R. (2018). Gardening for health: A regular dose of gardening. *Clinical Medicine*, 18(3), 201–205. https://doi.org/10.7861/clinmedicine.18-3-201

Van Den Berg, A. E., & Custers, M. H. G. (2011). Gardening promotes neuroendocrine and affective restoration from stress. *Journal of Health Psychology*, 16(1), 3–11. https://doi.org/10.1177/1359105310365577

White, A. (2022, March 31). *Plant nutrients: What they need and when they need it*. Gardener's Path. Https://gardenerspath.com/how-to/composting/plant-nutrients/#Amendments-Can-Affect-Soil-Conditions

Zick, C. D., Smith, K. R., Kowaleski-Jones, L., Uno, C., & Merrill, B. J. (2013). Harvesting more than vegetables: The potential weight control benefits of community gardening. *American Journal of Public Health*, 103(6), 1110–1115. https://doi.org/10.2105/ajph.2012.301009

www.ingramcontent.com/pod-product-compliance
Lightning Source LLC
Chambersburg PA
CBHW062116020426
42335CB00013B/986